BARNET & HADLEY
THROUGH TIME

Robert Bard

AMBERLEY PUBLISHING

Dedicated to Leslie Abrahams for his enthusiastic assistance

First published 2013

Amberley Publishing
The Hill, Stroud, Gloucestershire, GL5 4EP
www.amberley-books.com

ISBN 978 1 4456 1093 1

British Library Cataloguing in Publication Data.
A catalogue record for this book is available from the British Library.

Typesetting by Amberley Publishing.
Printed in Great Britain.

Introduction

In putting together a series of 'then and now' illustrations for Barnet and Hadley, I was keenly aware that what is now the Borough of Barnet is a large, all-embracing area. So within the limitations of this short history and series of pictures, I have cherry-picked from what I found to be the most visually and historically interesting that related to Barnet, Hadley, East Barnet and Arkley. The town of Barnet, now referred to officially as Chipping Barnet, is best known as the location of one of the key battles in the Wars of the Roses, which took place approximately a mile north of the town, where it adjoins Hadley. Barnet itself was primarily a single-street, prosperous town that owed its success to being located close to London on the Great North Road. A London history published in 1880 describes Barnet as the

> small busy town of High Barnet [which] stands at a fork where the road to Elstree and Watford branches off from the Great Northern Road, along which Dick Turpin used to ride; and the long High Street still shows marks of having been a street of inns and posting-houses as being in the old coaching days the first stage out of London on the road both to York and Manchester, for those roads diverge just beyond the northern end of the town.

Conjuring up a Barnet more suited to Jane Austen's Yorkshire Moors, the history continues:

> The town stands high and wind-swept extending along a ridge which commands distant views in every direction, and it is from this circumstance that it acquired the prefix of 'High'. The town is also called Chipping Barnet, from its market, 'which Henry II granted to be kept in this town; famous for cattle, and fairs held on every Monday', abbots of St. Albans.

The geography of Barnet was no less confusing in the nineteenth century than it has been in the twentieth century and beyond. The same 1880 history informs us that

> Barnet is considered to belong to Hertfordshire, but not all the town is in that county, nor does the town lie in a single parish ... There is, in fact, great confusion, because there are two Barnets, two miles apart – East Barnet and Chipping Barnet, or, as it is commonly called, High Barnet; and to these must be added third, 'New' Barnet, which lies between them both, and is rapidly being

> covered by modern streets and villas, of the common suburban type. Lying as it does, for the most part, between two lines of railway – the Great Northern main line and the Finchley and High Barnet branch – this central district enjoys the advantage of very frequent communication with London, and therefore is a favourite abode of City men.

There are a number of suppositions as to where the name 'Barnet' originated. Village London is of the view put forward by 'some antiquaries' that the word derives from the same word as 'Brent'; 'the river which rises in the valley between the town and Totteridge.' It continues to observe that Barnet appears in very early deeds as 'Betgnet', 'from the high situation thereof for the word "Bergnet" in the Saxon language signifies *munticulus*, a little hill'.

By the latter half of the nineteenth century, with High Barnet station well established, Barnet, Hadley, and the surrounding district was on the verge of rapid growth, after a period of decline as the stagecoach business decreased. The census return for 1871 gave the number of houses in High Barnet as 601, and the number of inhabitants as 3,375. By 1881, it was 4,283. At the beginning of the nineteenth century, the population was around 1,000 souls. Barnet was best known for its annual September horse and cattle fair. *Village London* (1880) tells us that the event takes place near the station at High Barnet:

> many thousand head of cattle from the Highlands change hands here. Even Cossacks from the neighbourhood of the Don, in Russia, have been known to attend the fair, clothed in the costume of their native country. The horse and cattle fair used formerly to be bound up with a pleasure fair and races, which became very popular with London roughs; but on the formation of a railway, in 1871, the racecourse was broken up, and the races were of necessity abandoned – an event on which the good people of Barnet may well be congratulated.

Of the oldest still-standing structures are three churches. Firstly, St John the Baptist in Barnet High Street, which originally dated from the thirteenth century and, despite extensive renovation in the fifteenth and nineteenth centuries, still retains reminders of its earliest past. Church Passage immediately to the north of the church has been much modernised, and is almost certainly the location of the execution by burning of William Hale under the English Catholic monarch Mary I during the period of the Protestant persecutions. Those that died for the Protestant cause were listed in John Foxe's *Book of Martyrs,* published after Mary's death in 1563. Hale's entry reads,

> William Hale of Thorp in the county of Essex, who likewise being examined with the rest the twelfth of July, received with them also the sentence of condemnation; giving this exhortation withal to the lookers-on: 'Ah, good people,' said he, 'beware of this idolater, and this antichrist;' pointing unto the bishop of London. And so was he delivered to the sheriffs as a heretic to be burned, who sent him to Barnet, where, about the latter end of August, he most constantly sealed up his faith with the consuming of his body by cruel fire, yielding his soul unto the Lord Jesus, his only and most sure Redeemer.

Secondly, of tremendous beauty and approximately a mile north in Hadley, is St Mary the Virgin church. Above the main door, the date 1494 is carved. Brasses dating from an earlier period confirm that there has probably been a church here since Norman times. The tower boasts an iron beacon, which is a replacement for the earlier beacon, probably used to warn of invasion, and to assist travellers across Enfield Chase. The earlier beacon was blown down on 1 January 1779, when it was repaired and replaced.

Finally, probably the best preserved in the sense of preserved original features, is another St Mary the Virgin, in Church Hill Road, East Barnet. The 1908 *Victoria County History* describes this well-preserved, atmospheric Norman church as, 'The old parish church of East Barnet [which] stands almost forsaken on the western slope of the valley of Pymme's Brook. There are a few residences in this valley and a number of large houses in their parks and grounds on the eastern ridge standing a little back from the highroad.'

The graveyard is wonderfully secluded and overgrown. It overlooks Oak Hill Park and Oak Hill House. A number of former inhabitants now occupy the cemetery. The haunting atmosphere lends itself to a recent description by an author on the Battle of Barnet:

> East Barnet is one of the most haunted spots in the country, Church Hill Road having been famously described as 'The Ghosts' Promenade', such is the volume of its spectral traffic. There have been sightings of a phantom knight in armour in Oak Hill Park, but this is believed to be the ghost of Geoffrey de Mandeville, whose sole tenuous connection with the Battle of Barnet is as founder of Walden Abbey and, as a consequence, Monken Hadley church.

The Battle of Barnet took place on 14 April 1471 on or around Hadley Common, and was one of the most decisive battles of the Wars of the Roses, with the defeat and killing of the leading protagonist, the Earl of Warwick. His place of demise is marked by an obelisk erected in 1745. The truth is that we know very little about where the battle lines were situated, despite a number of early and contemporary sources. There are tantalising clues as to where many thousands of the dead lie buried on the battlefield, but as yet nothing has been found. With the support of the Battlefield Trust, hopefully this will soon be uncovered. Barnet and Hadley are fortunate in being steeped in a well-preserved, and cared for, history.

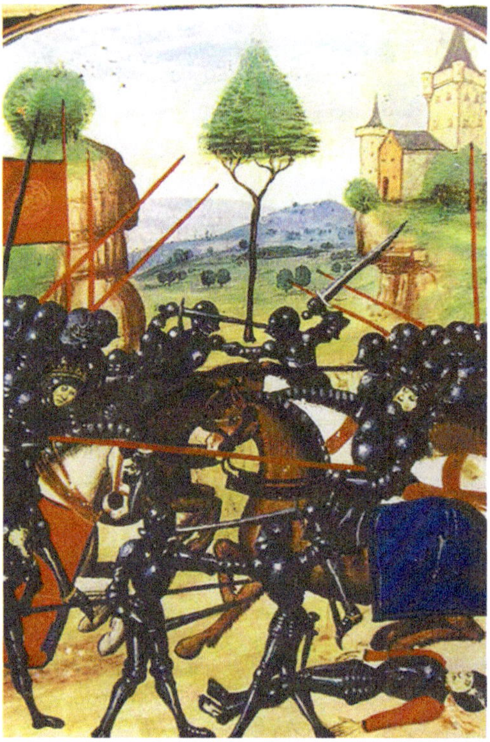

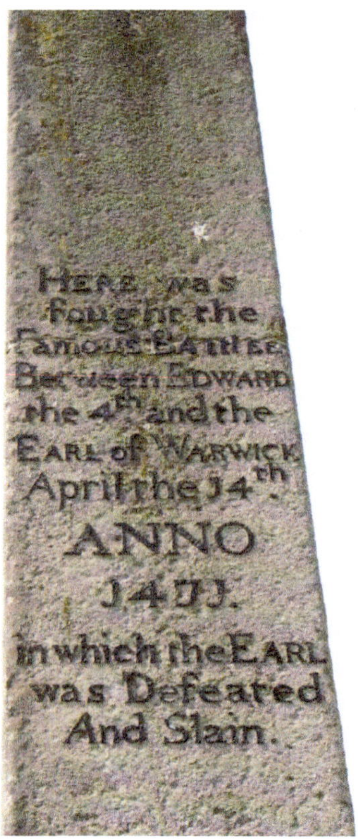

Battle of Barnet

The Battle of Barnet was one of the key encounters of the Wars of the Roses. It took place on a foggy Easter morning on 14 April 1471 between approximately 10,000 Yorkists, led by Edward VI, and 15,000 Lancastrians, led by the Earl of Warwick. Warwick (The Kingmaker) was slain along with a large number of nobility. Three Kings of England were present on the field at Barnet – Edward VI, Richard III and Henry VI. The illustration is contemporary but highly inaccurate.

The obelisk is said to mark the spot where the Earl of Warwick was killed. Apart from the obelisk not being in its original position, there is no evidence that he died on this spot, although it was undoubtedly nearby. His body was stripped naked, put on a cart, taken to St Paul's in London and put on display as proof of his demise. From there he was taken to Bisham Priory in Berkshire and buried.

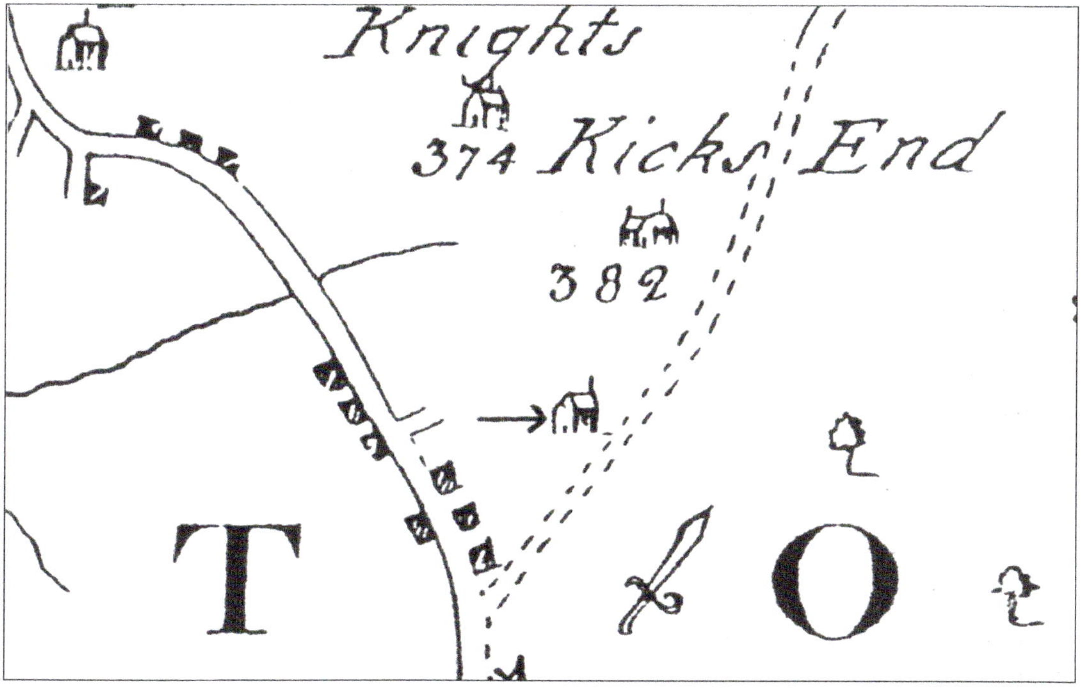

Battle of Barnet Layout
John Warburton's map of Middlesex (*above*) shows a chapel marked by an arrow. Early sources tell us that a chapel was built shortly after the battle for the souls of those that were killed. The chapel was probably situated on land that is now part of Wrotham Park. The lower illustration shows a conventional view of the opposing armies.

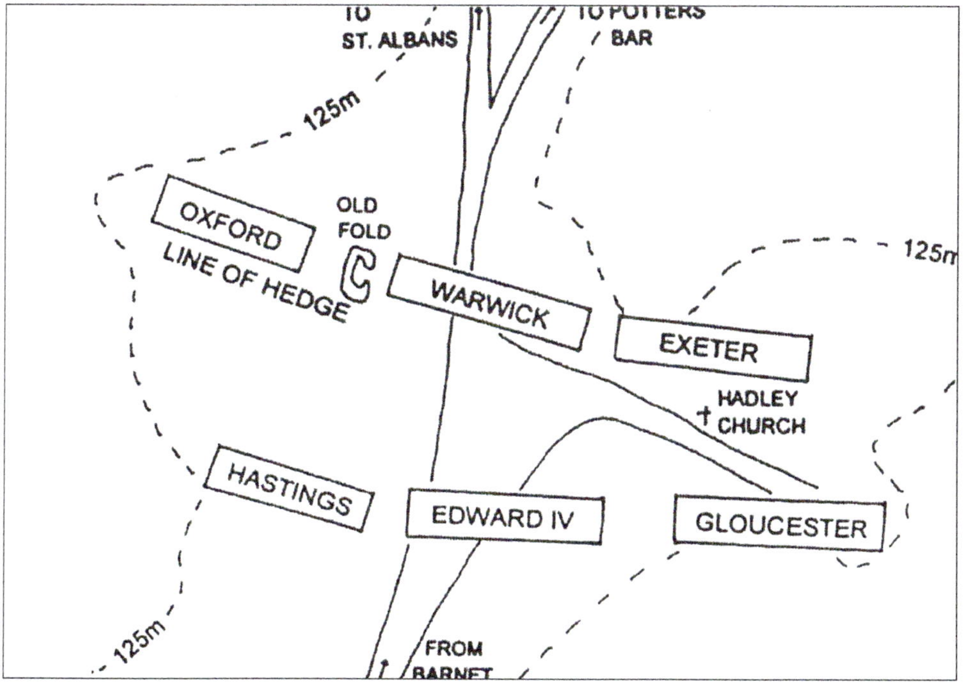

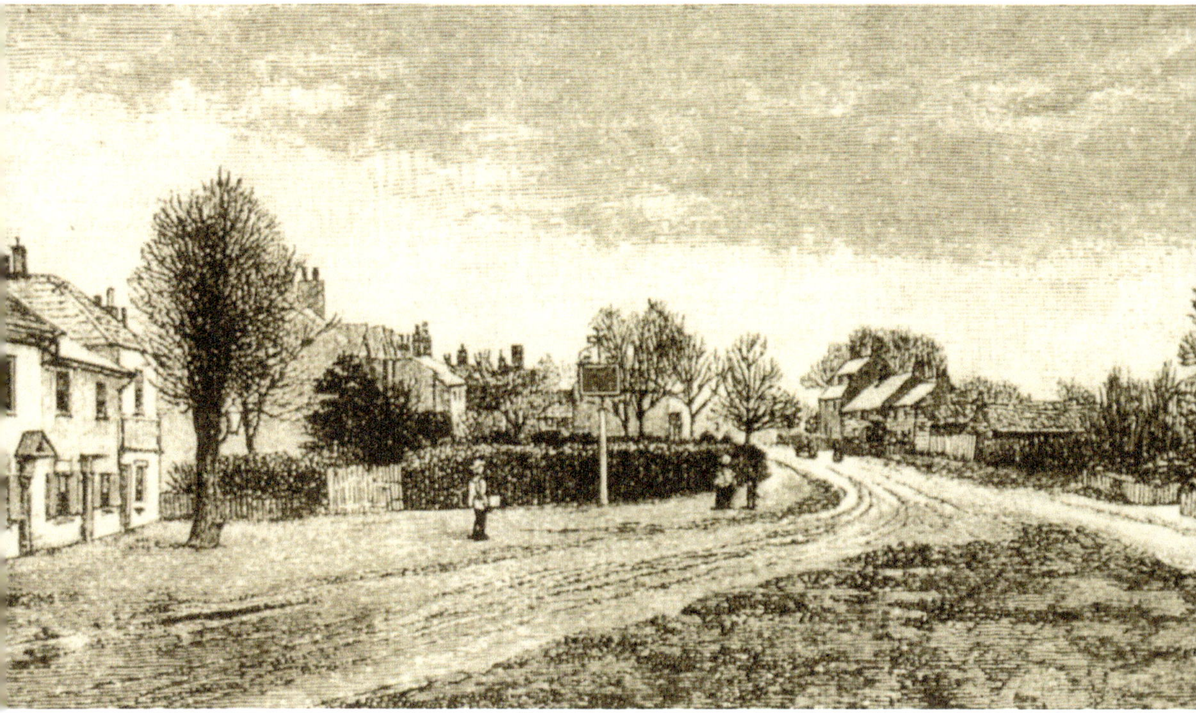

View from Warwick Obelisk

A mid-nineteenth-century view looking south from where the Warwick obelisk stands. Below, the same view in 2013.

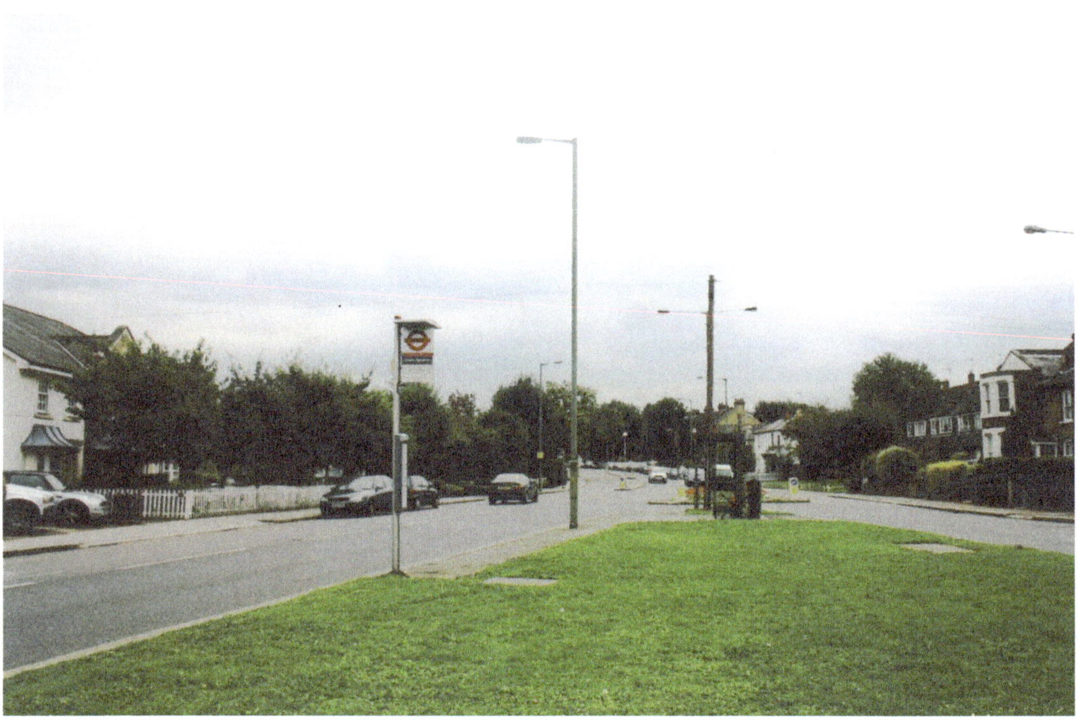

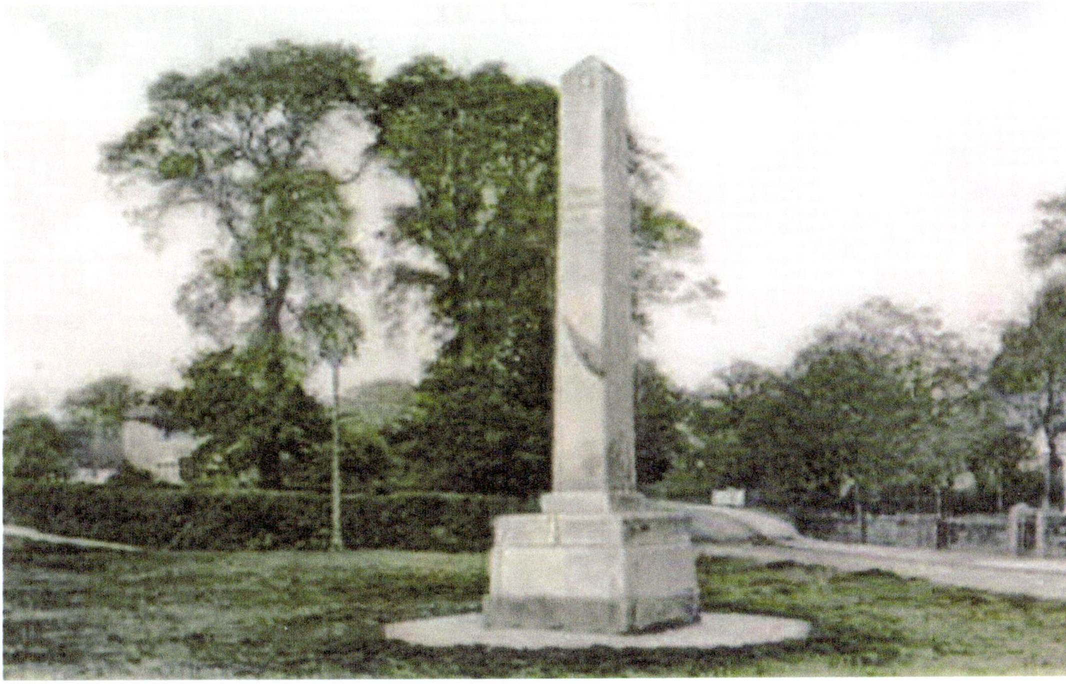

Warwick Obelisk

A photograph dating from *c.* 1905, looking to the north with Barnet behind, where the road splits. Below, the same view in 2013.

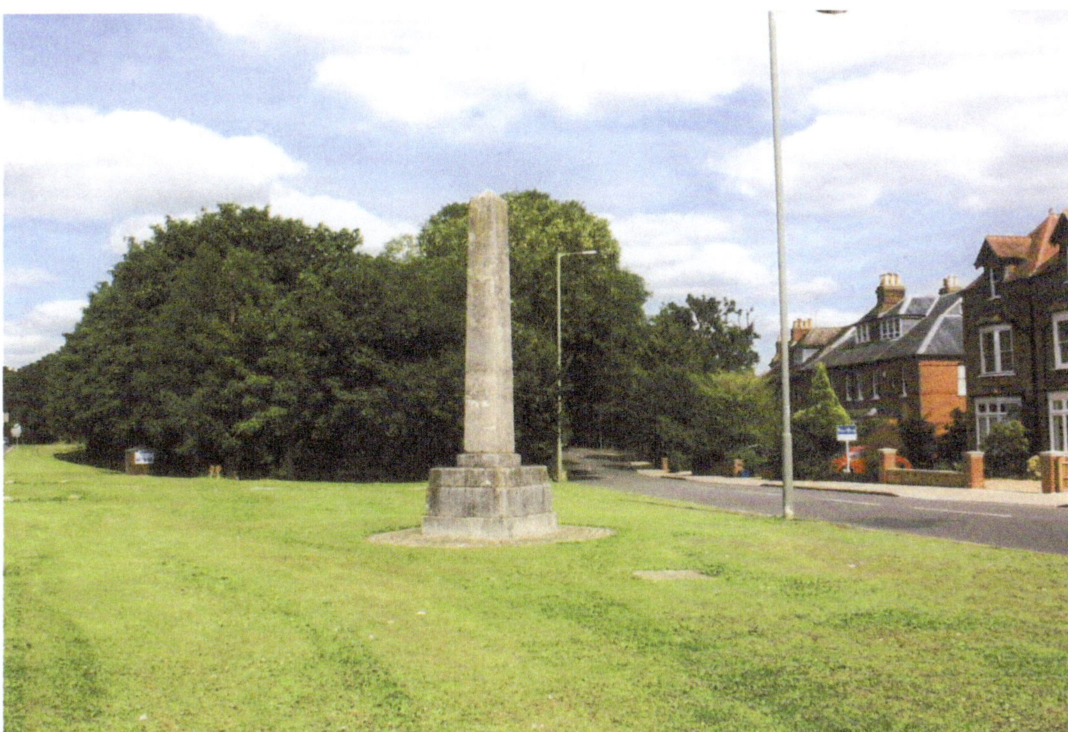

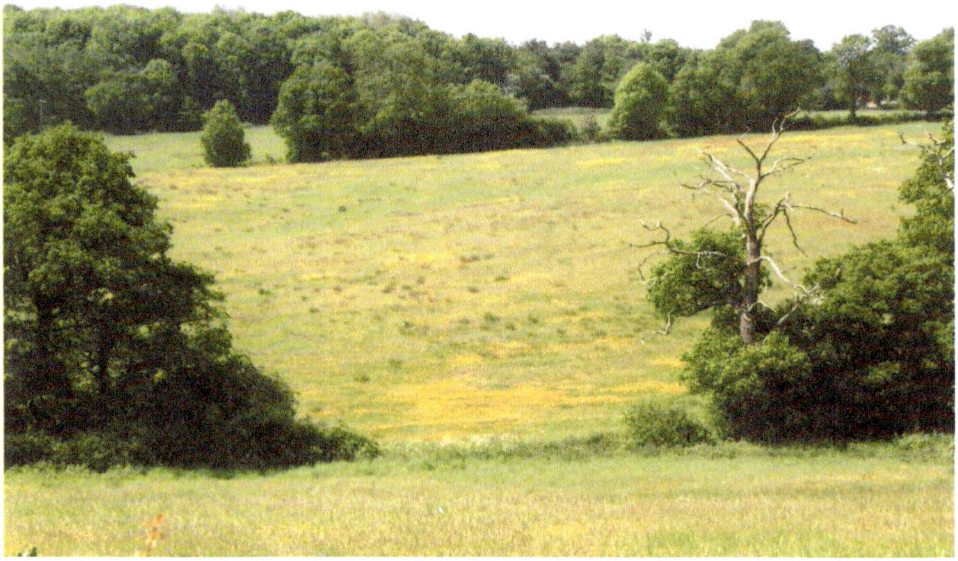

Where the Forgotten Lie

The Battle of Barnet is believed to have claimed somewhere between 1,500 and 4,000 lives. Apart from the well-to-do and nobility whose bodies were removed and given proper burials, the bodies of the common soldiers who were buried on the battlefield have yet to be found. Above is Dead Man's Bottom, looking south towards Barnet, which is believed to be a contender for the site of burial, but this is unlikely. It is more likely to be this moated area on the Wrotham Park estate (*below*) where the possible 4,000 forgotten dead lie.

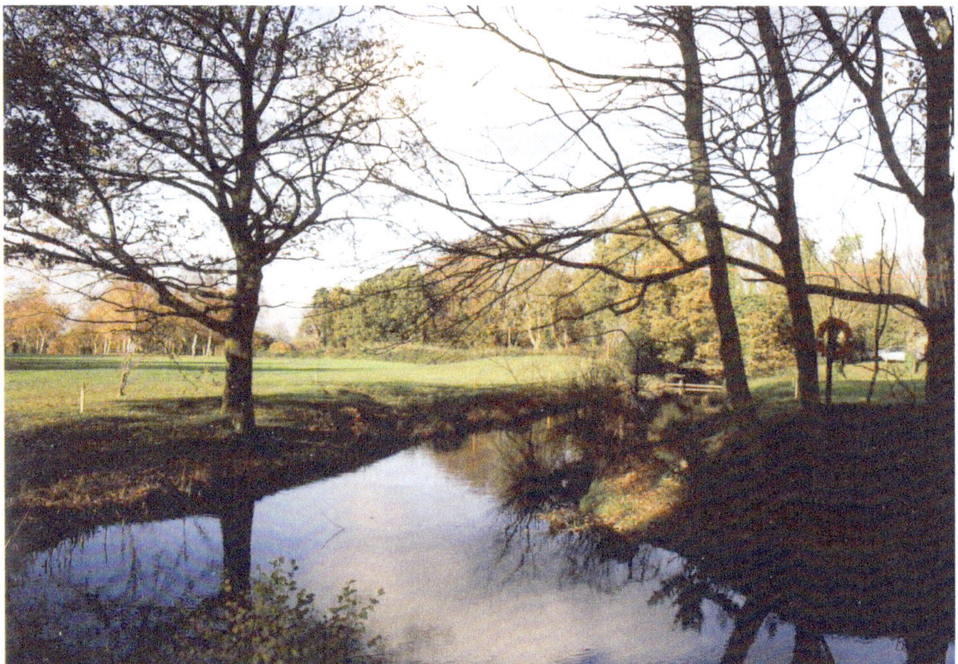

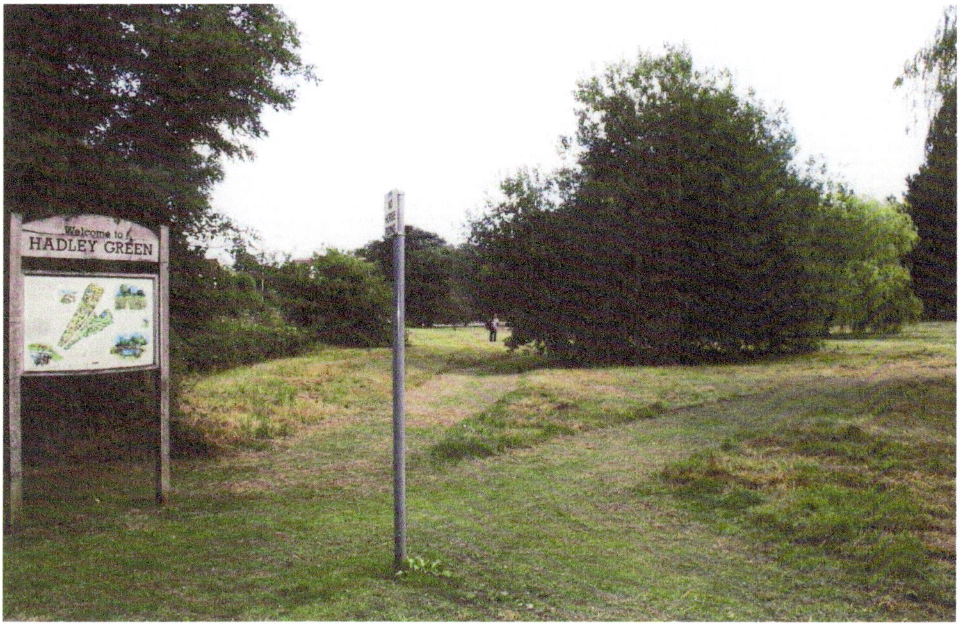

Hadley Green

On Hadley Green, the Battle of Barnet board offers a diagram of the probable layout of the opposing armies. A contemporary of the 1471 battle wrote that 'Warwick and his liegemen and followers, who had been at Coventry, pitched camp a mile beyond the said village [Barnet], right beside the St Alban's high road, on a broad green.' A letter from a combatant, Sir John Paston, written four days after the battle, refers to the battle being fought half a mile from Barnet. It is possible the armies faced each other on an east–west axis, not north–south.

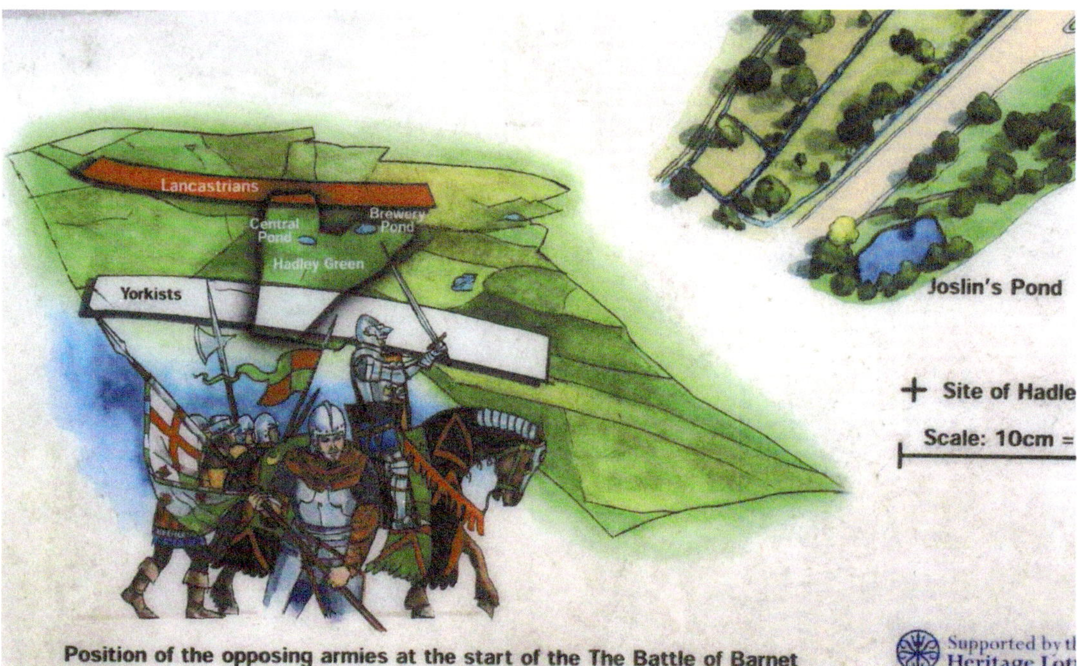

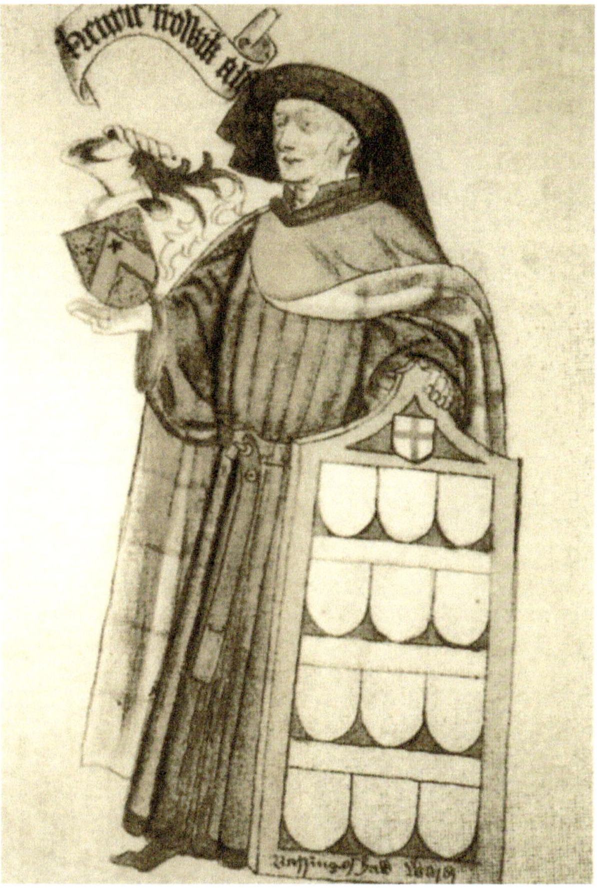

Old Fold Manor

A nineteenth-century local historian believes that 'the moated manor-house of Old Fold belonging to the Frowykes, may have been an important feature in the conflict'. He is referring to the building that stood on the site of the existing house. The moat from the earlier building is now part of the Old Fold Golf Club, contains water, and is still clearly visible. It is possible that the Earl of Warwick used the manor as his headquarters. The Frowykes were an important local family, with Henry Frowyke (*right*) a one-time Lord Mayor of London.

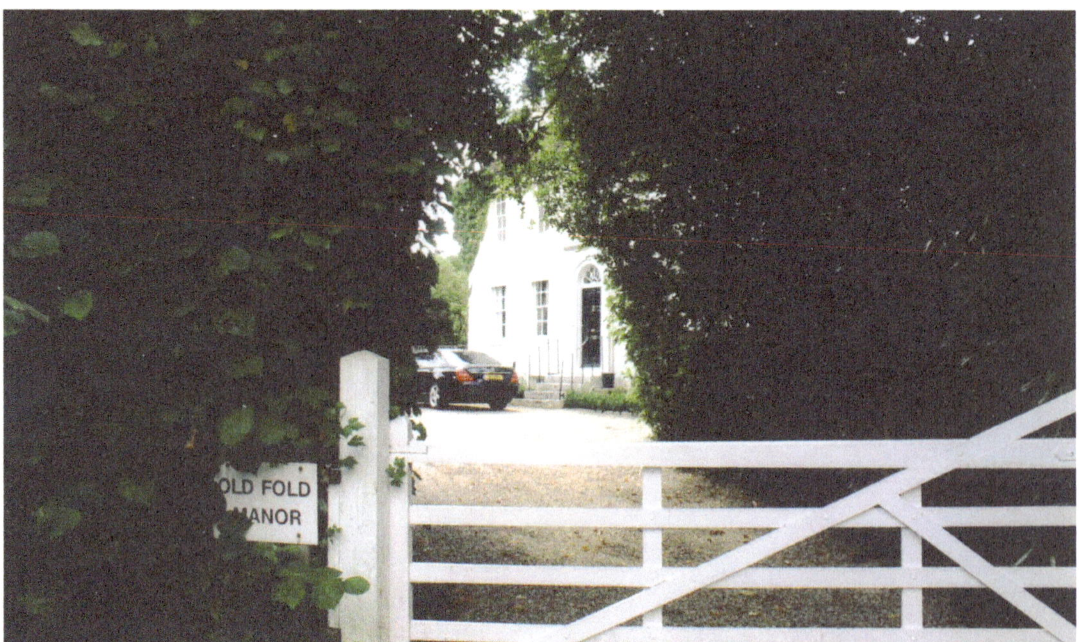

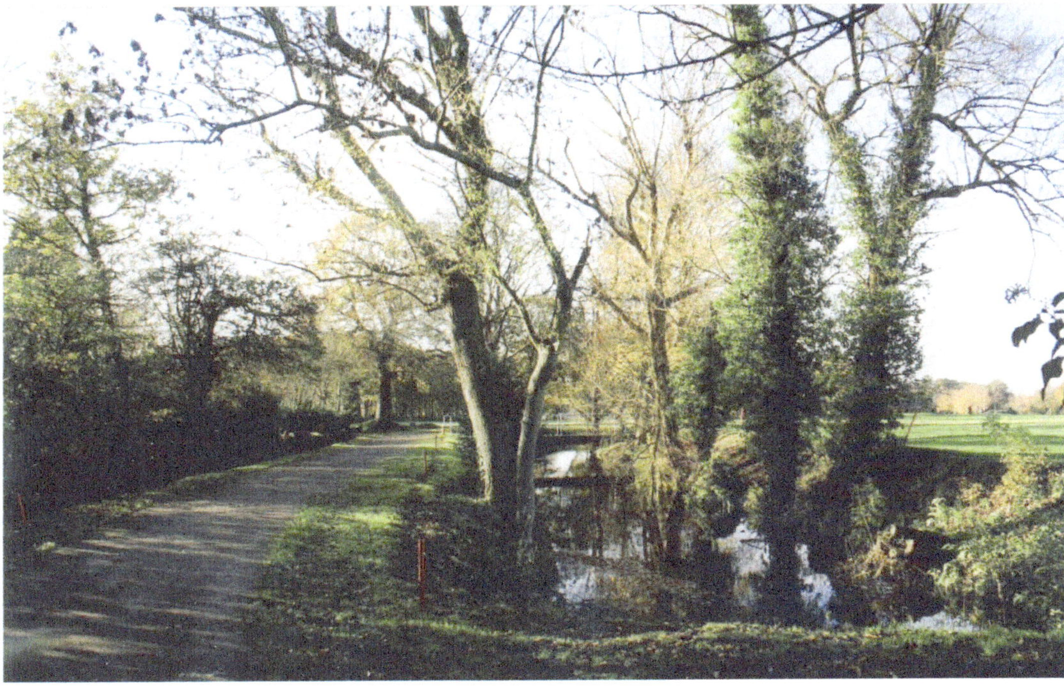

Old Fold Manor Moat and Great North Road

Above are the remains of the moat of Old Fold Manor, which is in the grounds of Old Fold Golf Club. The image below shows where the old Great North Road ran directly along where Old Fold Manor and the golf club now stand. Further down are some houses. This strip of road is part of the original road.

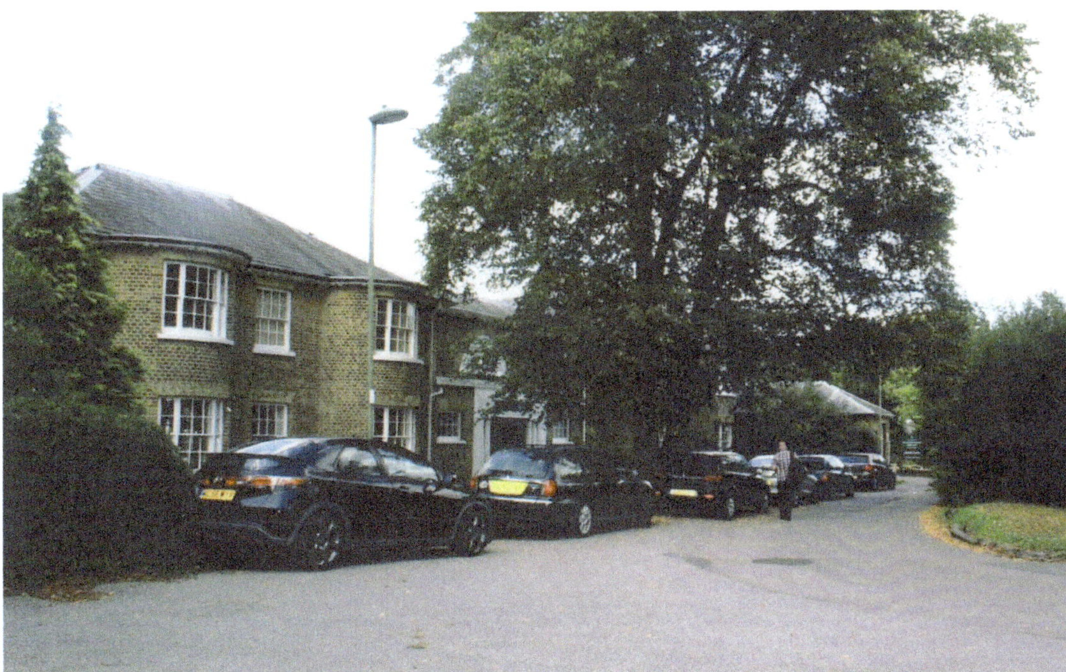

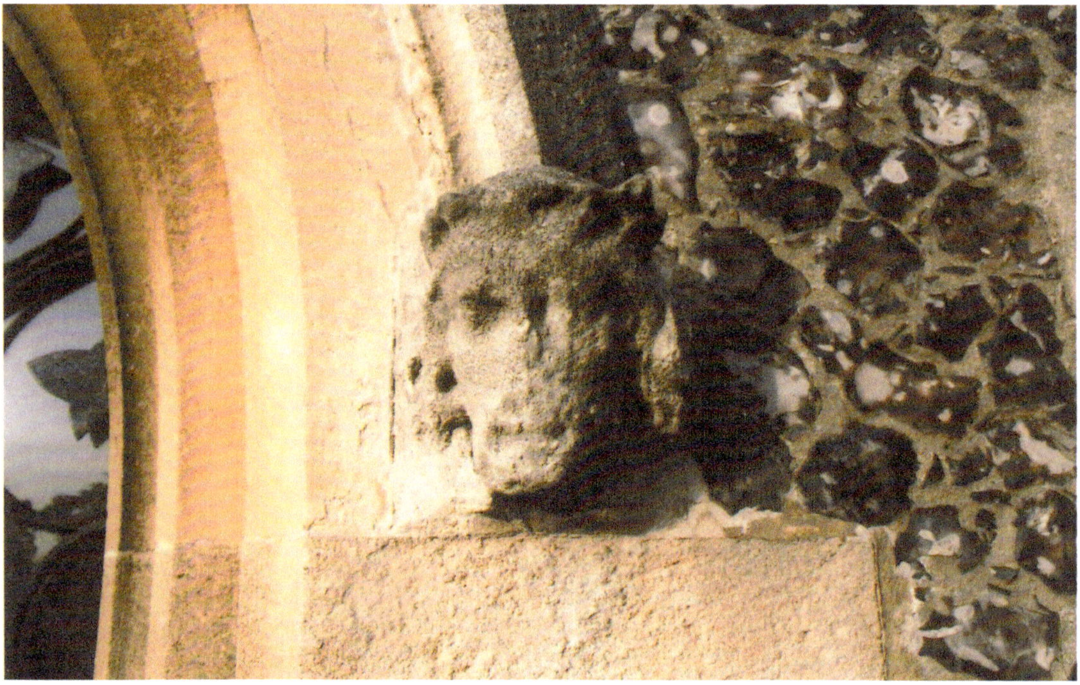

King Edward IV and His Queen

Over the entrance to St Mary's church, Monken Hadley, are two carved heads facing each other. It has been suggested that the two heads are Edward IV (*above*) and his wife, Elizabeth Woodville (*below*).

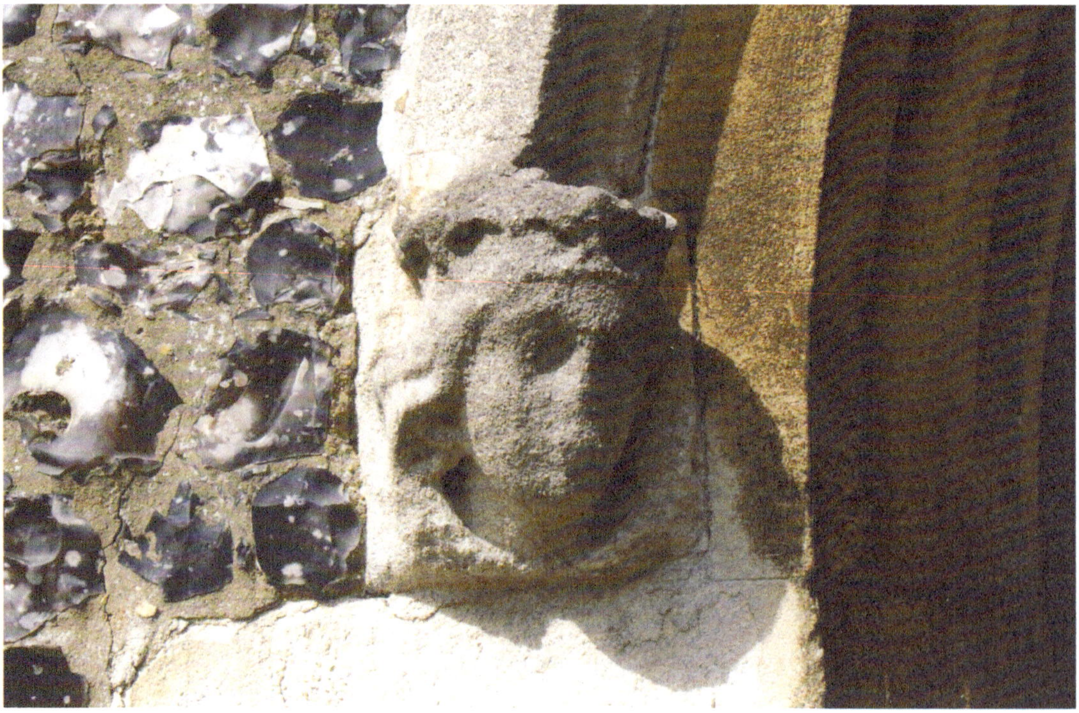

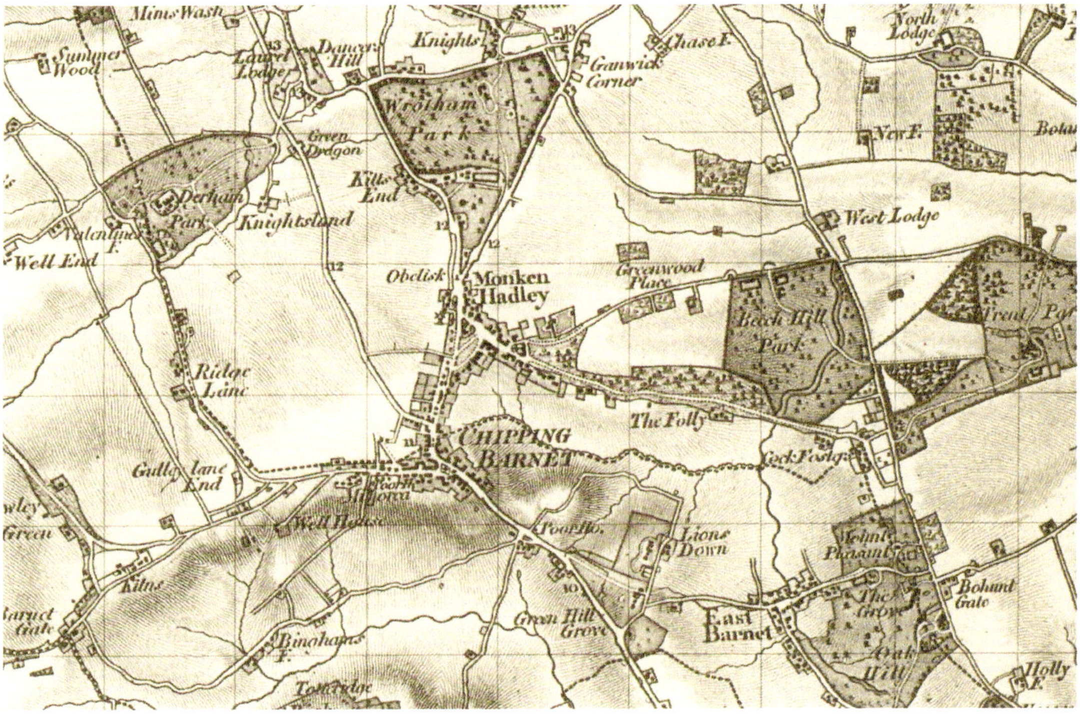

Rural Barnet

The Ordnance Survey map of London, 1805–22, shows the rural nature of early nineteenth-century Chipping Barnet. It was still a one-street town. By 1897 (*below*), the area was beginning to become the choice of residence for the well-off city and middle classes, with the arrival of High Barnet station, opened on 1 April 1872 by the Great Northern Railway on the site of the former Barnet Fair.

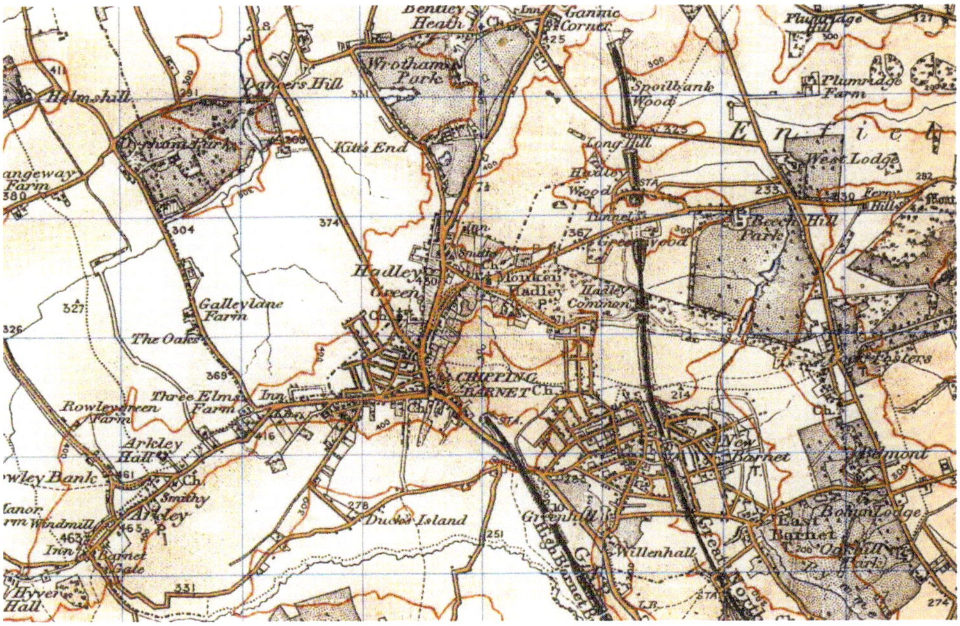

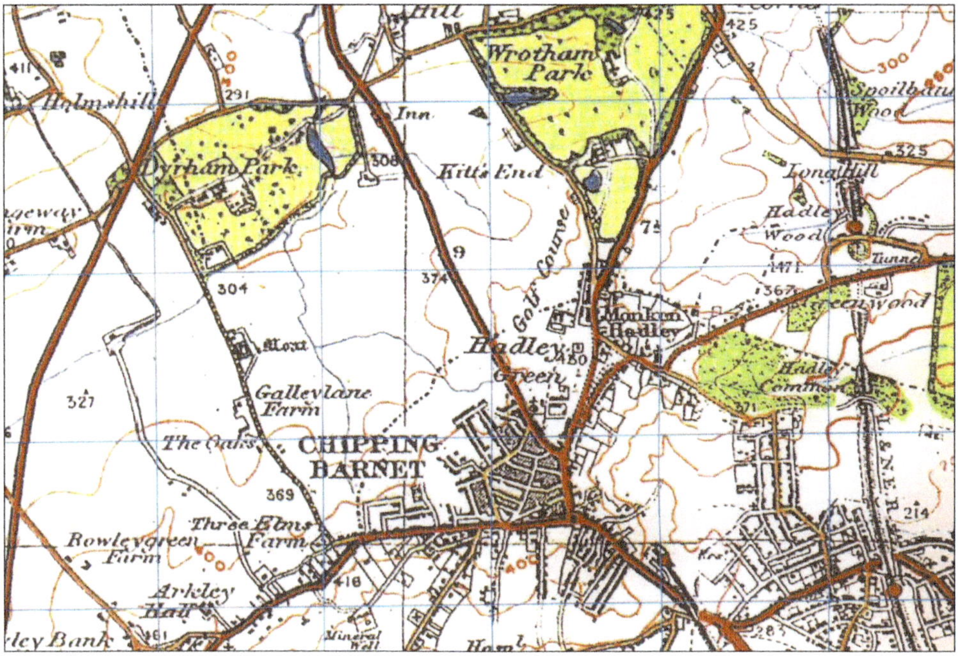

Map of Barnet and St Mary's Church

Detail from the Ordnance Survey map of 1920 (*above*) shows that the Chipping Barnet and Hadley areas had changed little since the 1897–98 map. The church of St Mary (*below*), said in 1504 to be dedicated to St Mary, was rebuilt *c.* 1494, on the site of an older building. It is situated in a prominent position on the edge of Hadley Common. It has been suggested that it was here that the mortuary chapel for the dead at the Battle of Barnet was built, but as with much to do with the battle, there is also much evidence to the contrary.

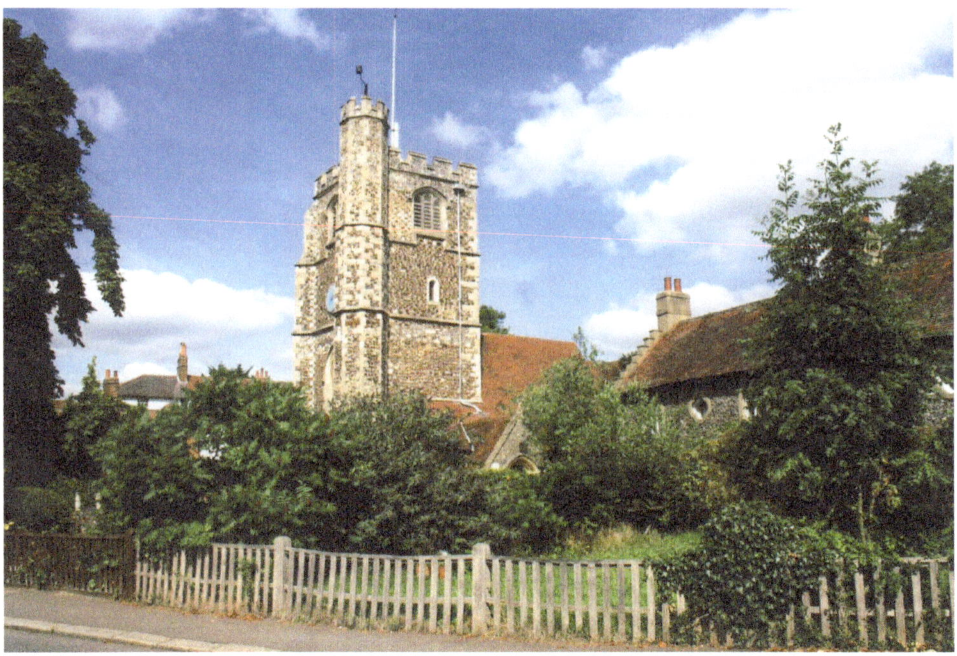

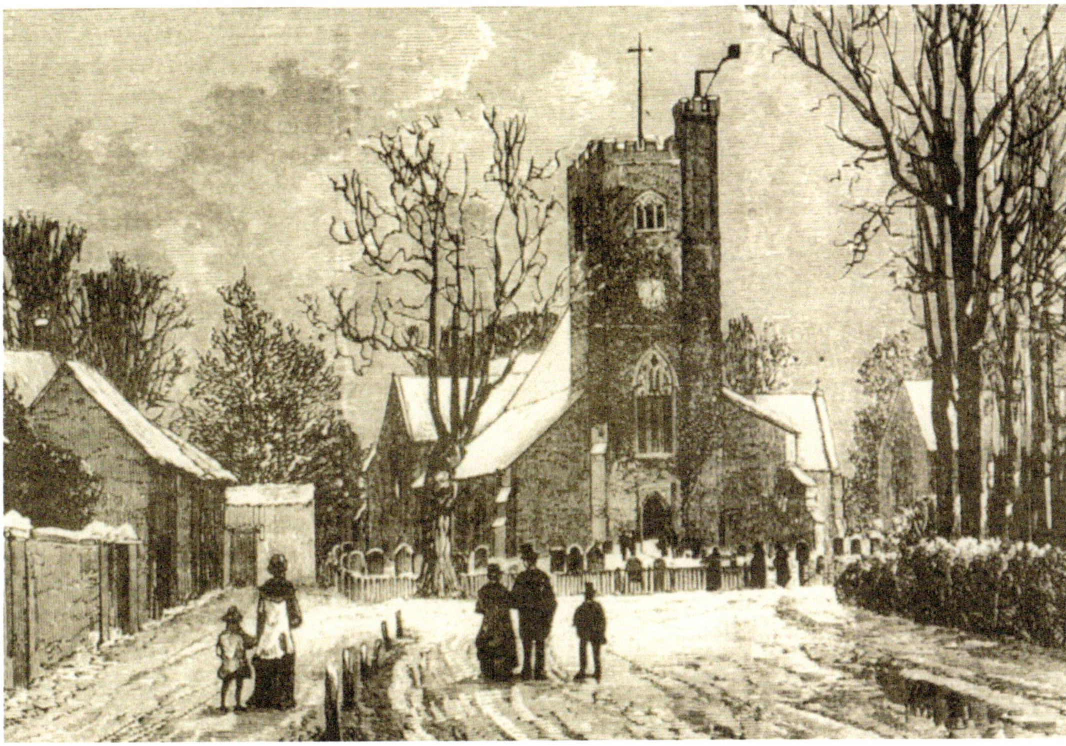

St Mary's Church

Above, the church of St Mary in Hadley, *c.* 1860. The preservation of the village makes the view in 2013 (*below*) instantly recognisable, although some of the buildings on the periphery are not the same.

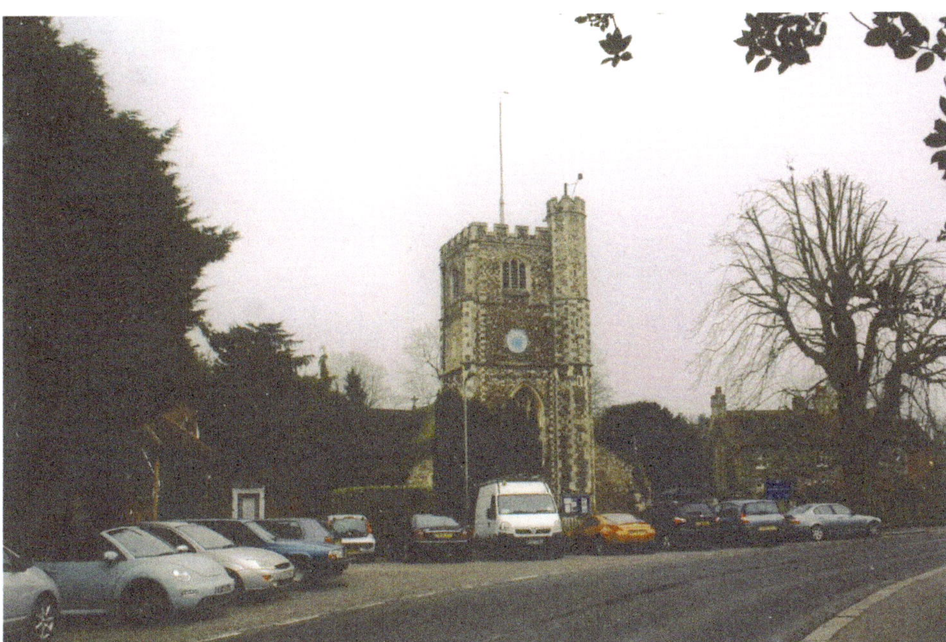

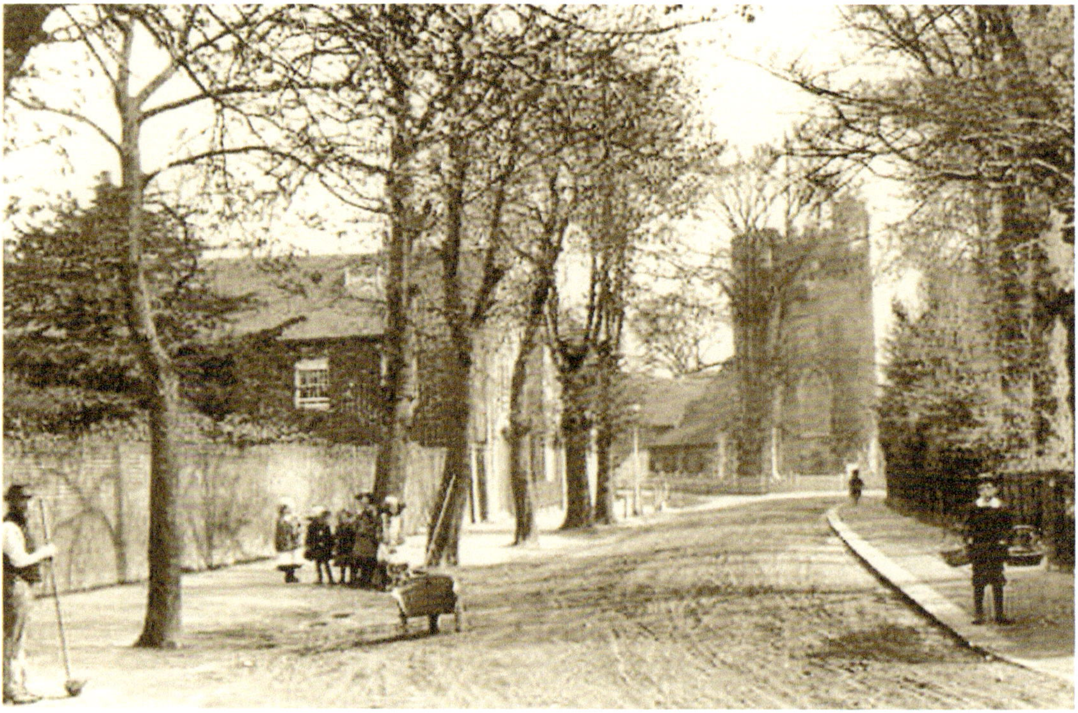

St Mary's Church

Two old views of St Mary's church, Hadley. The above image dates from around 1890, and below from the 1920s.

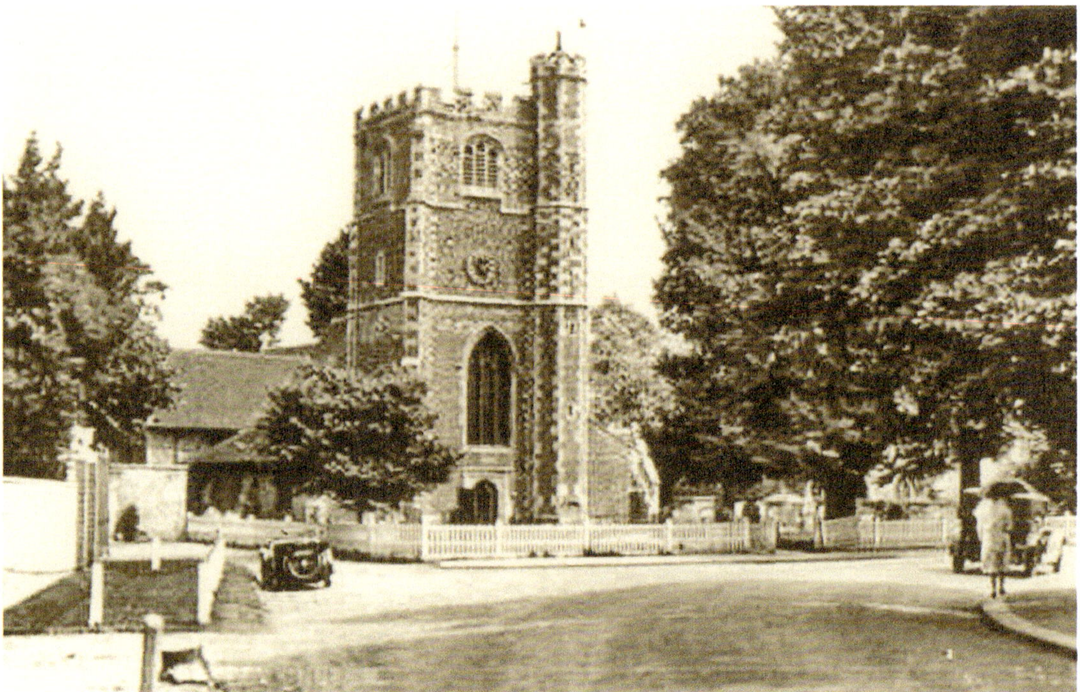

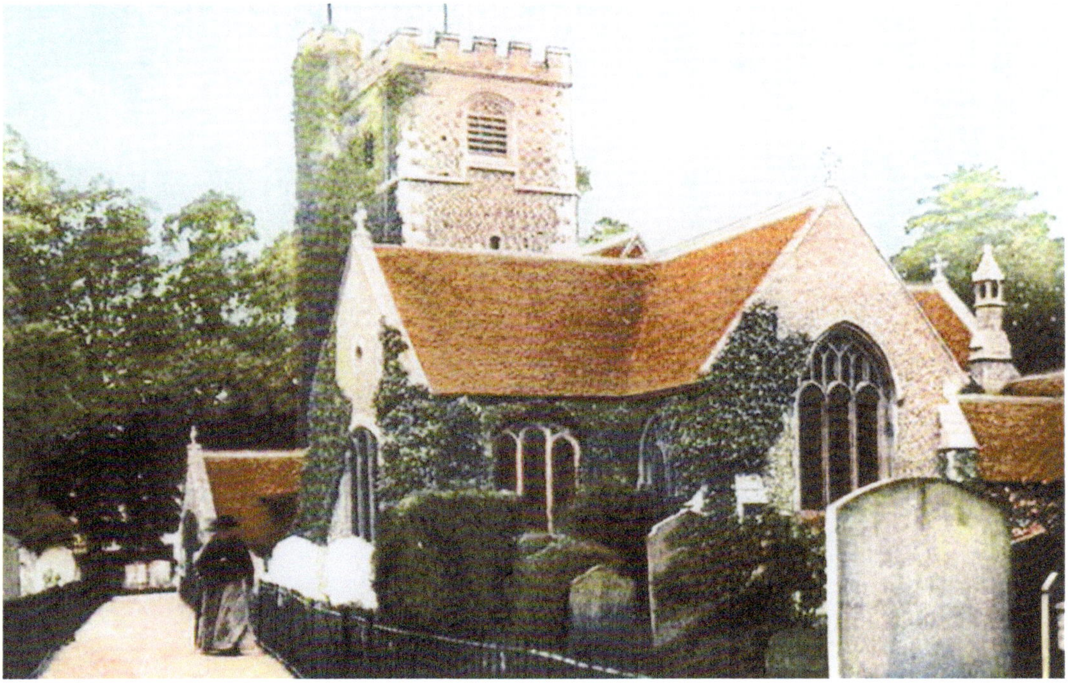

St Mary's Church

A colour photograph of the graveyard side of St Mary's church, Hadley (*above*), showing a woman in Edwardian dress. The picture dates from *c.* 1905. Apart from removal of the ivy, the addition of lighting and removal of the railings, little has changed in over a century.

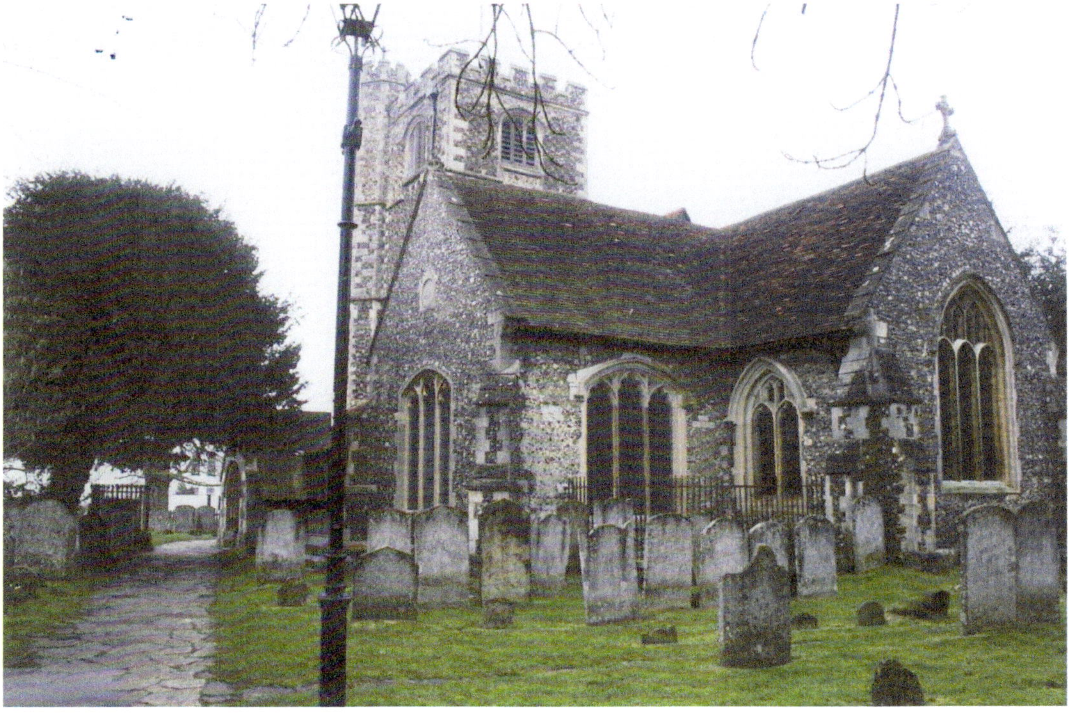

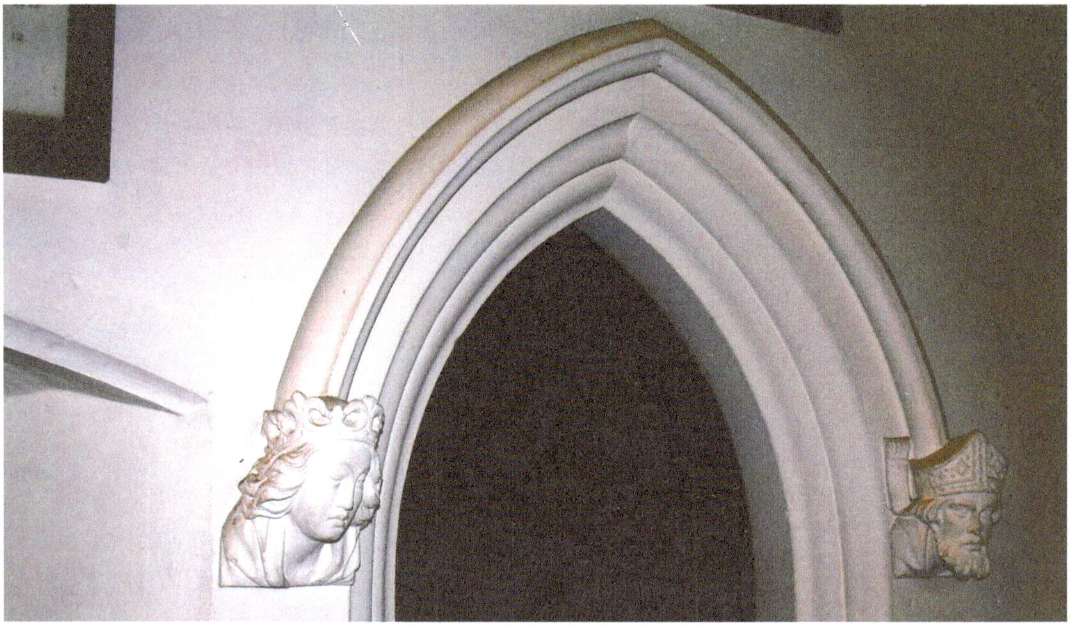

St Mary's Church, Interior

In 1848, G. E. Street replaced the old interior. The pulpit, galleries and plastered ceiling were moved, and the chancel floor, which had been below that of the nave, was raised a step above it. The church contains a number of ancient brasses, the oldest dated 1442, dedicated to Philip and Margaret Green and Margaret Somercotes. They are evidence of the earlier building. A wall monument to Sir Roger Wilbraham (*d.* 1616), by the elder Nicholas Stone, and one to Henry Carew (*d.* 1626) and his mother Alice Stanford (*d.* 1573), are of exceptional quality and poignancy.

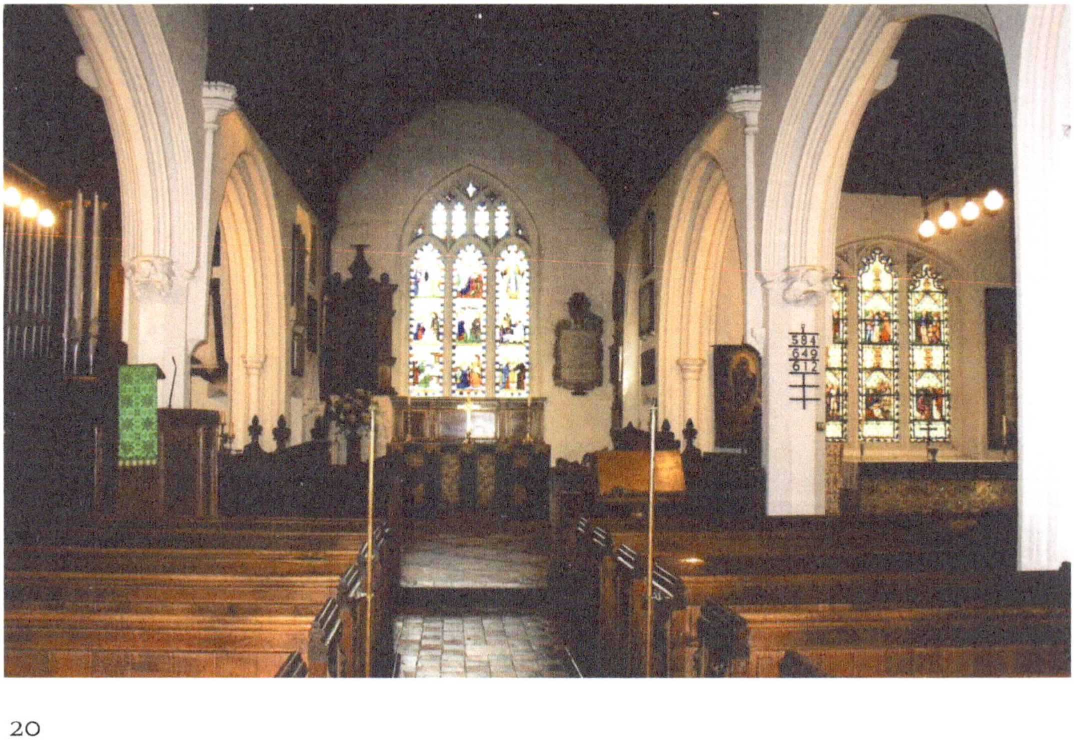

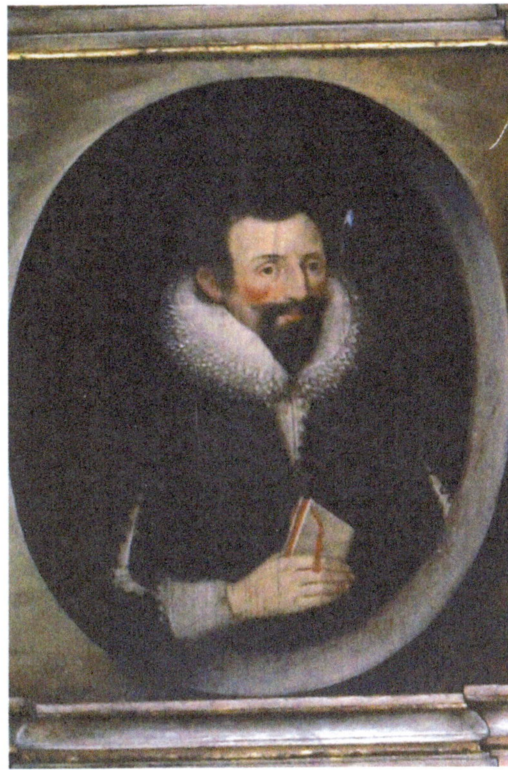

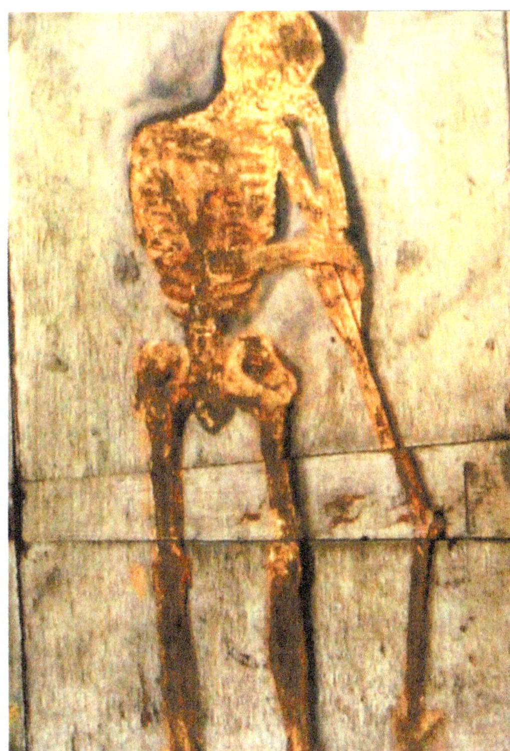

Henry Carew Monument
The monument to Henry Carew (1560–1626) and his mother Alice Stanford (*d.* 1573) contains a painted portrait of the son within an oval surround. The skeleton and skull motifs were very popular at that time, and were meant to act as a reminder of mortality and our ultimate fate. The mourning skeleton figure (*below*) is a detail from Carew's memorial.

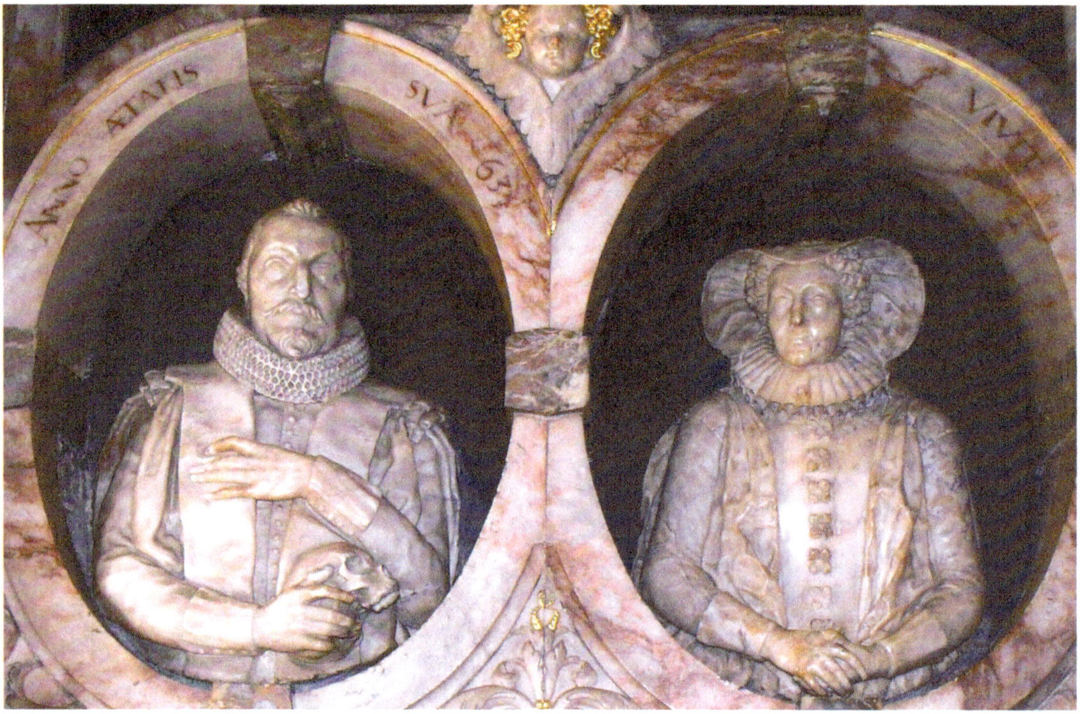

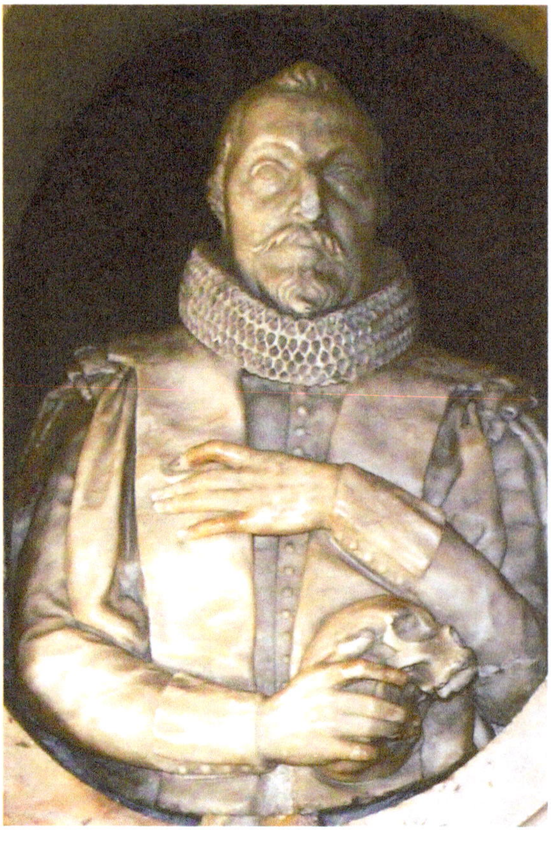

Roger Wilbraham Monument

Roger Wilbraham was born in Nantwich, Cheshire, in 1553. Wilbraham became a lawyer, and was admitted to Gray's Inn in London in 1576. On 13 February 1585, he was appointed Solicitor-General for Ireland, a position he held for fourteen years. He was elected a Member of Parliament for Callington in 1604, and returned as Knight of the Shire (MP) for Cheshire in 1614. He received a knighthood before 1613. In Monken Hadley, he founded the almshouses for 'six decayed housekeepers' in 1616. He died on 31 July 1616 at Monken Hadley, Middlesex, of an acute fever, most likely malaria. His wall monument by Nicholas Stone commemorating Wilbraham and his family was erected in the church at Monken Hadley in 1616, at a cost of £80. It has busts of Wilbraham and his wife, as well as figures of their daughters.

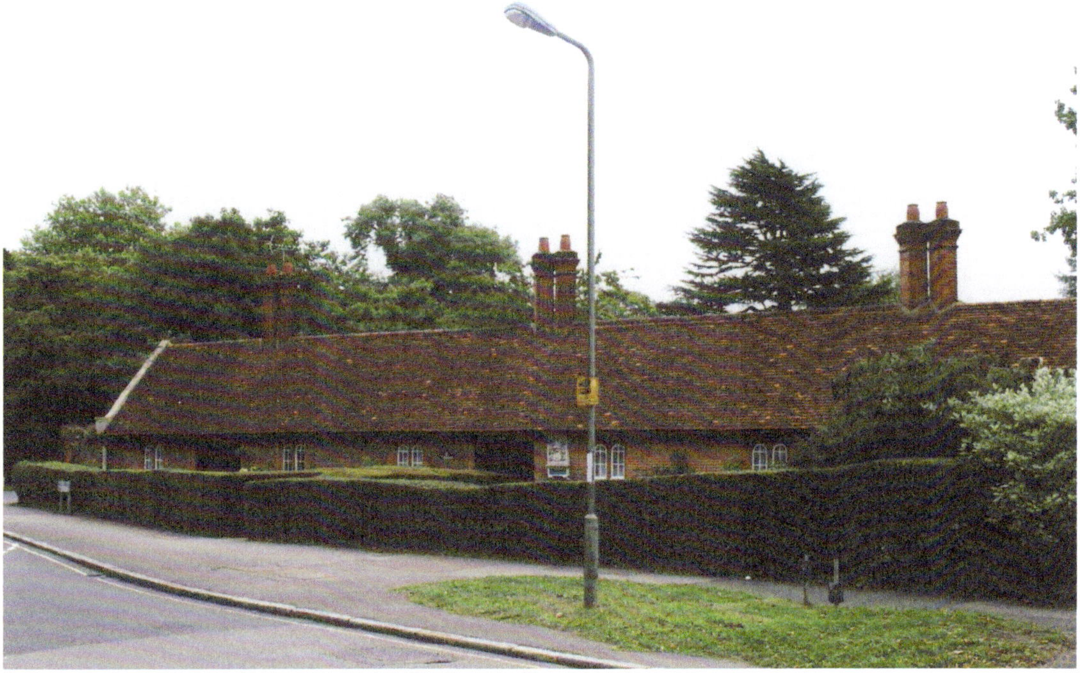

Almshouses

Above, the almshouses Sir Roger Wilbraham founded for 'six decayed housekeepers' in 1616. They are situated on the corner in Hadley Green Road, and are Grade II listed. Below is a photograph dating from *c.* 1905 with Hadley Common behind, and the church is on the right through the gates.

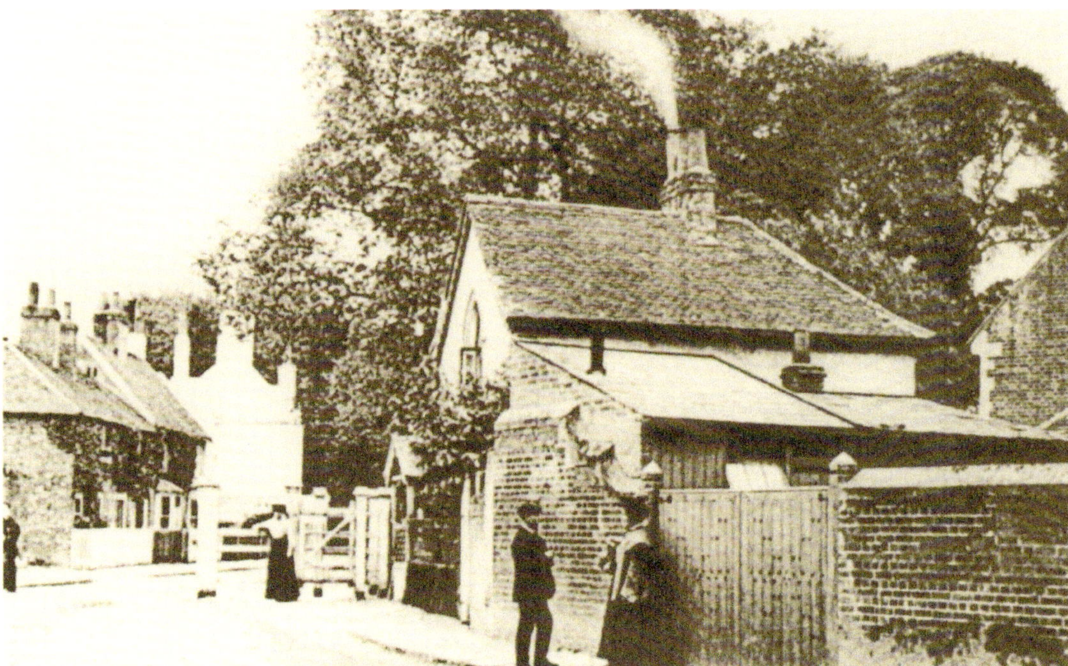

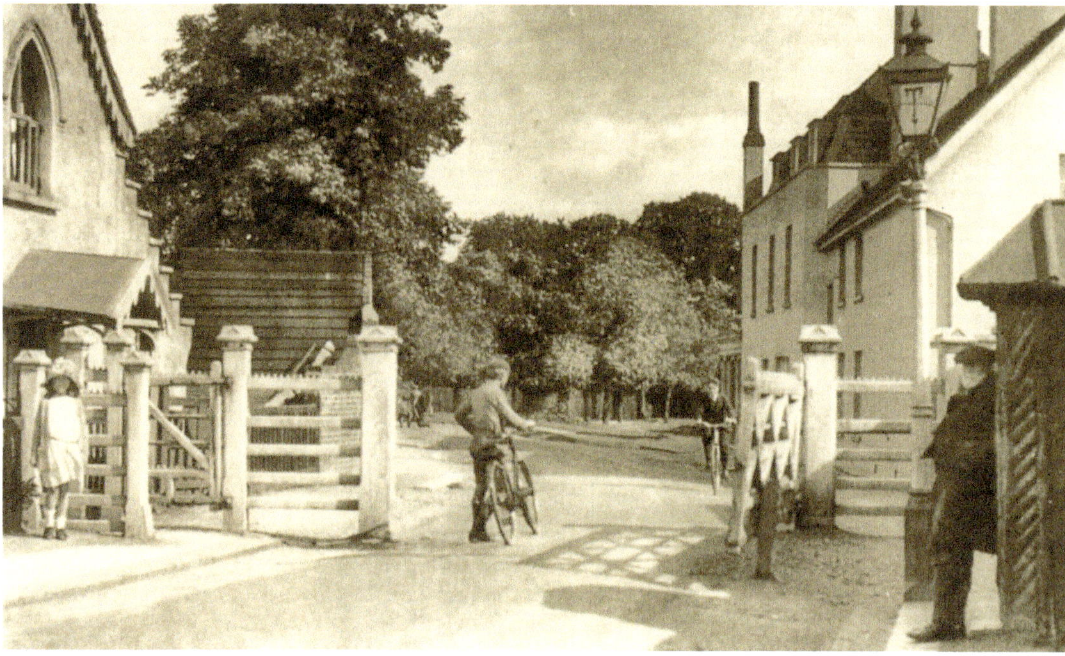

Hadley Lodge

The photograph above dates from *c.* 1920. Through the gate to the right can be seen Hadley Lodge, parts of which dated from the seventeenth century, which was destroyed in a fire on 19 April 1981. Below can be seen the replacement, which was finished in 1996.

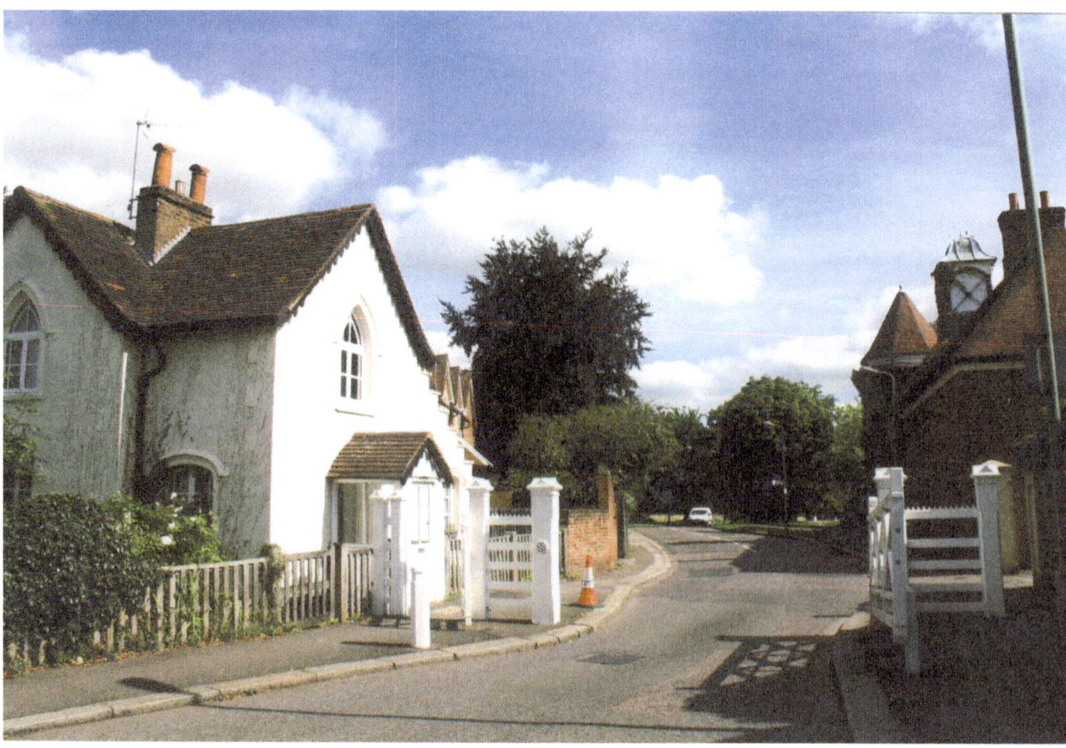

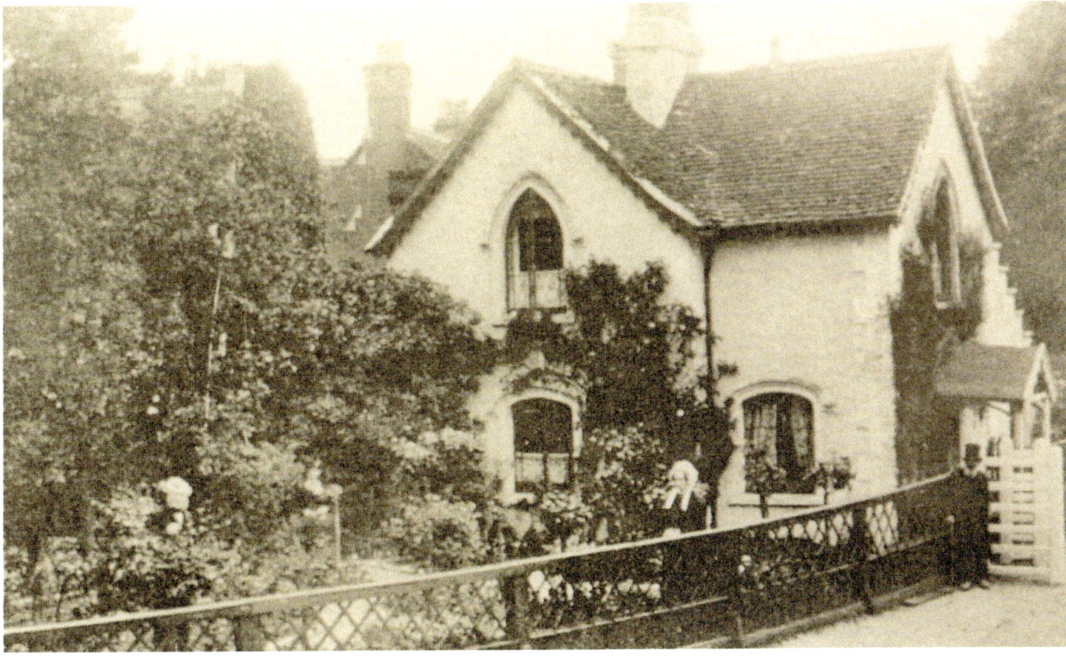

The Gate House
The gates seen here were not toll gates. This is a view of the Gate House from where the verger lived, taken around 1900.

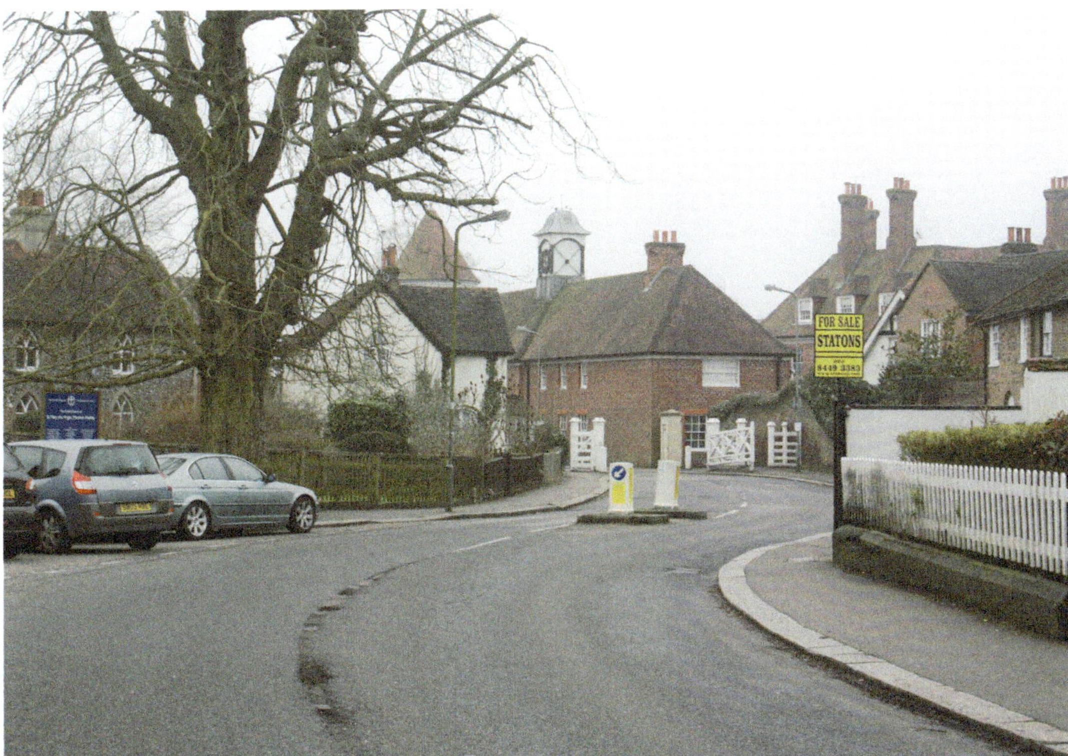

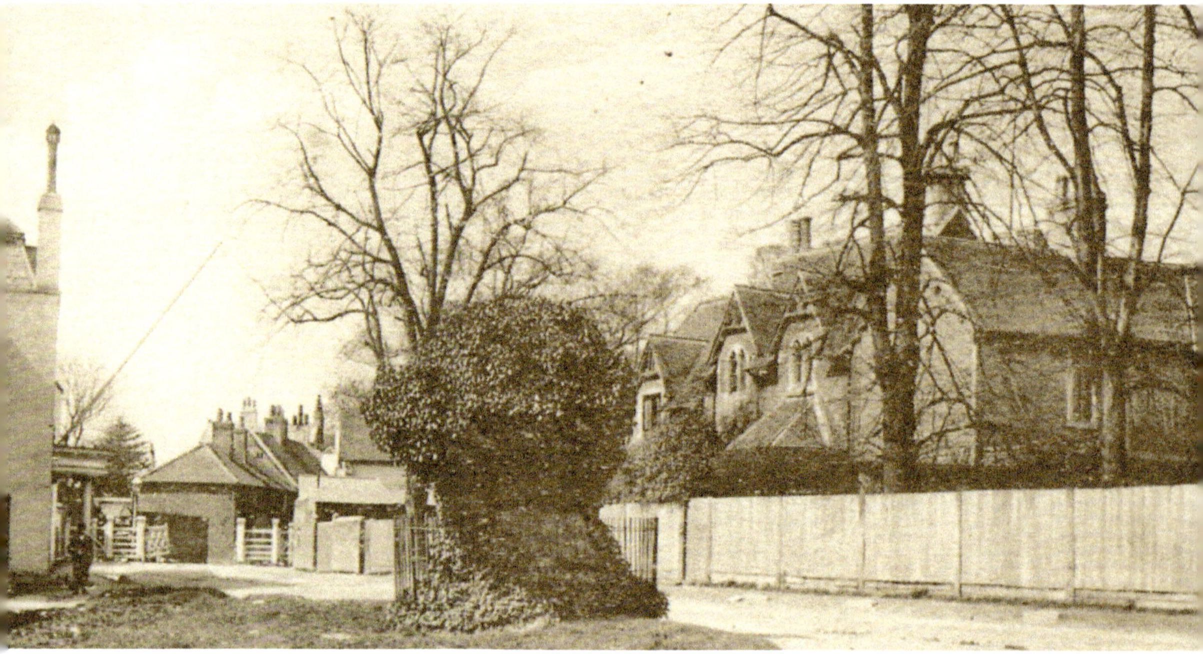

Warwick's Oak

Above is a picture of what was known as Warwick's Oak, and it survived until the railings were removed in 1941. It stood opposite the gate to Hadley Rectory, and in 1903 was recorded as having a circumference of 27 feet (8.23 metres). The tree reputedly marked the spot where the Earl of Warwick (The Kingmaker) was killed at the Battle of Barnet in 1471. It stood approximately where the modern tree is standing in the 2013 photograph below.

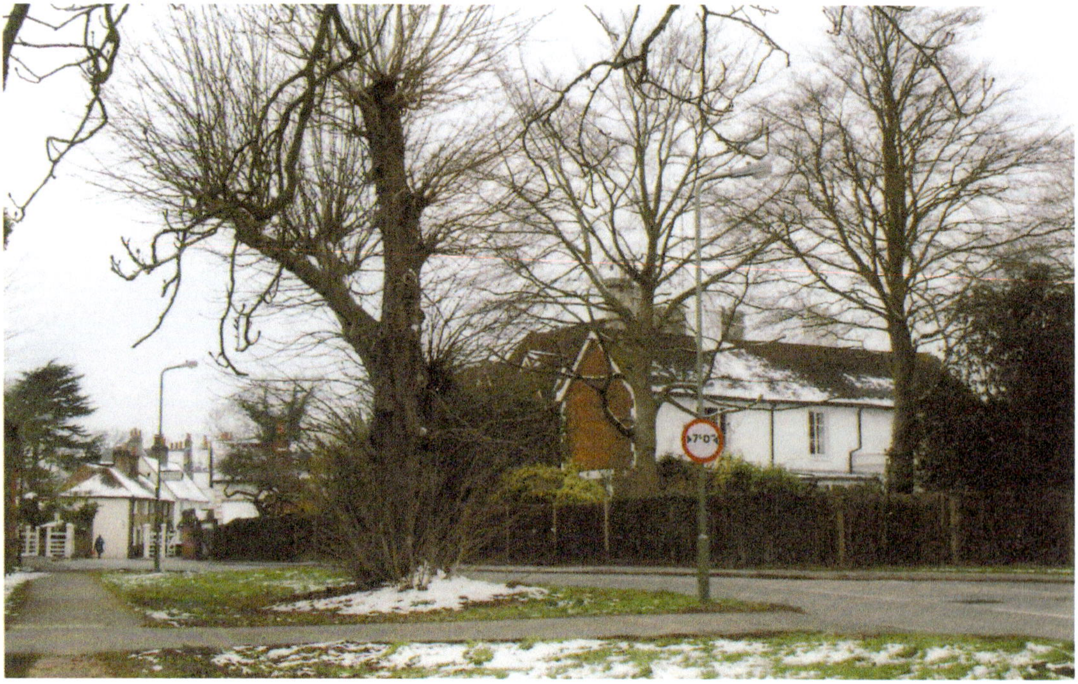

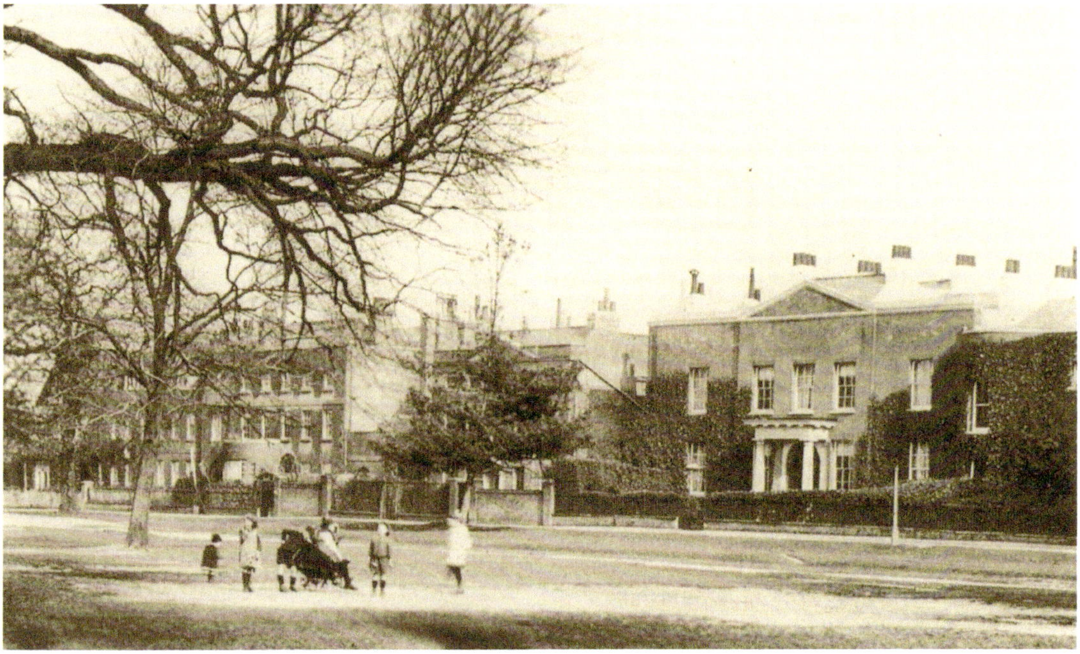

Hadley Green

On the south-east side of Hadley Green are a number of magnificent mid-Georgian and Georgian-style houses, which have housed a number of well-known persons over the centuries, as well as those passing through. In 1558, Elizabeth I stayed at Hadley manor house on her journey from Hatfield to London. The novelists Anthony Trollope (1815–82) and William Makepeace Thackeray (1811–63) had close connections with Hadley. The picture above dates from around 1905.

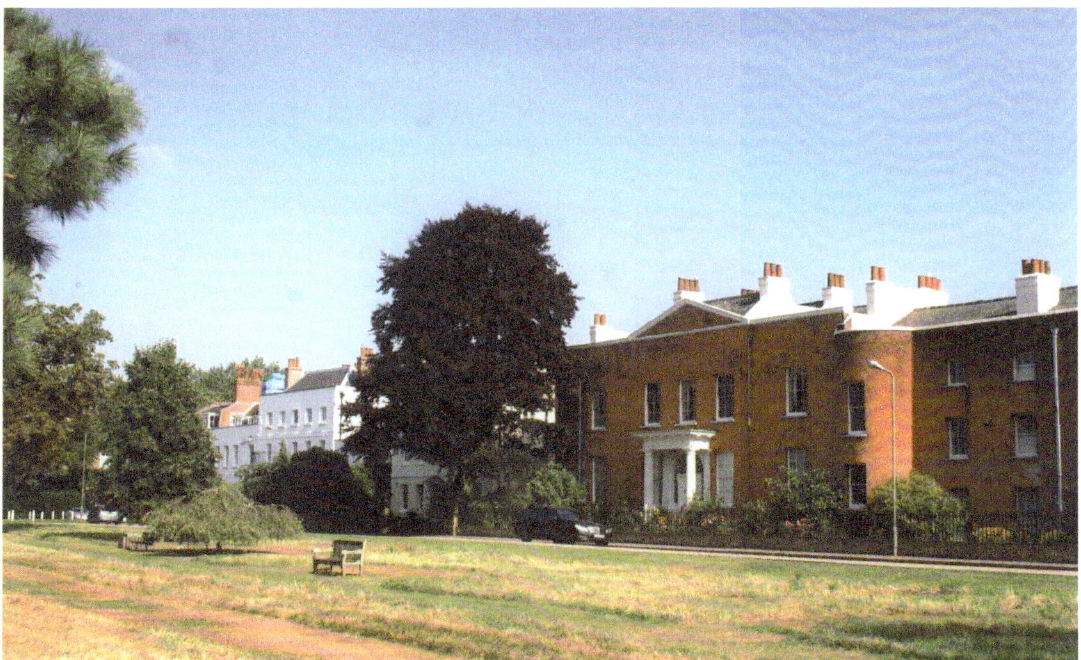

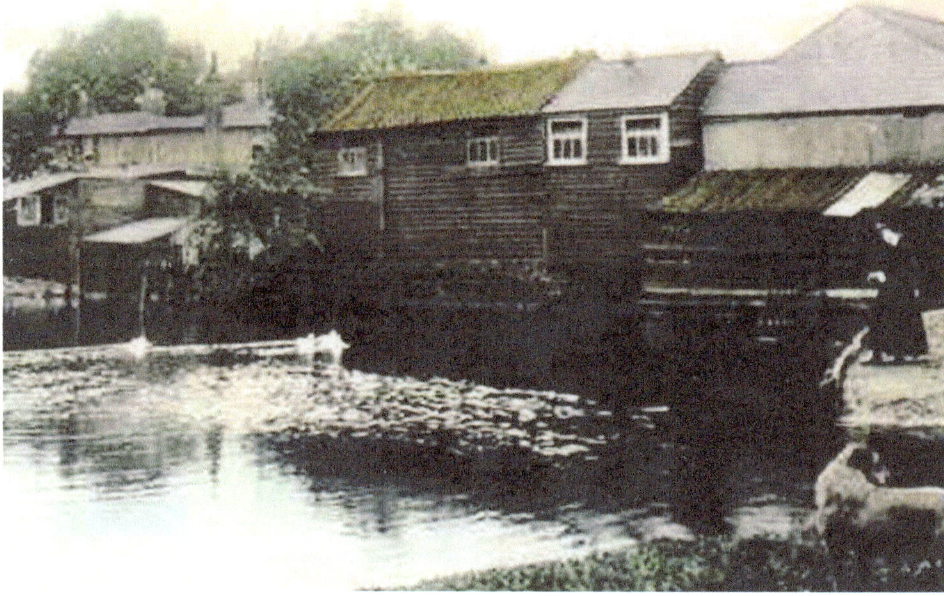

Hadley Brewery

In 1795, Hadley Brewery moved to a site at the northern end of Hadley Green. After changing hands a number of times it was acquired by Whitbread, who closed it down in 1969. It was demolished in 1978, and there are now houses built on the site, as seen below. The above picture dates from around 1900.

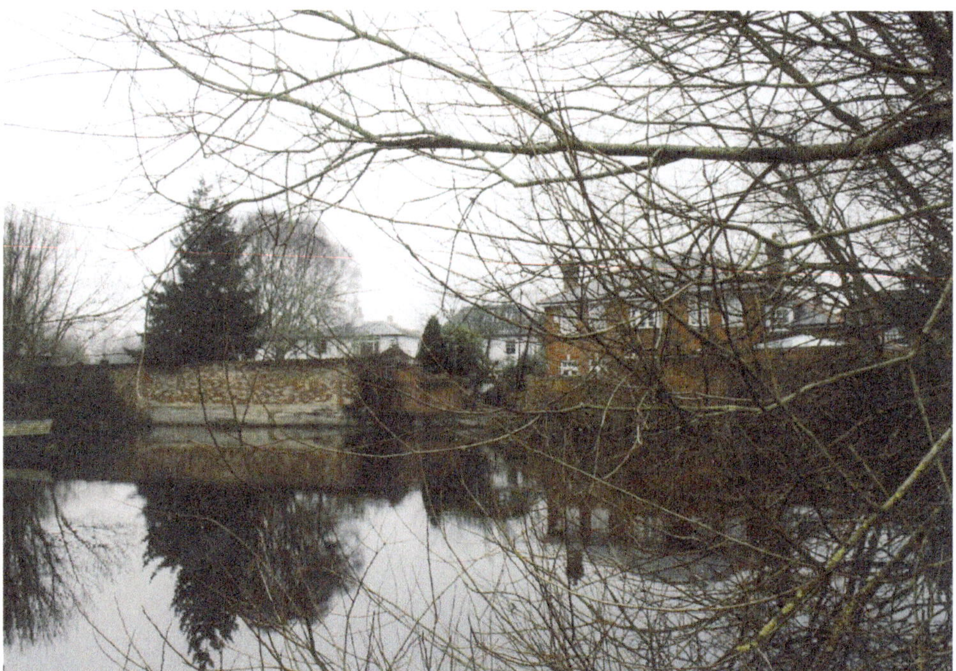

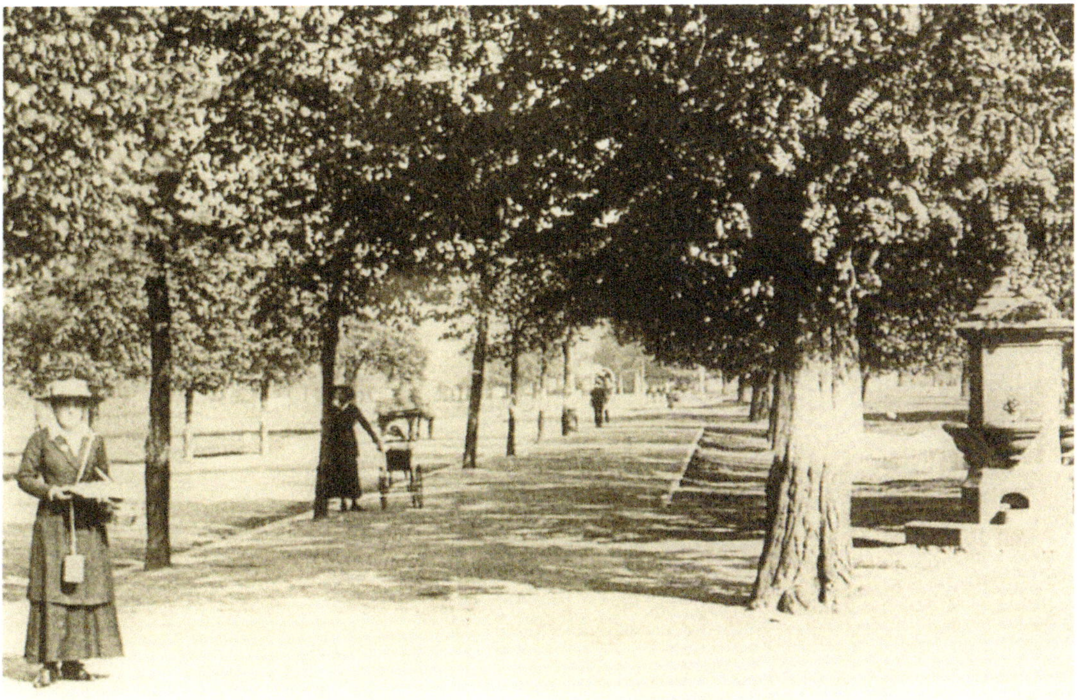

Great North Road

The Great North Road at Hadley. The picture dates from around 1910, and the drinking fountain was erected in 1885.

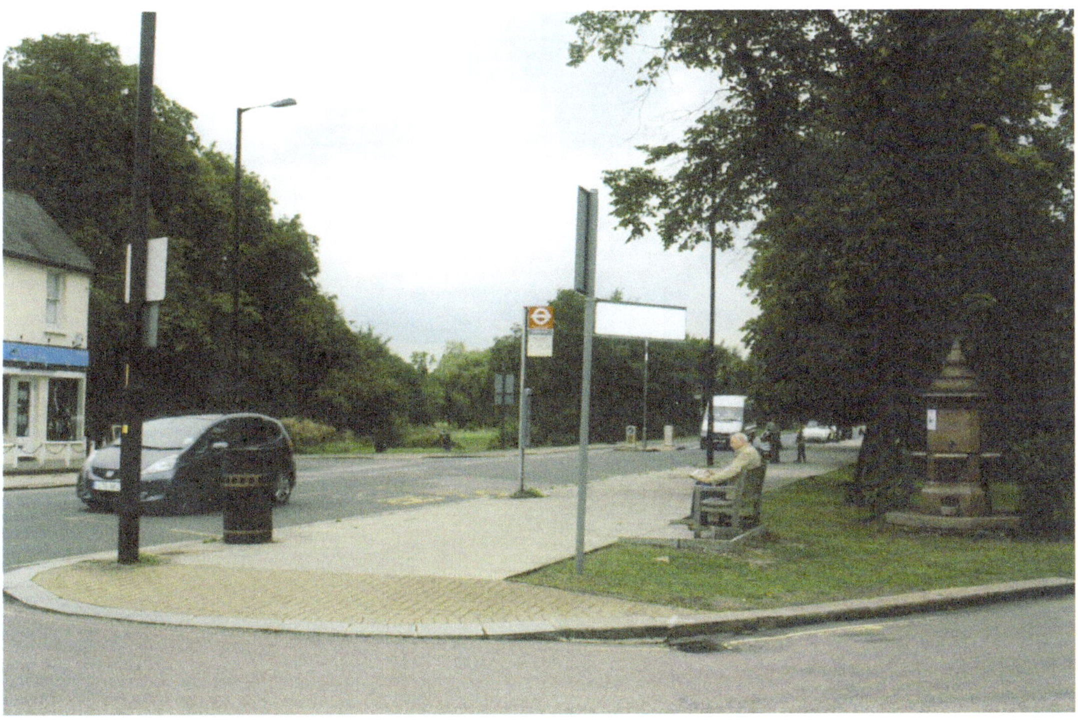

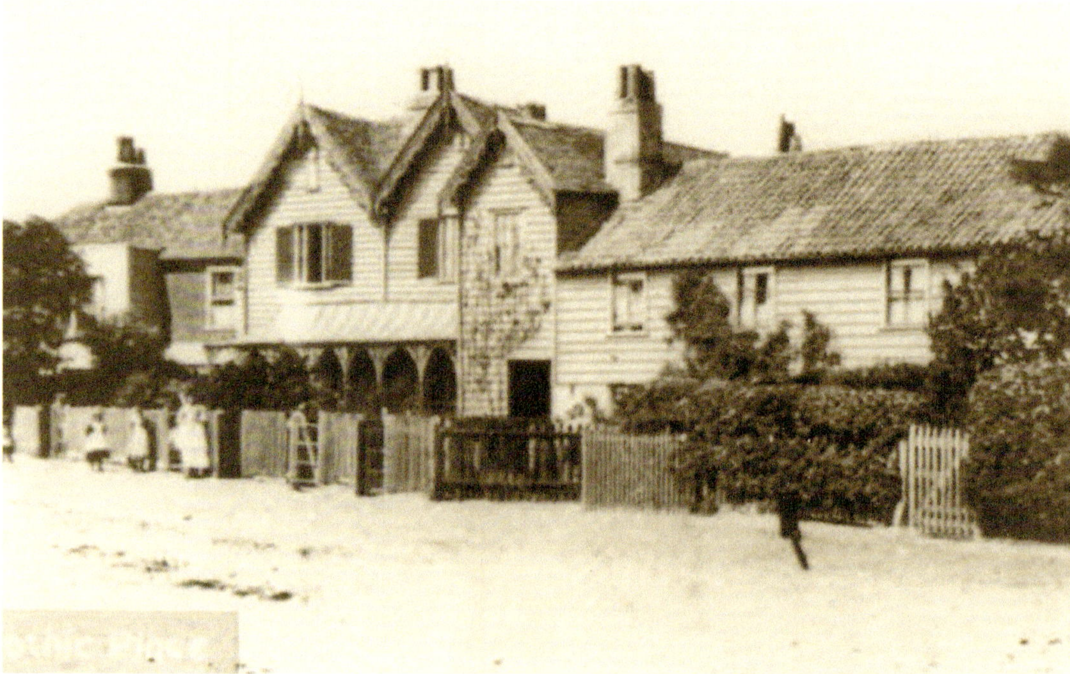

Gothic Place

Gothic Place in Drury Road around 1890. The building is still instantly recognisable in 2013, despite tree growth.

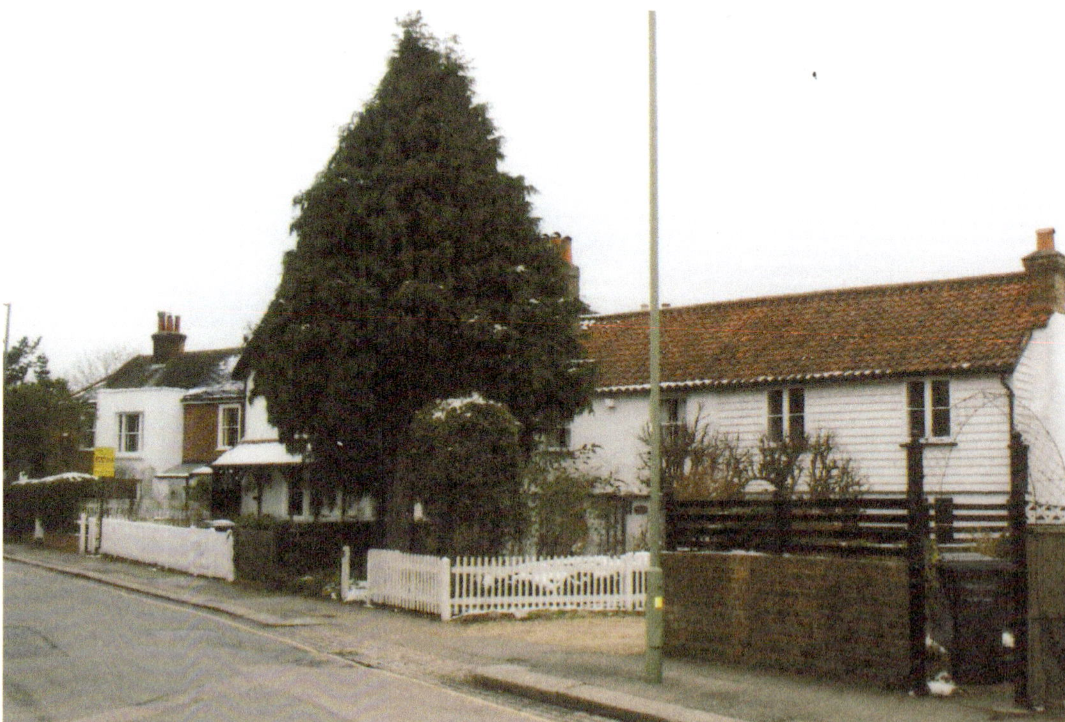

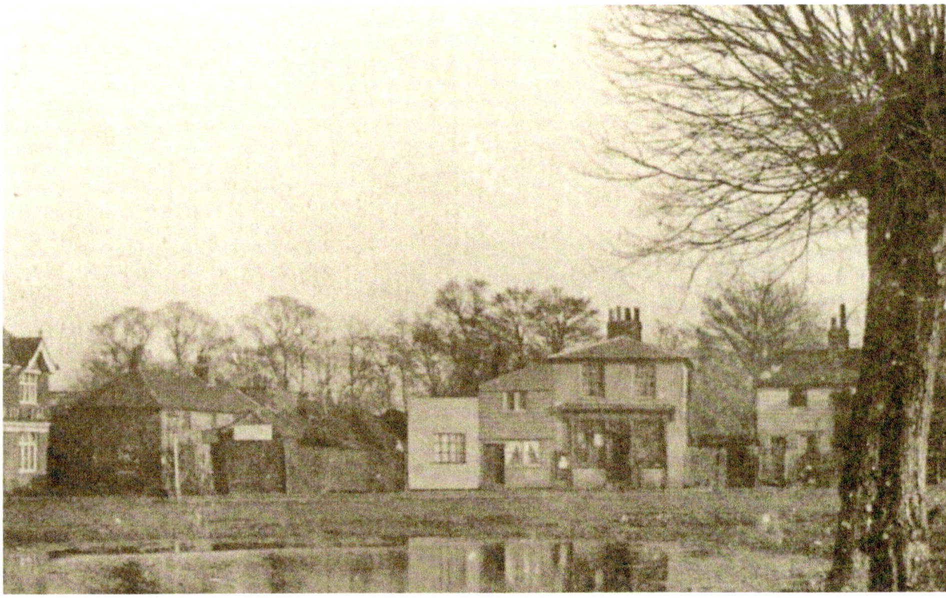

Hadley Green

The above photograph dates from around 1925 and shows the post office at Hadley Highstone. It was replaced by Hadley Green Garage, which is now closed. Below, looking north on Hadley Green in 2013.

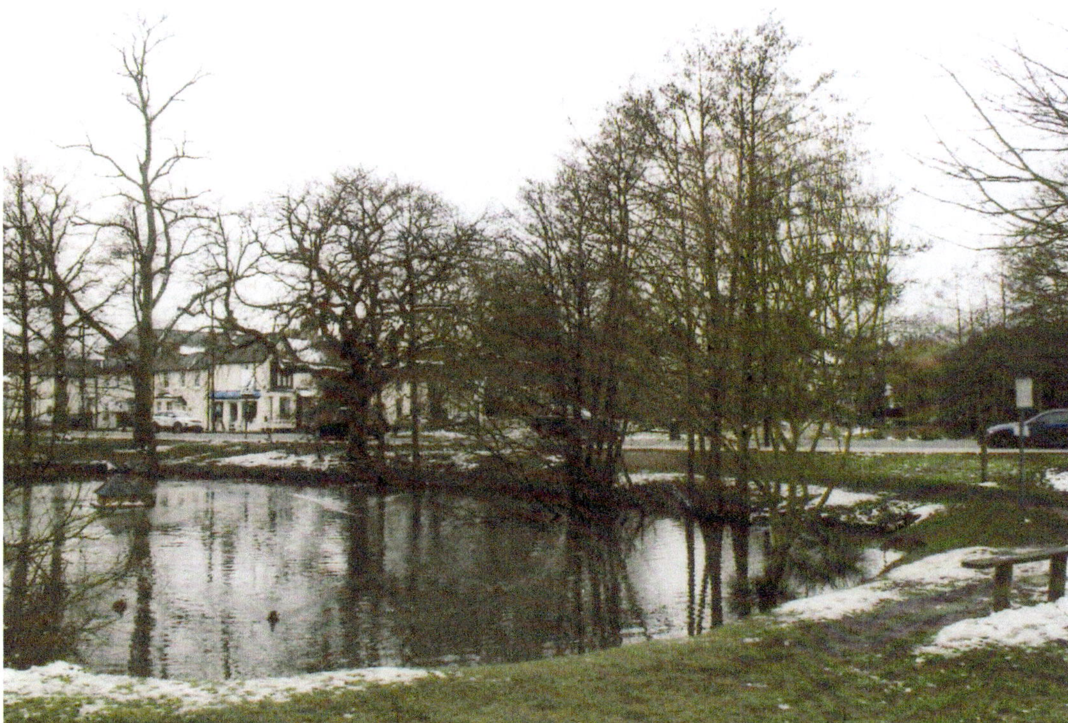

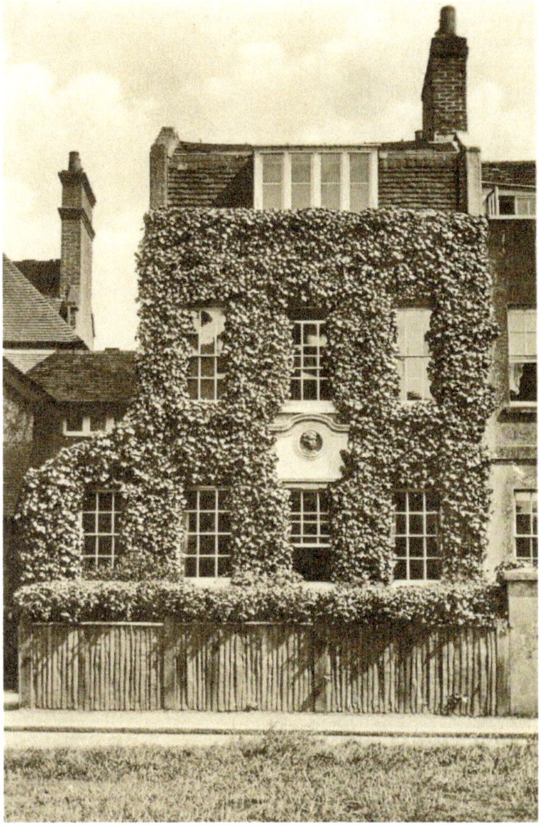

Livingstone Cottage

David Livingstone Cottage on Hadley Green dates from the middle of the eighteenth century. It was named after the brief residence of the Scottish missionary explorer, famous for his time in Africa. Livingstone stayed here in 1857/58, and wrote *Missionary Travels and Researches in South Africa*. He stayed for only nine months and later wrote, 'We spent no pleasanter time in England than the months in Hadley.' The house situated near the Wilbraham almshouses, externally at least, remains the same as in the old photograph.

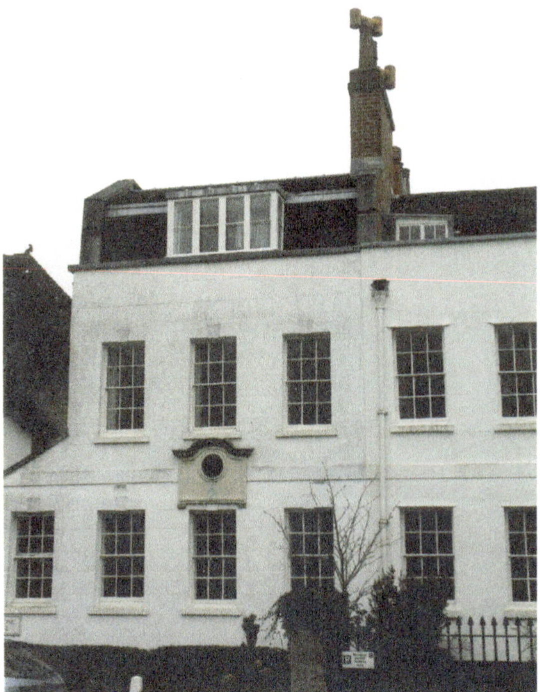

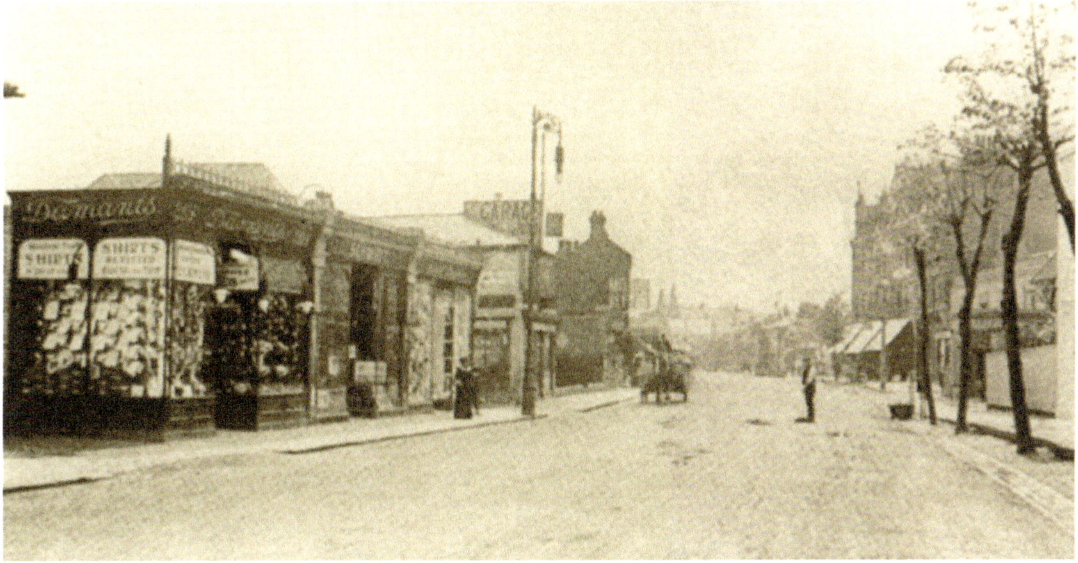

High Street, Barnet

The northern end of High Street, Barnet, looking to the south. The photograph above dates from around 1900. The photograph below, taken in 2013, shows the same shopping parade.

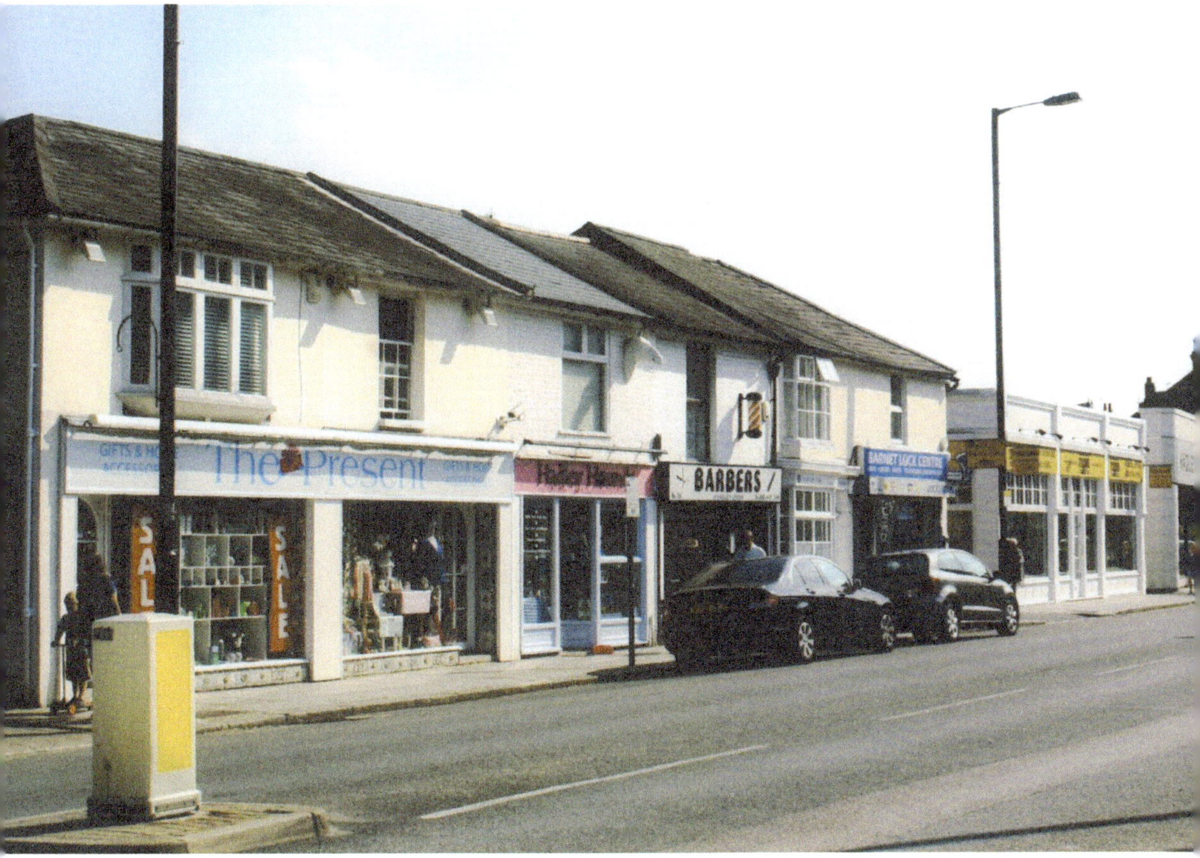

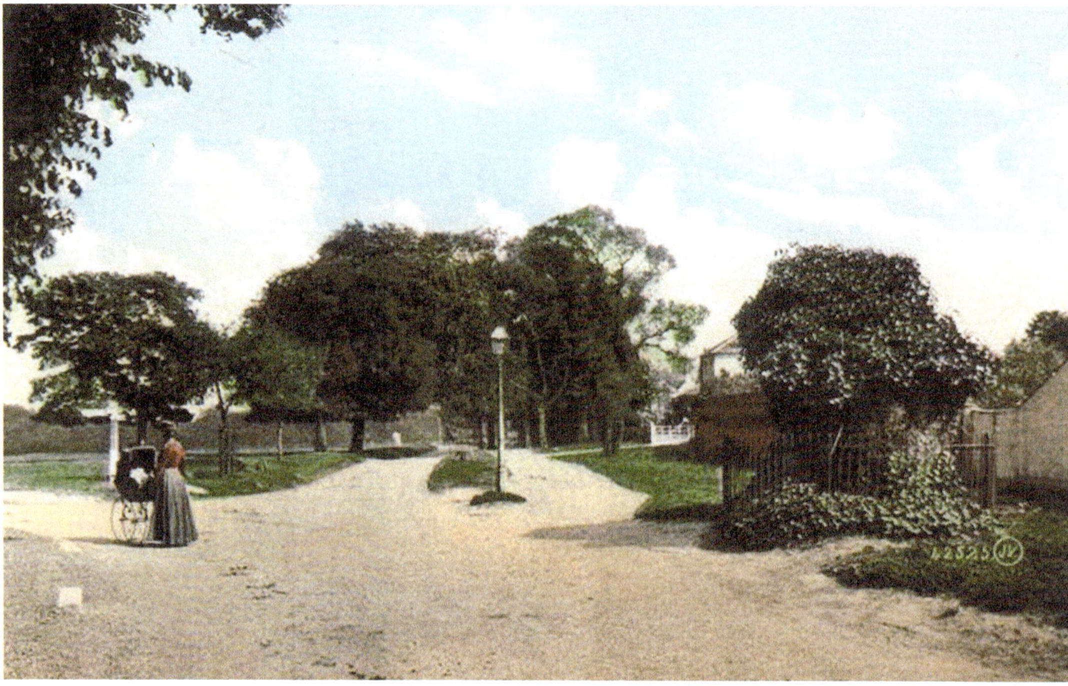

Warwick's Oak, *c.* 1900 and 2013

An Edwardian lady pushing a pram, *c.* 1900. Note Warwick's Oak behind the railings to the right. The gates leading to St Mary's church are directly behind the photographer. The same view is not easily recognisable in the 2013 view.

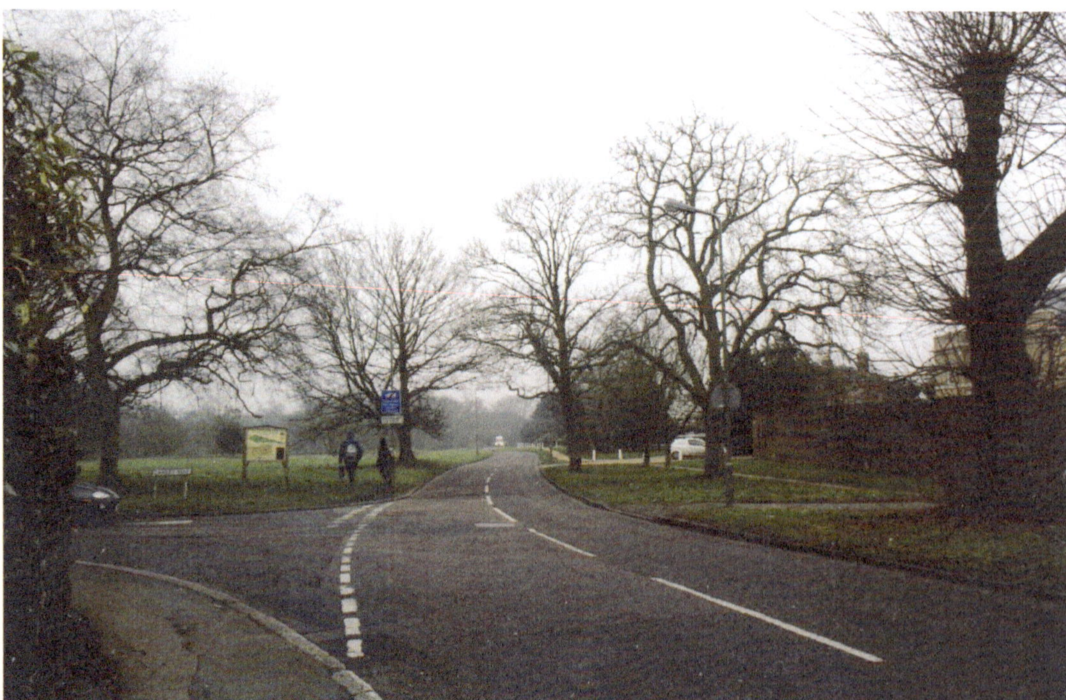

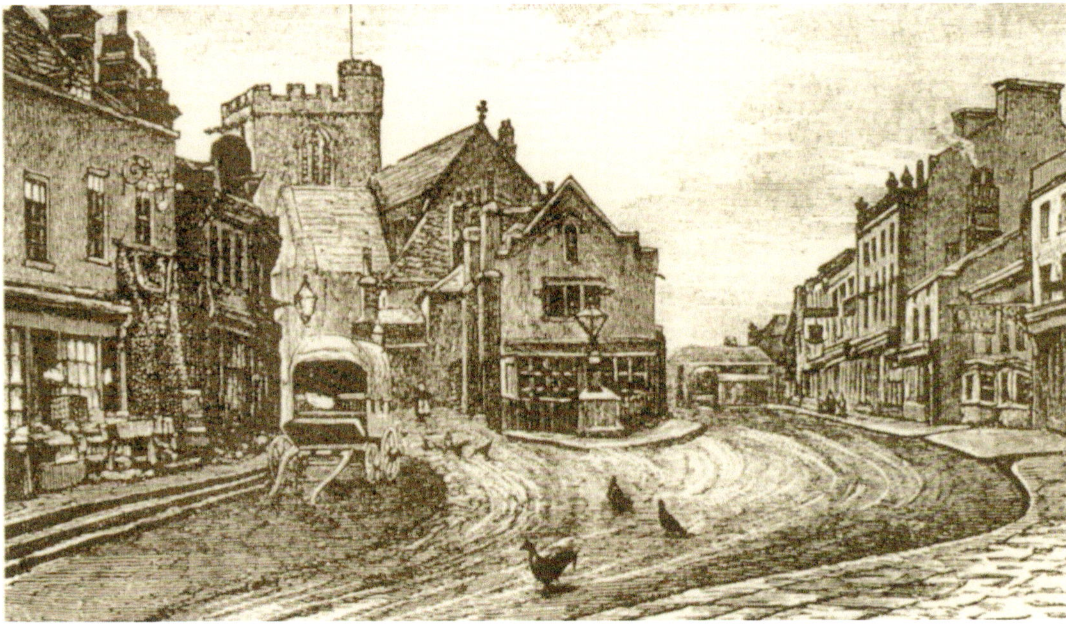

Wood Street and Middle Row

In 1817, Barnet was described as the 'second posting town in the kingdom, giving precedence in that line only to Hounslow'. With 150 coaches per day passing through, this was the peak. With the spread of the railways in the 1840s, it was clear that the end was in sight. A decline set in over the next few decades, which badly affected the numerous inns and businesses set up to serve the coaches. The sketch above shows a coach at the junction of Wood Street and Middle Row, the area immediately in front of St John's church. The sketch probably dates from around 1850. The photograph below was probably taken around 1885, as the building in the foreground burned down in 1889.

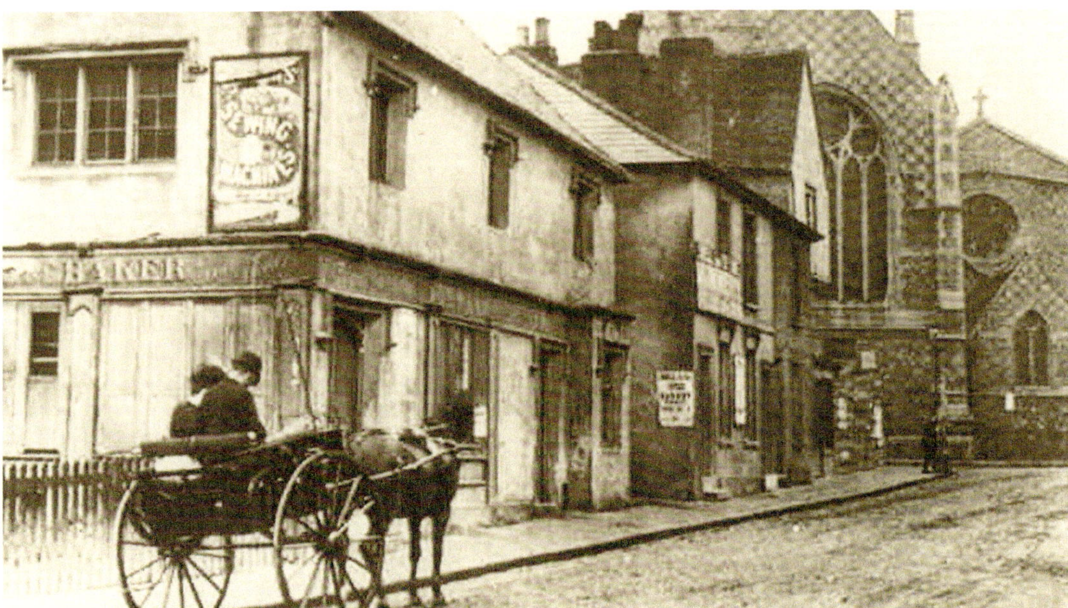

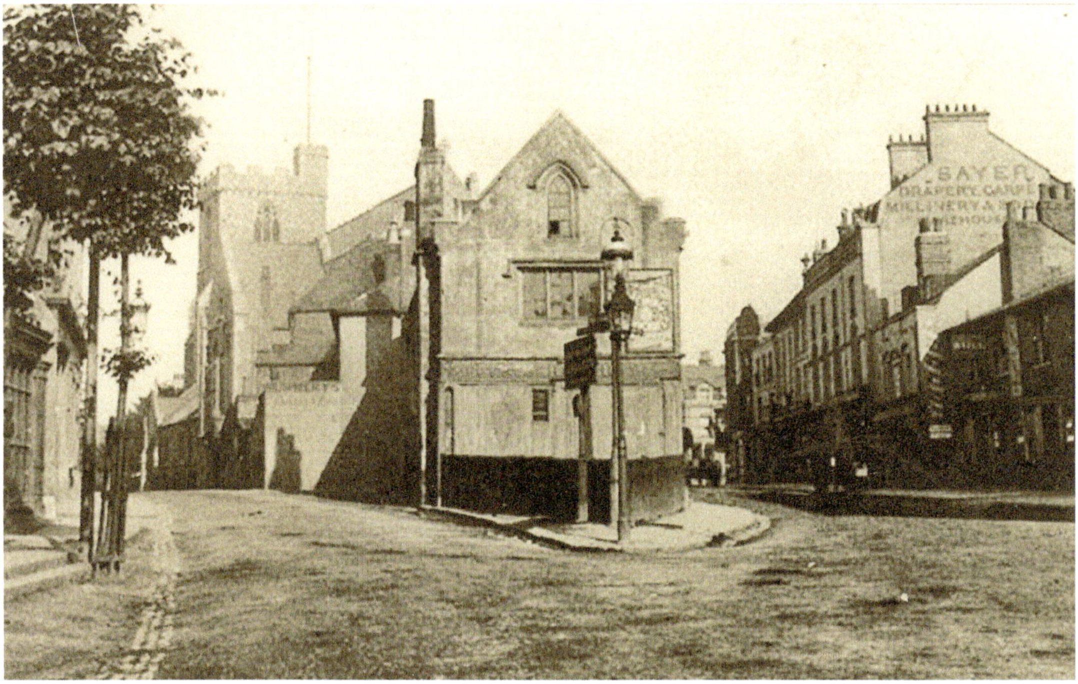

Barnet High Road

The photograph above predates 1889, when the old market building (*centre*) burned down and Middle Row was demolished, but comes after the installation of gaslights in Barnet High Road, *c*. 1870. The road to the left is Wood Street, and to the right is Barnet High Road looking from south to north. Below, the same view in 2013.

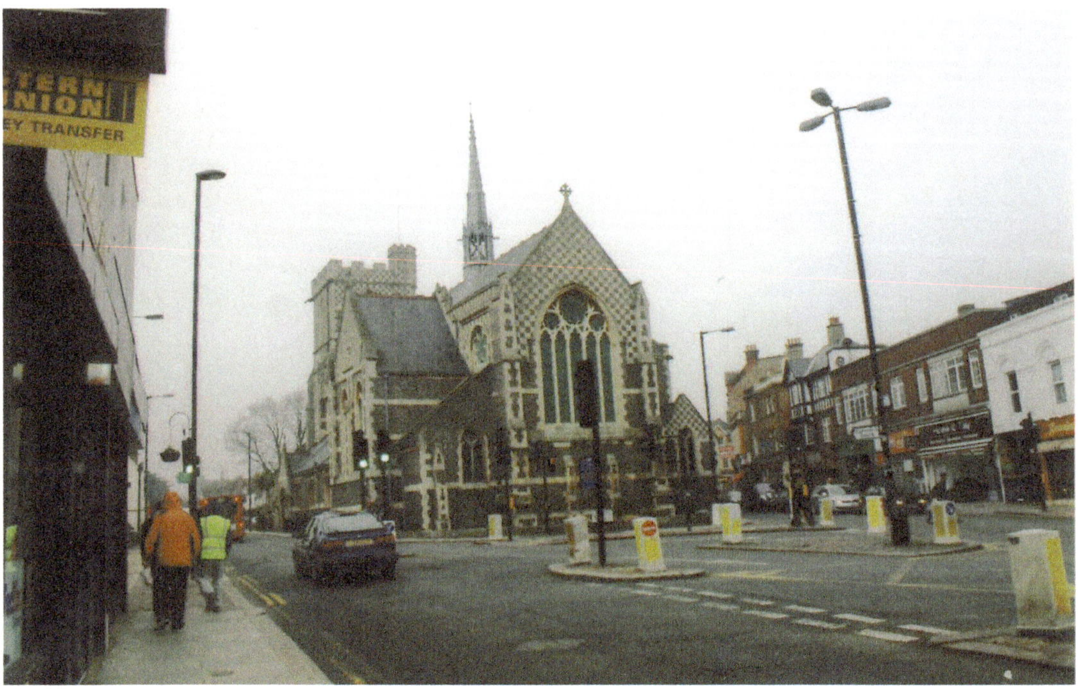

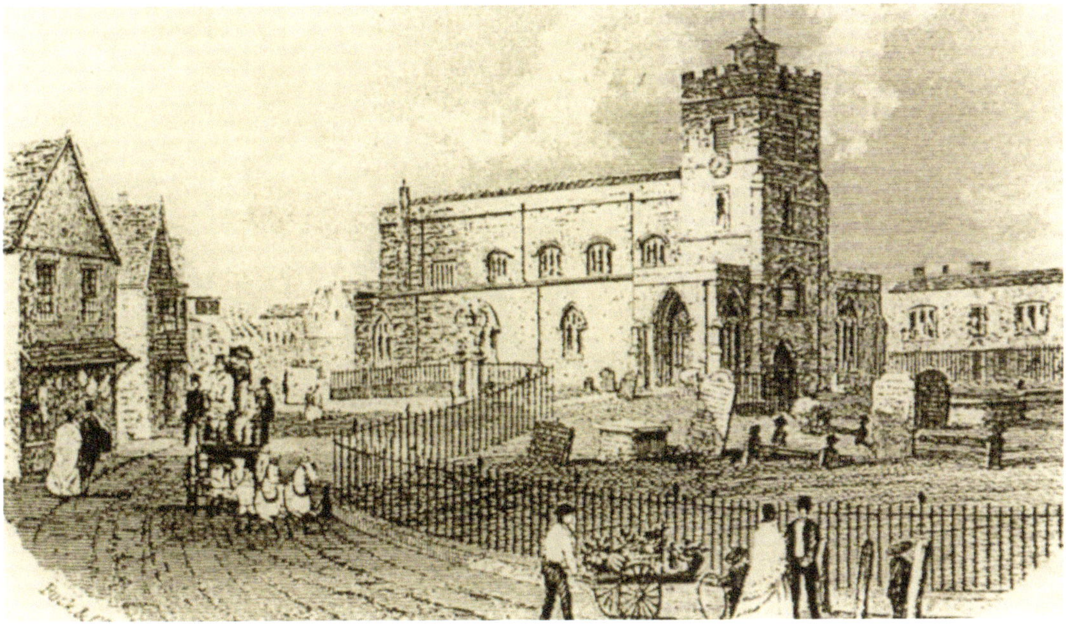

St John's Church

St John's church is referred to in a papal bull of 1157, and again in a court roll entry of 1276, which refers to it as 'the church of Barnet'. The mother church was St Mary's in East Barnet, which still retains much of its original character. St John's has been heavily restored, once by John Beauchamp, who died in 1453, and again during the latter quarter of the nineteenth century. What we see now dates mostly from the 1870s and 1880s, but there are a number of features from the mid-fifteenth century. The illustration above shows a stagecoach approaching the High Street, and the extent of the original cemetery, most of which is now paved over. The view is from north looking south in Barnet High Street in 1860.

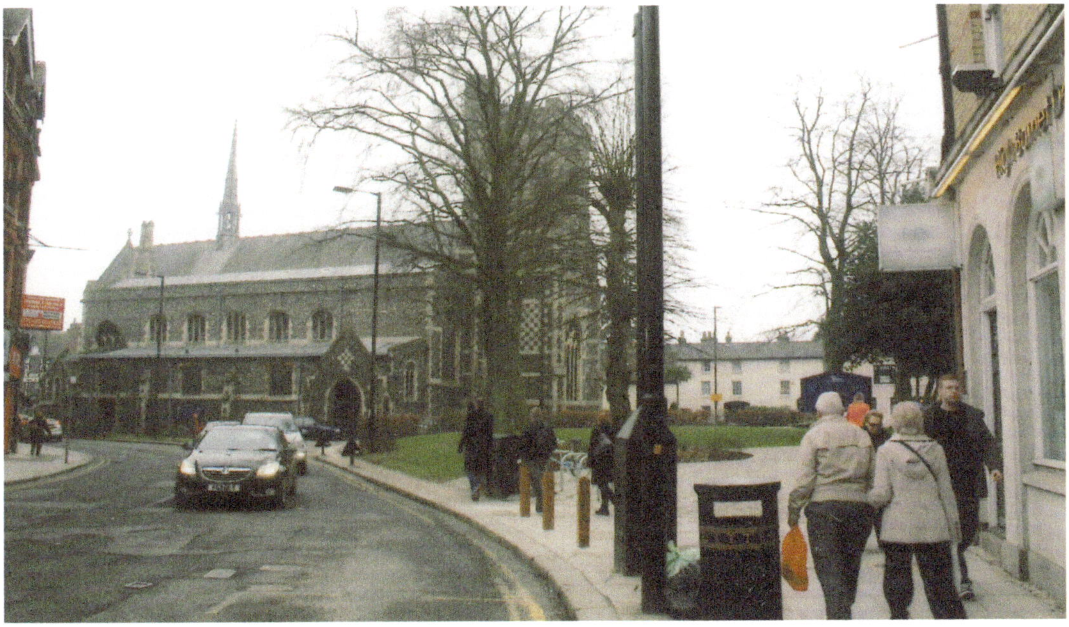

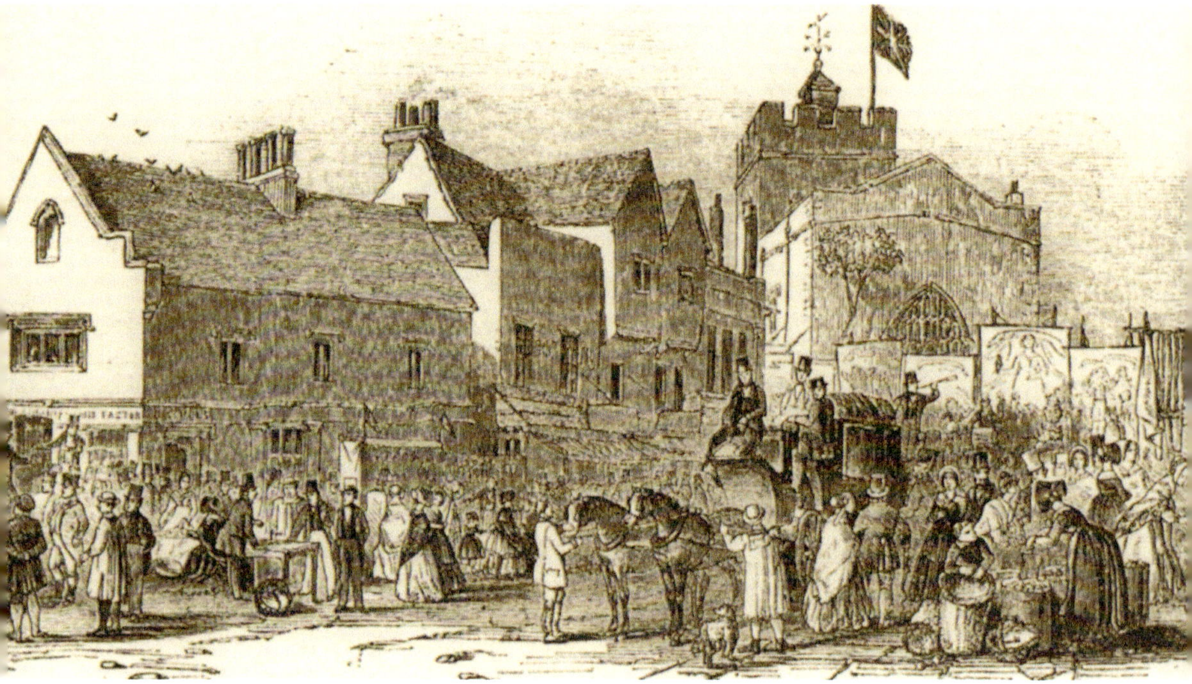

Barnet Market

The above illustration shows the market that took place in front of St John's church. The illustration dates from 19 April 1845.

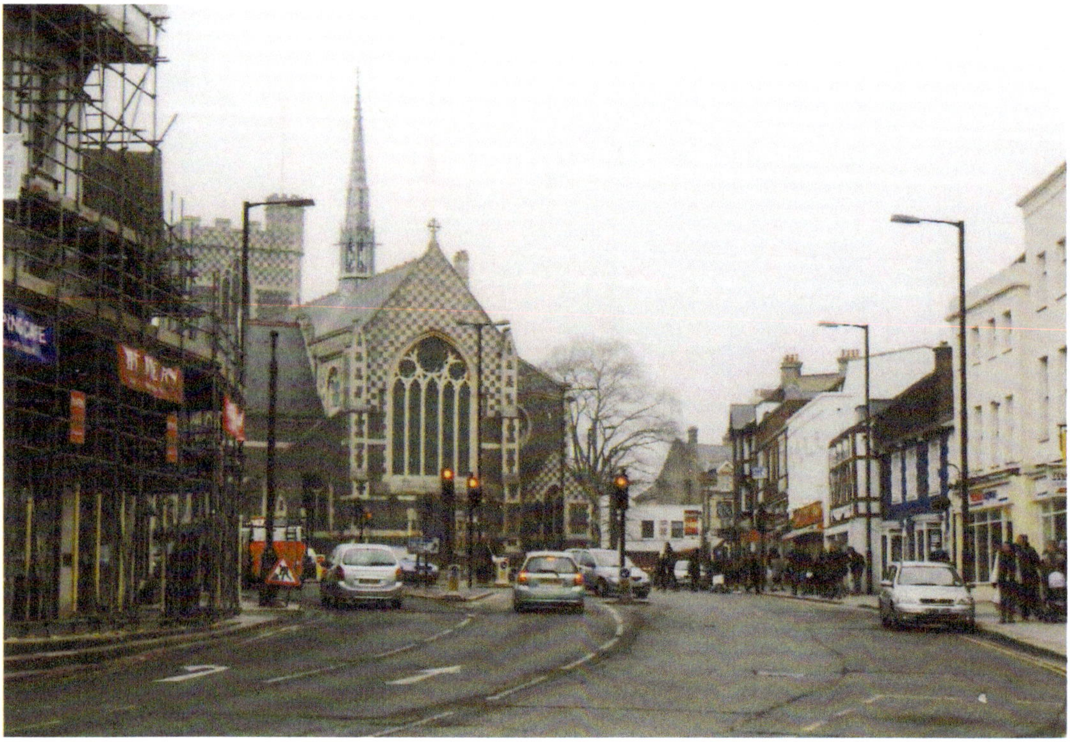

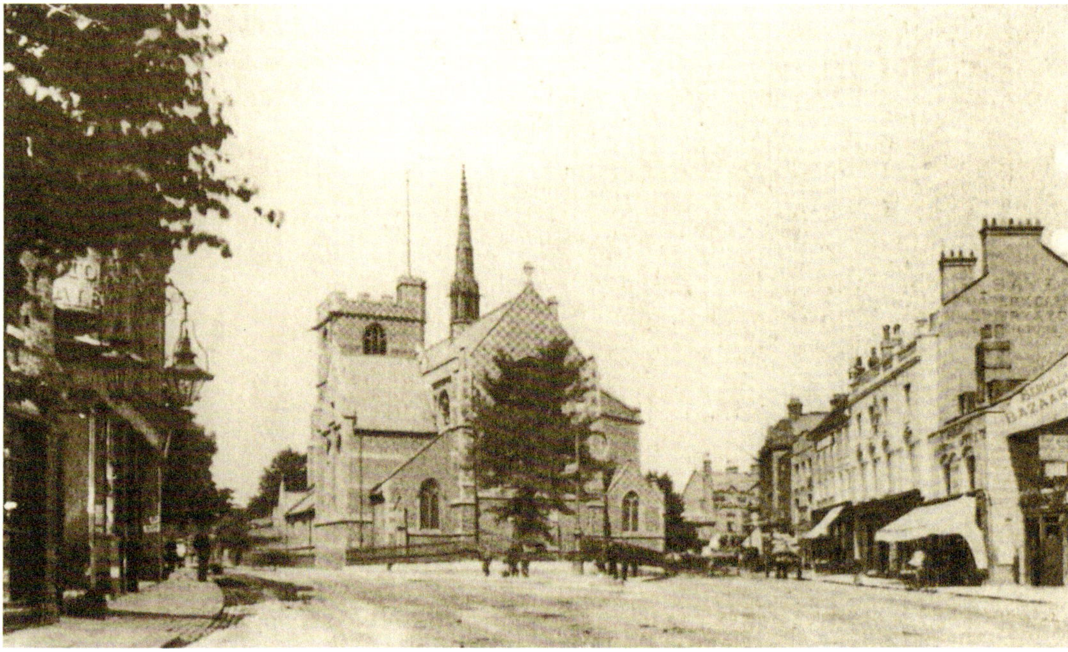

Great North Road

The illustration above dates from the period after Middle Row was cleared in 1889 and before the First World War memorial was dedicated on 3 April 1921. The memorial was moved to its present position in 1937. This area of the Great North Road had always been a problem. An Act in 1763 allowed a widening of the road 'by reason of the many great loads and carriages of goods and the many passengers and droves of cattle which daily pass therein'. It describes the difficulty and dangers of using this narrow and 'ruinous' stretch of road.

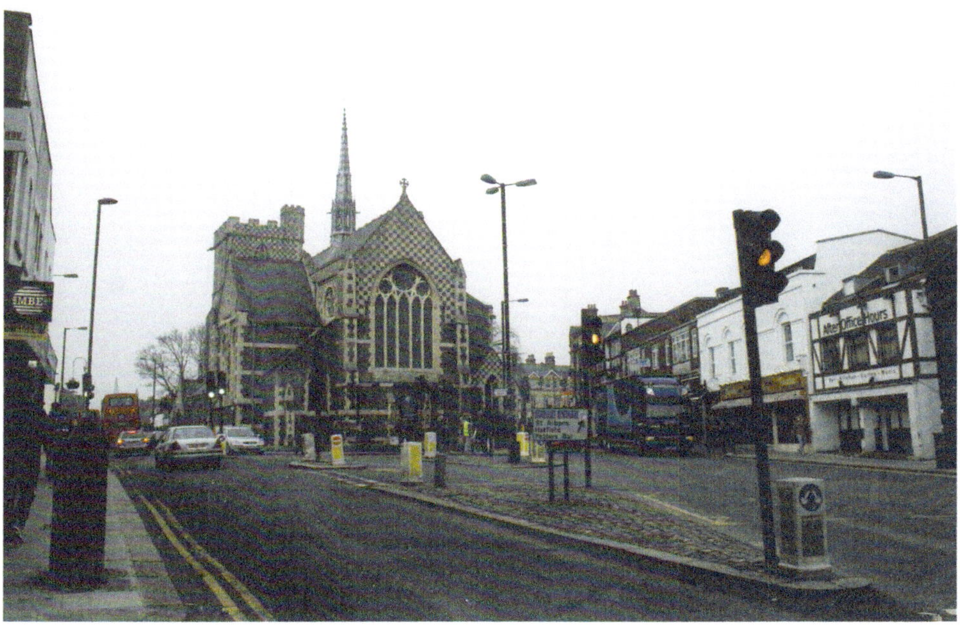

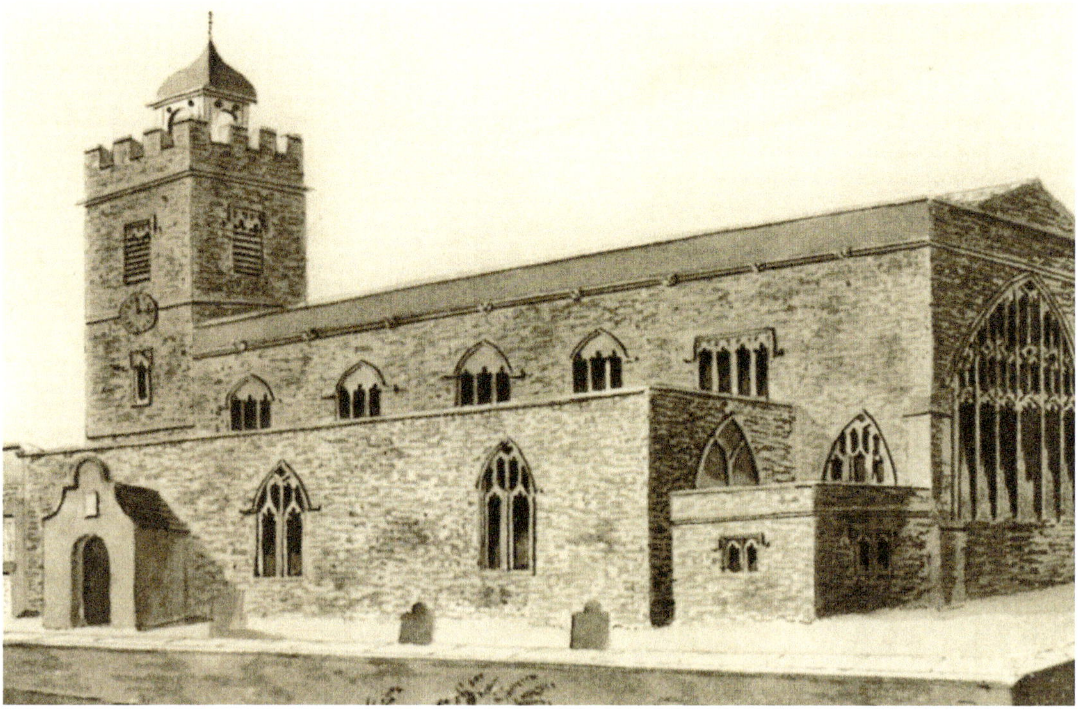

St John's Church and Ravenscroft Tomb

The above illustration of St John's in Chipping Barnet dates from around 1800, before the major alterations of the 1870s and 1880s took place. Below is the tomb of Thomas Ravenscroft.

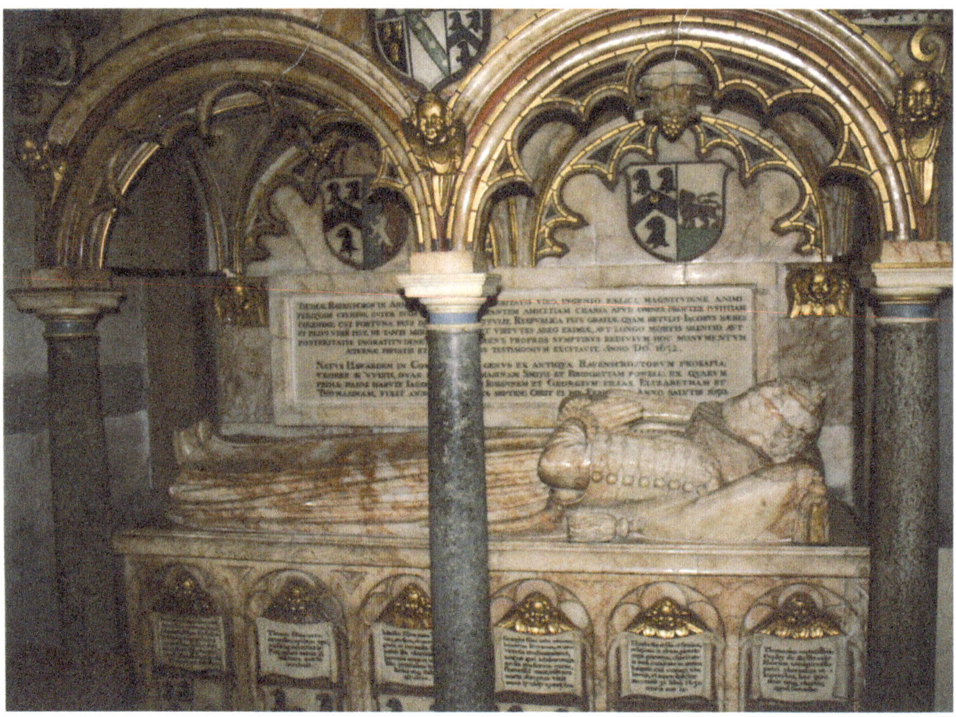

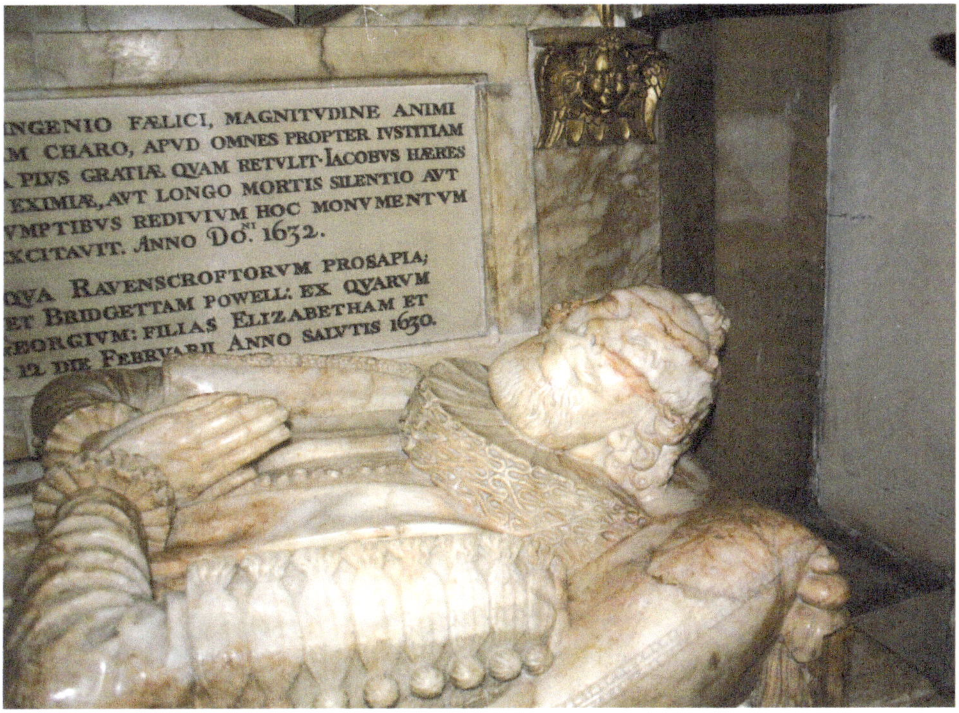

Ravenscroft Tomb

Above is detail from the Ravenscroft tomb. It resides in a small chapel built to contain the monuments of the Ravenscroft family, moved from their place in the old chancel. Thomas Ravenscroft died in 1630 and the tomb was set up in 1632. Below is the interior of St John's church in 2013.

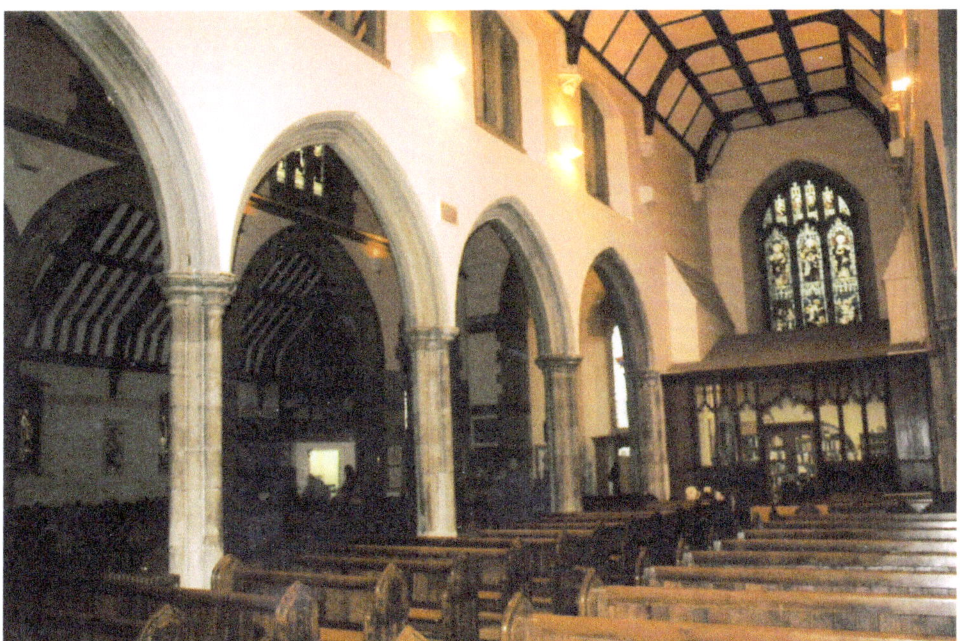

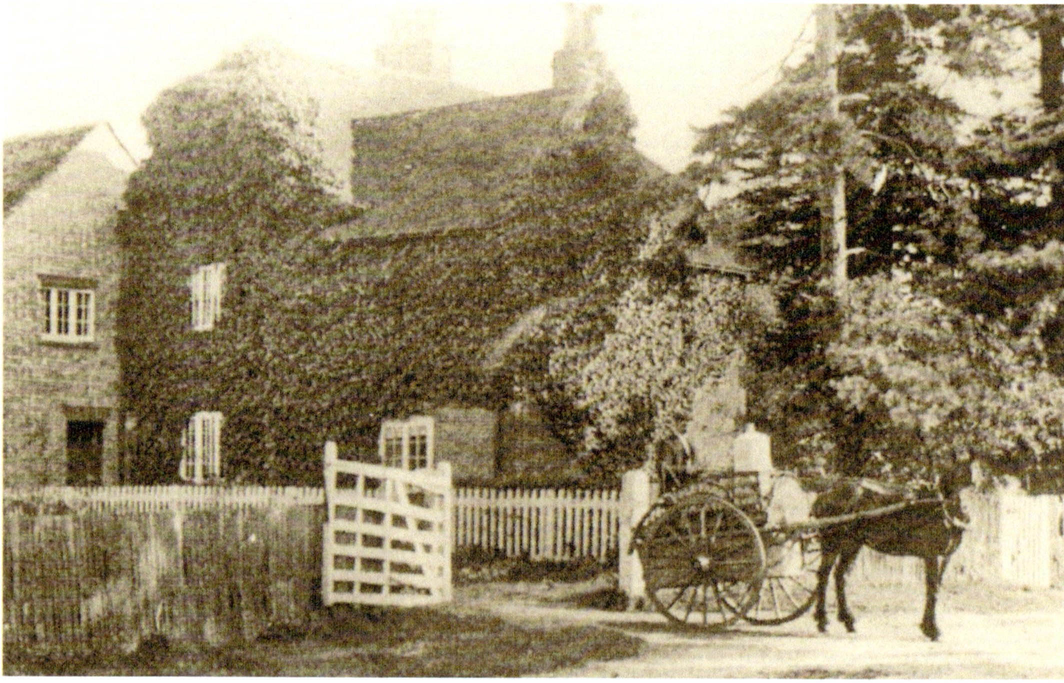

Fold Farm

Above, the Fold Farm in Galley Lane, off Wood Street, sits on the site of James Ravenscroft's seventeenth-century farm. The photograph dates from around 1900. Below is Fold Farm in 2013.

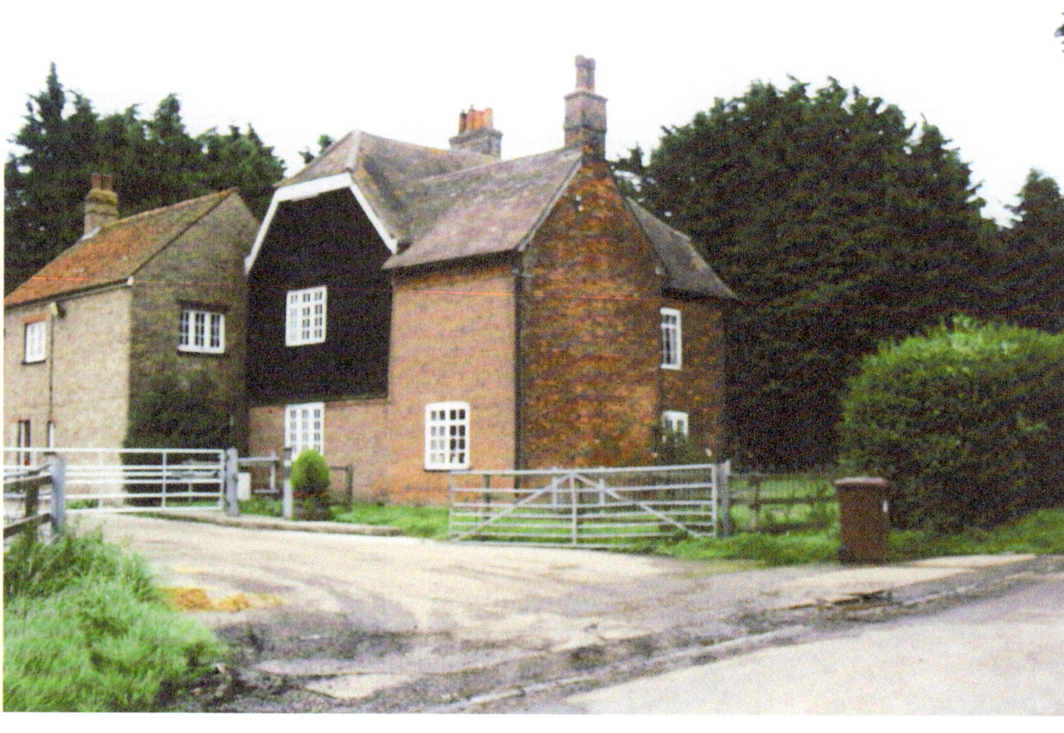

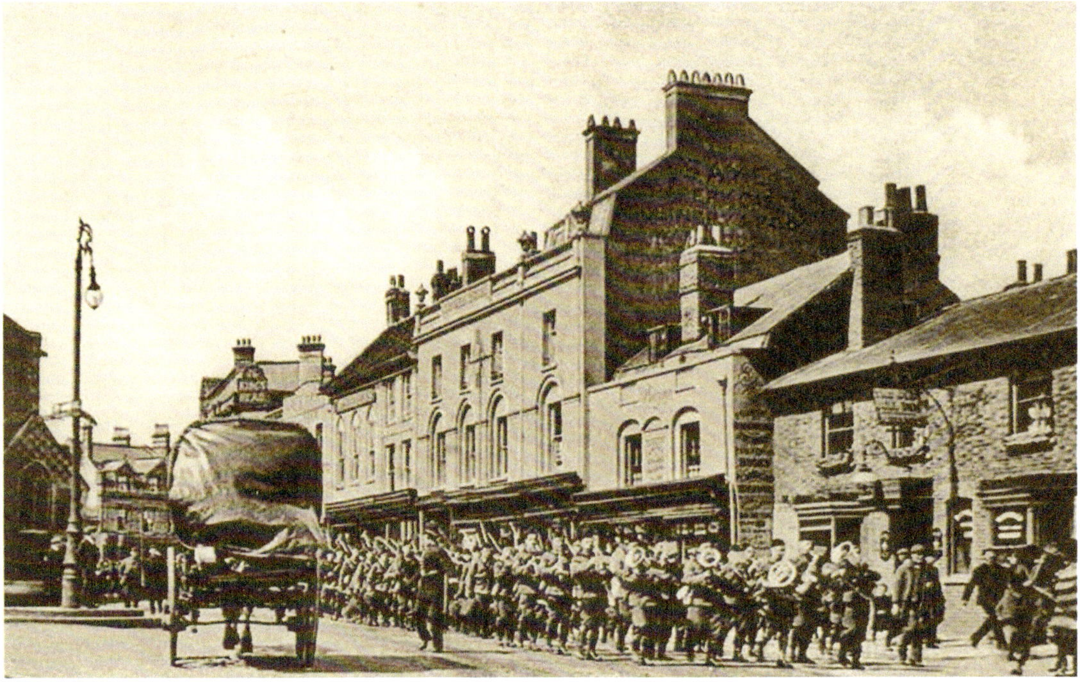

Middlesex Battalion

The 7th Middlesex in Barnet High Street, *c.* 1900. They were the first territorial battalion to leave for the front in August 1914, but were instead sent to Gibraltar. They returned to England in February 1915 and were sent to Flanders in March.

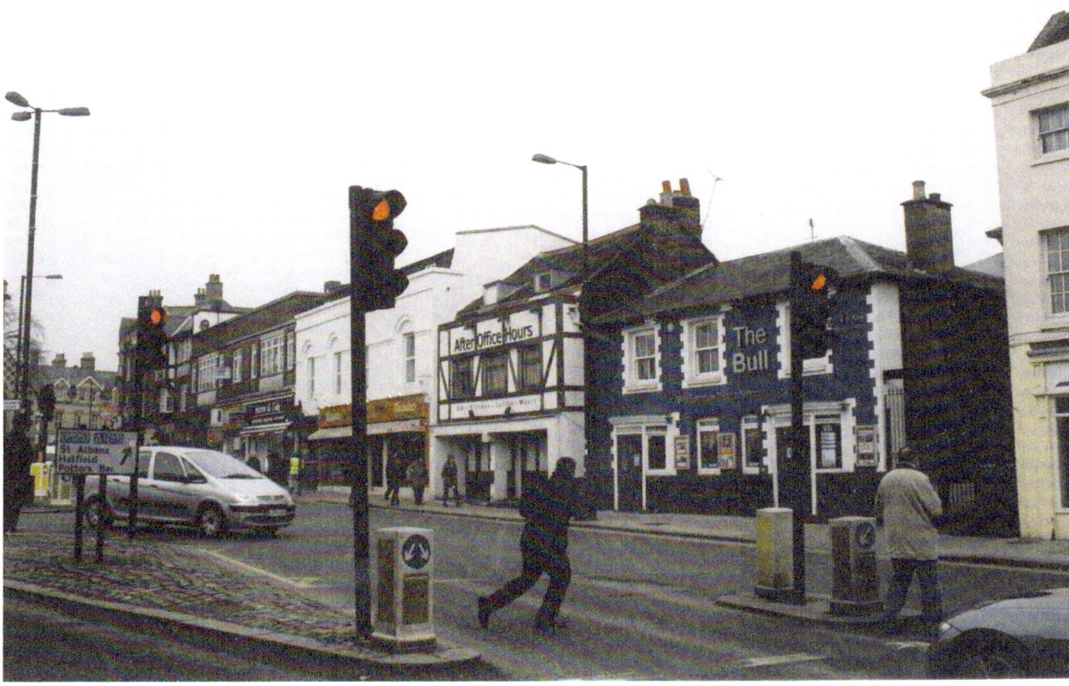

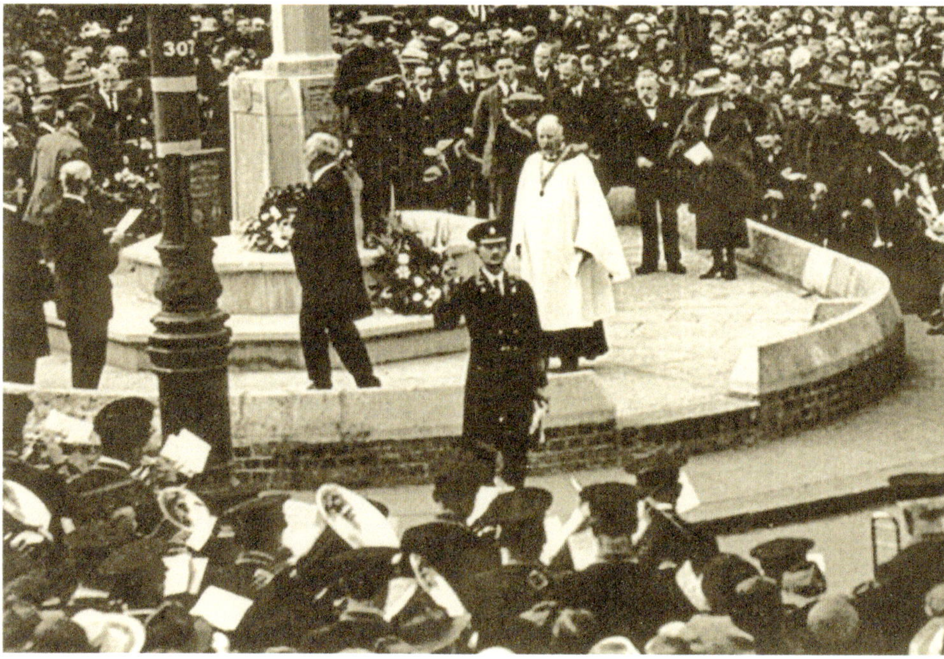

War Memorial

The First World War memorial was unveiled on 3 April 1923, and was located in front of St John's church where the elongated traffic island still stands. It was moved to its present position on the other side of the church in 1937.

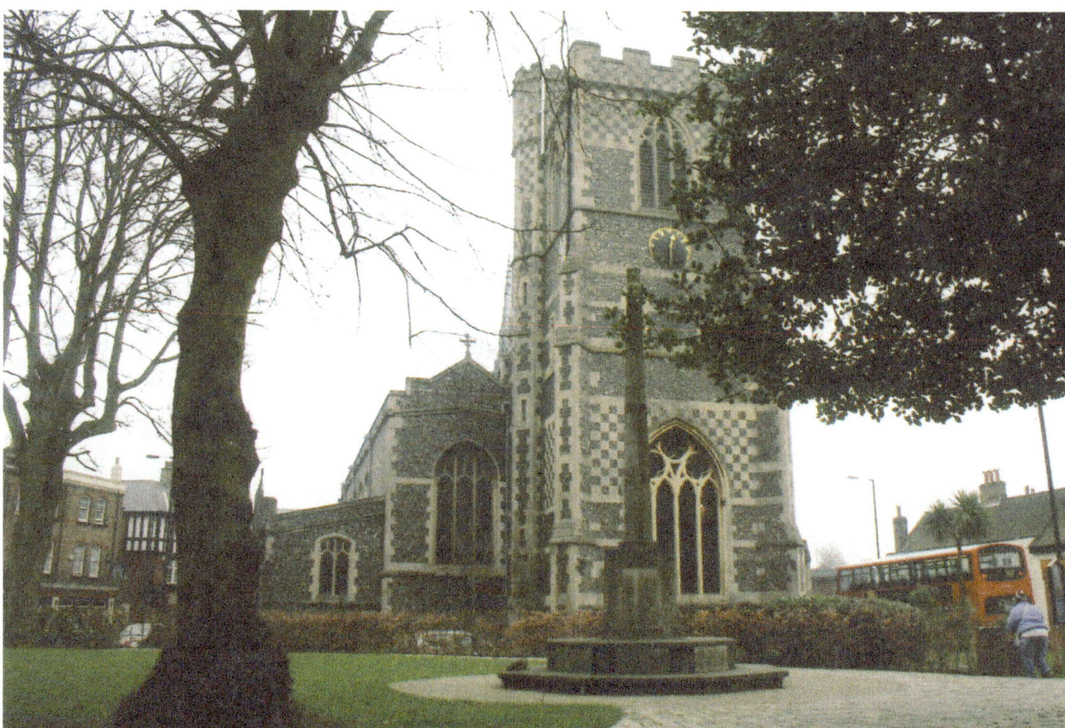

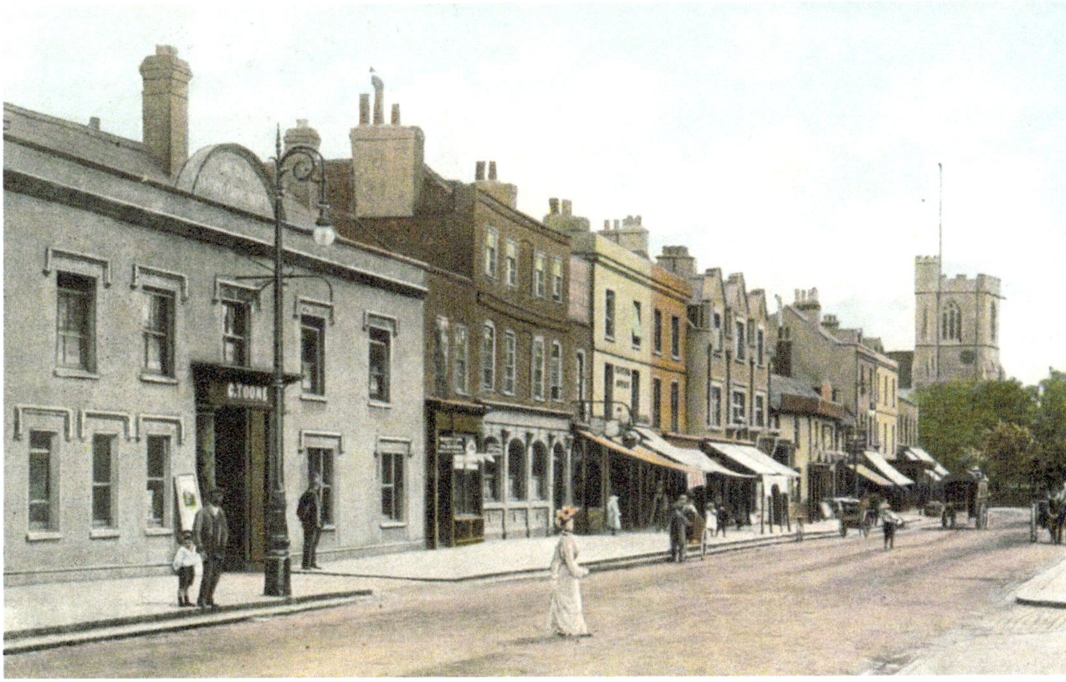

Barnet High Street

The above picture was taken near where the post office in Barnet High Street is situated, looking to the south in around 1905. The picture below is taken slightly closer to the church and is of a slightly earlier date but post 1875, as the Hertfordshire spike is missing from the church tower.

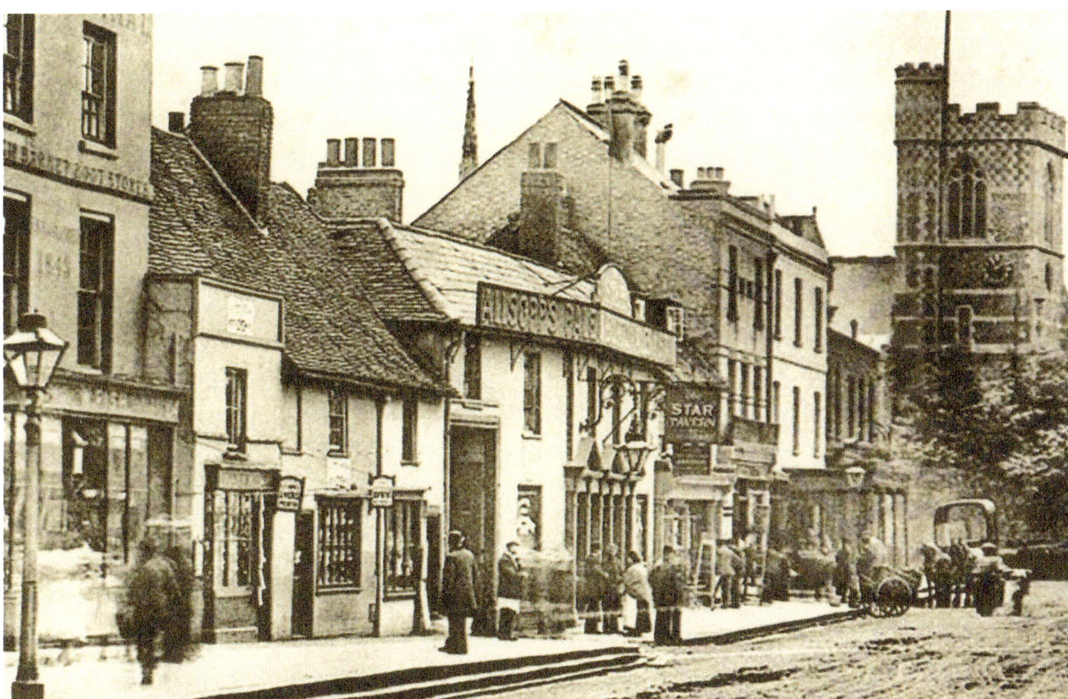

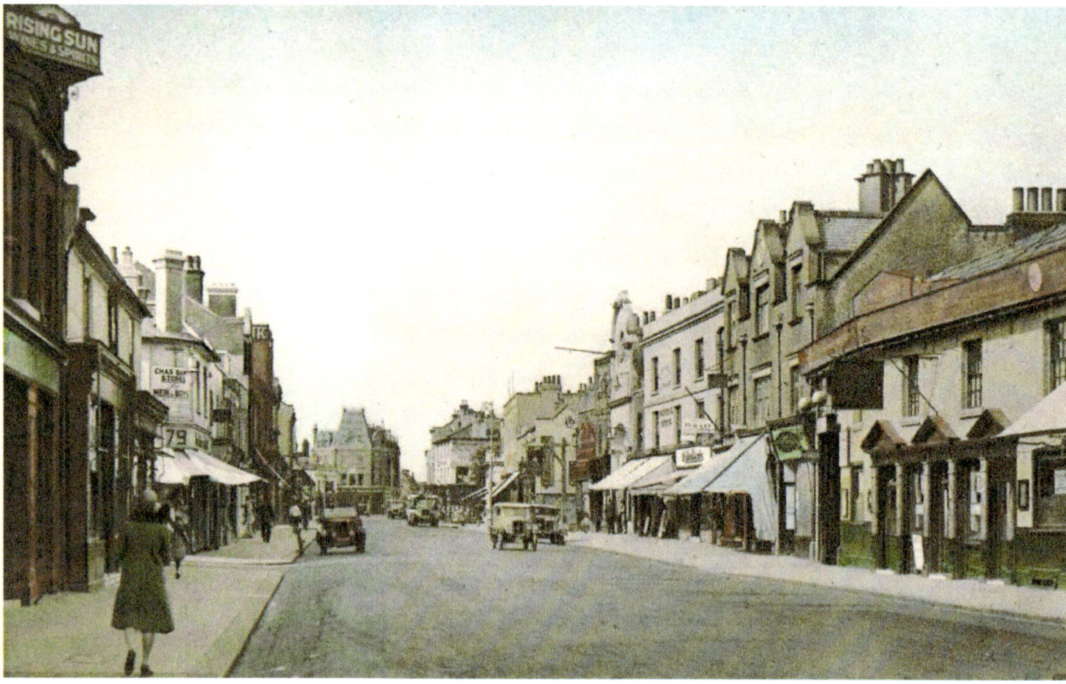

Barnet High Street

These two photographs were taken in the vicinity of where the entrance to the spires stand today in Barnet High Street looking north. Both date from the 1920s.

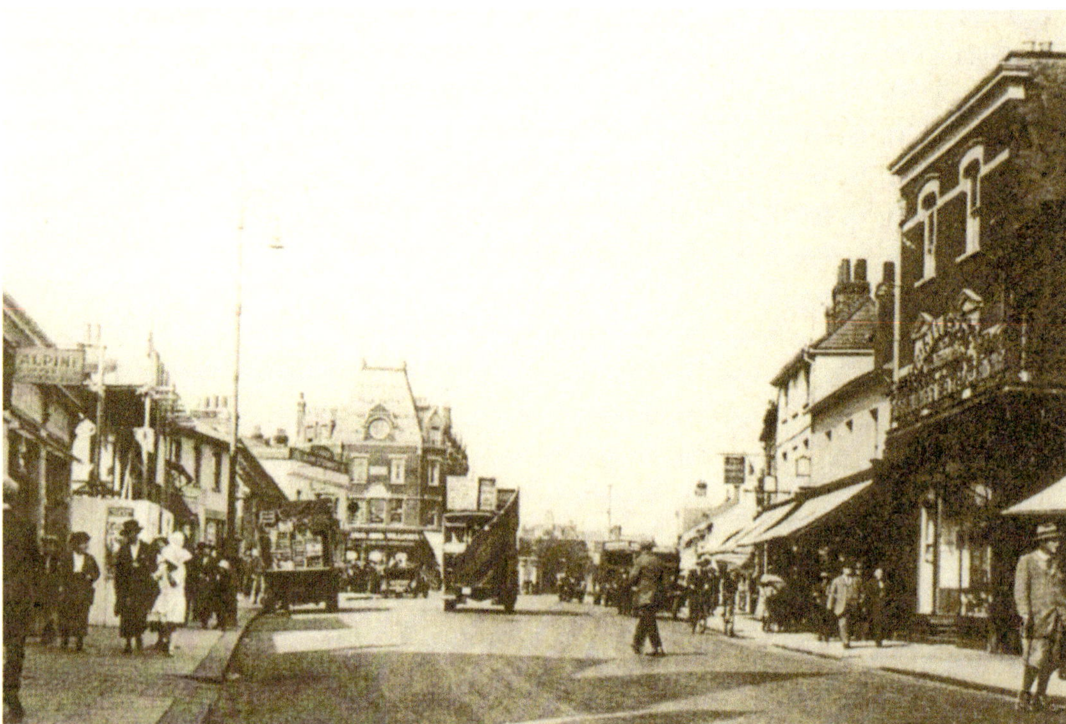

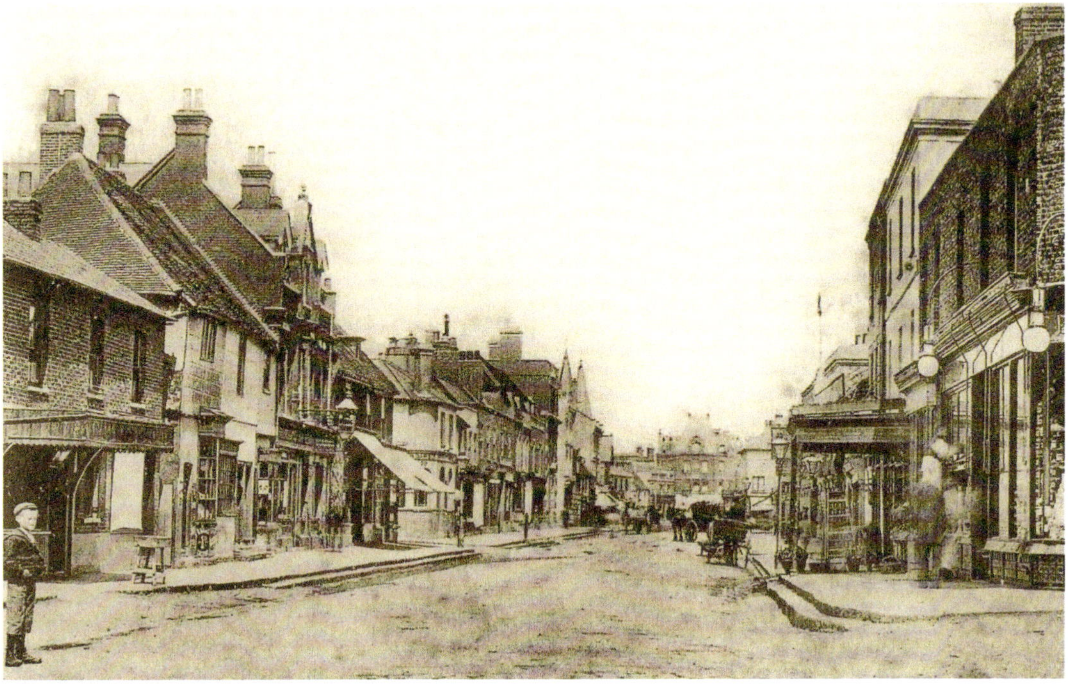

Barnet High Street

Above, an atmospheric picture of Barnet High Street looking north. In the middle can be seen the church spires that are still preserved as the entrance to the modern Spires shopping centre. The above picture dates from around 1900.

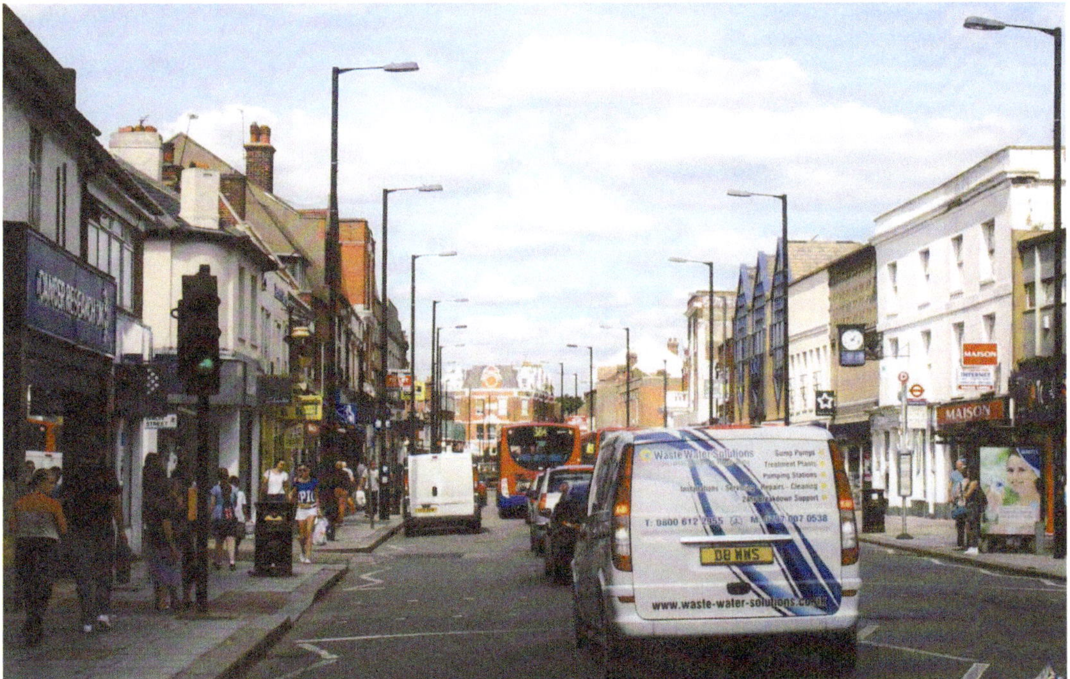

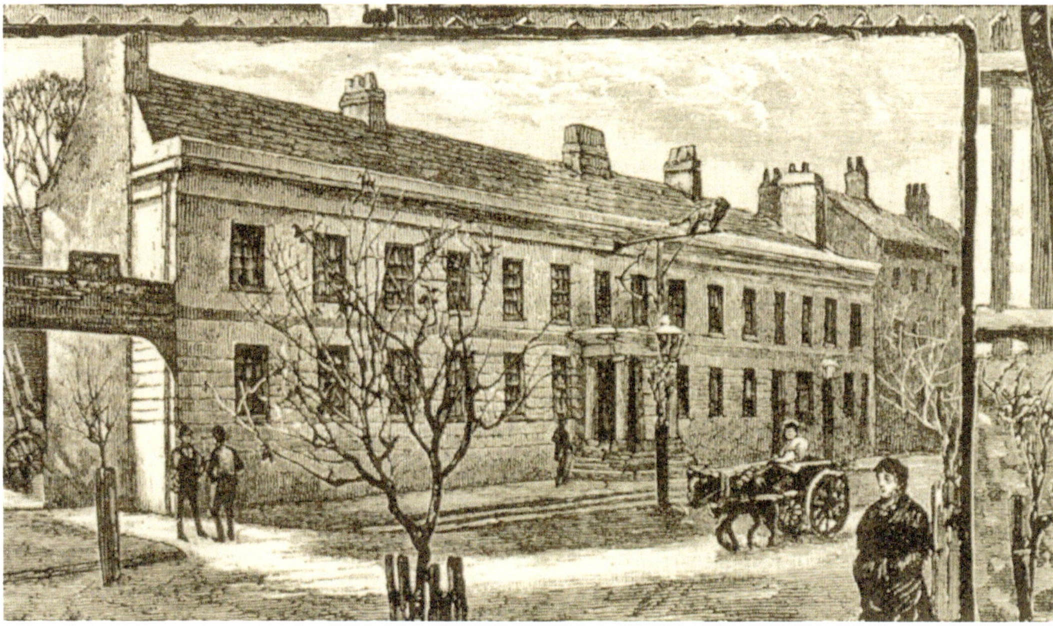

The Red Lion

The Red Lion was one of Barnet's major coaching inns, though with a series of rebuilds. The earlier Red Lion was halved by the building of Fitzjohns Avenue in around 1907. In 1667, Samuel Pepys claimed to have eaten the best cheesecake of his life at the Red Lion. Below, the modern Red Lion with the original Victorian lion.

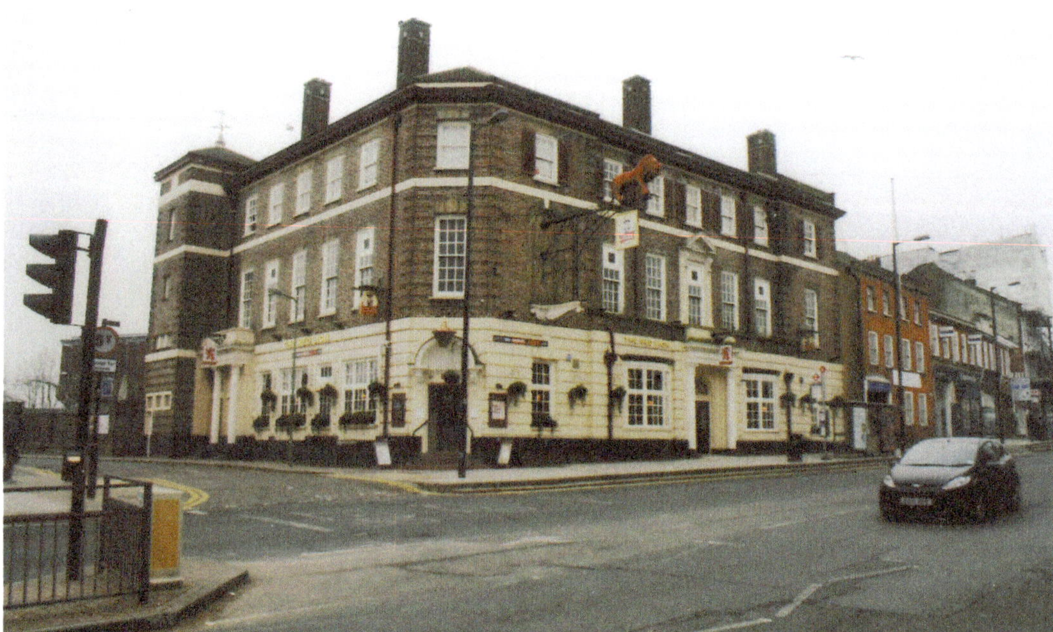

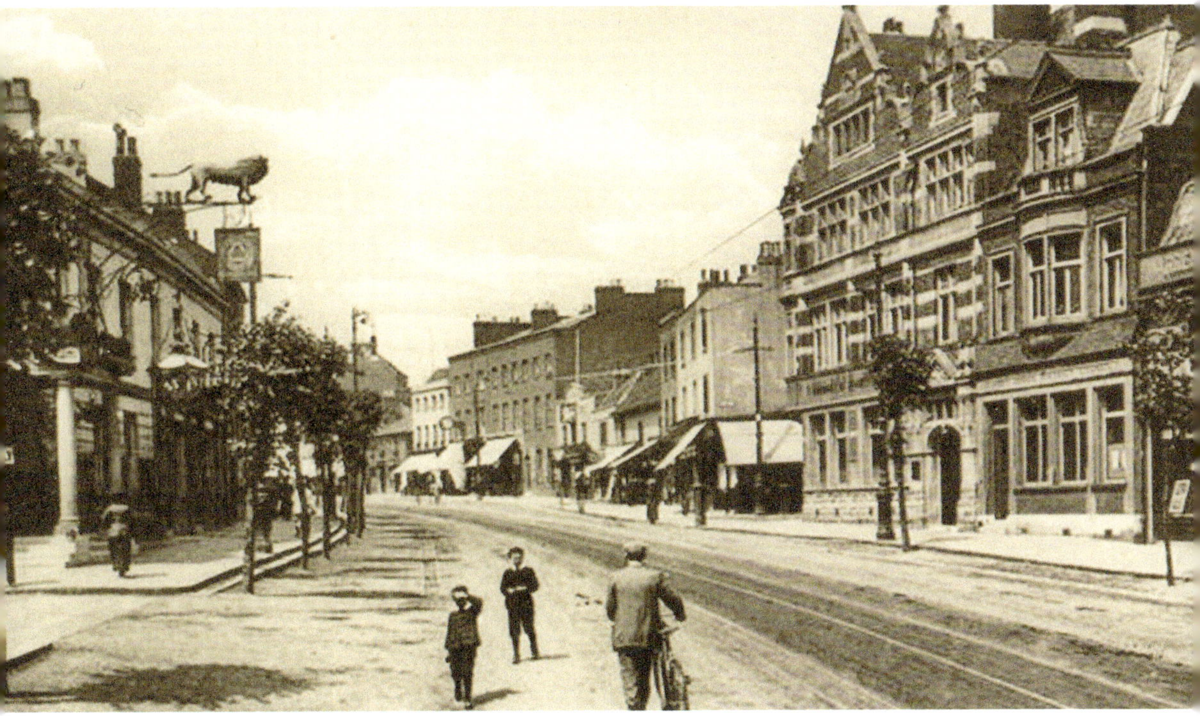

Barnet Hill

Two comparative views with the Red Lion on the left looking from the bottom of Barnet Hill. The above view dates from around 1910 while below is the view today.

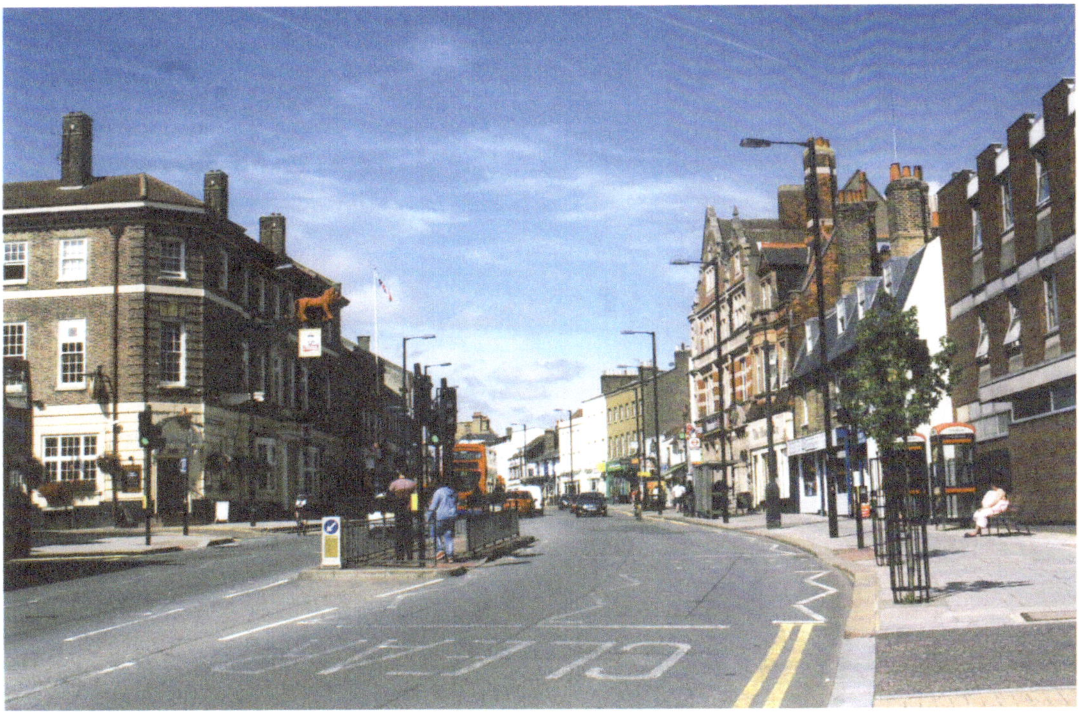

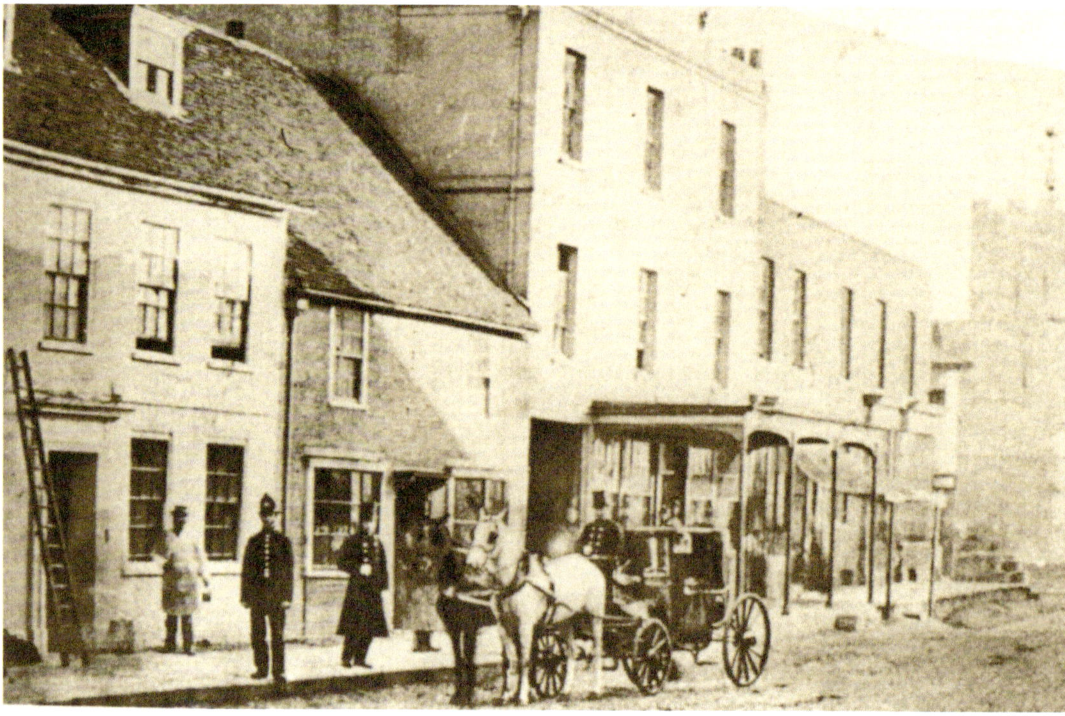

Barnet High Street

A very early view of Barnet High Street looking south towards the church. It was taken before 1875. Below, the same view is almost unrecognisable in 2013.

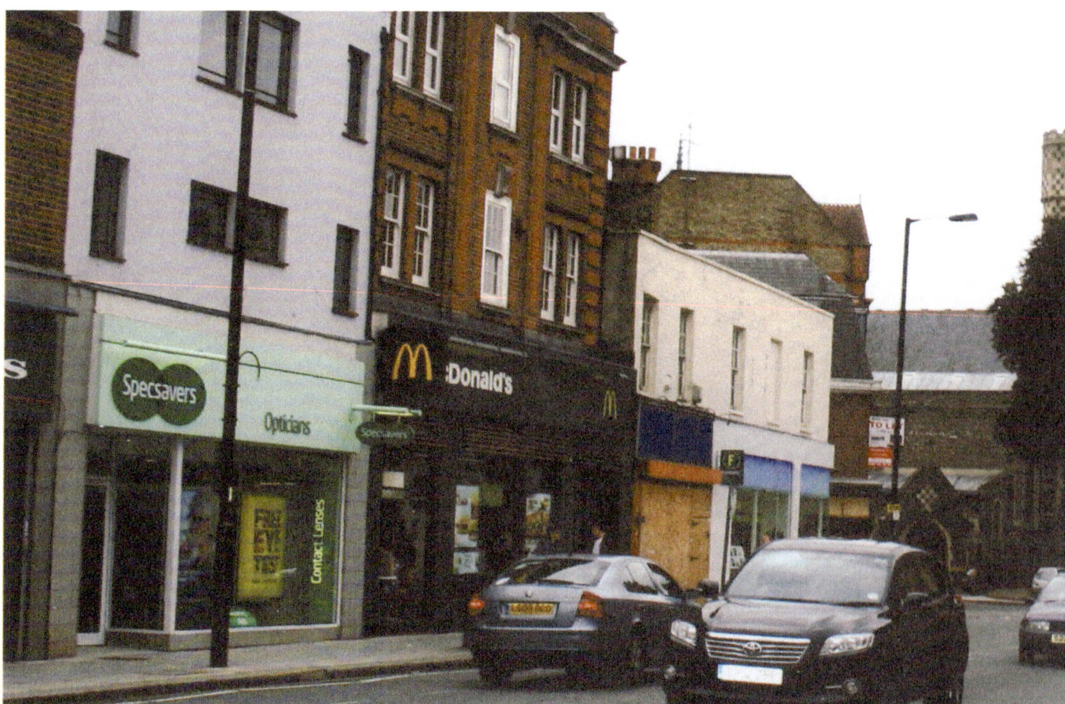

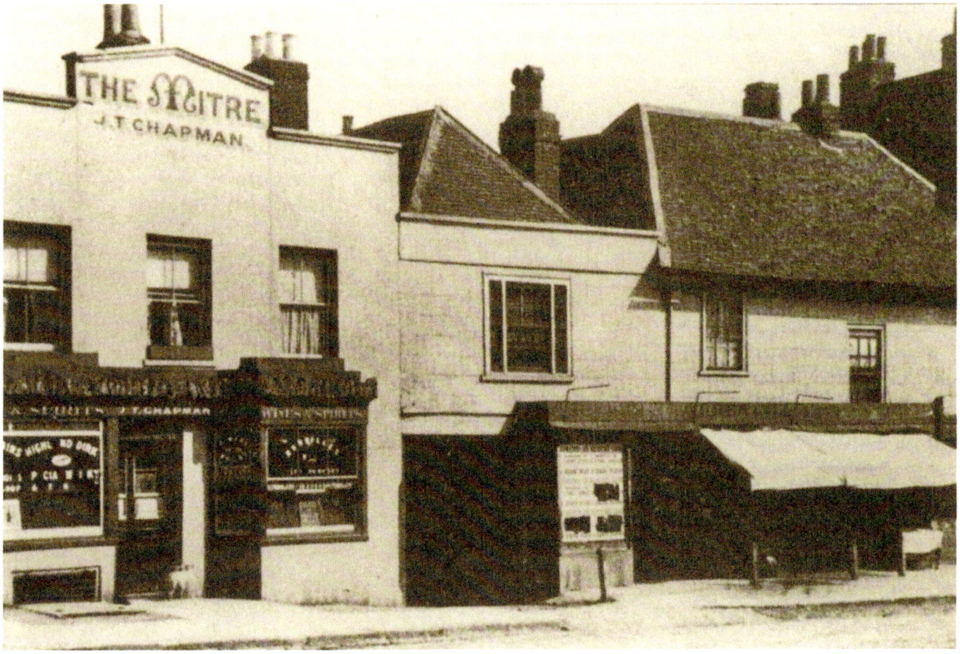

The Mitre Inn

The Mitre Inn, situated on Barnet Hill just south of St John's church, existed in 1633 and is possibly the oldest remaining coaching inn building. In 1660, General Monck stayed at the Mitre on his way to London to restore Charles II, after the Commonwealth of Oliver Cromwell. His 5,000 troops had to camp on Finchley Common. The building we see now was described as 'new built' in April 1785, with 'stabling for upwards of one hundred horses' and 'roomy conveniences for carriages' in 1790. The photograph above dates from around 1880. Below, the Mitre Inn in 2013.

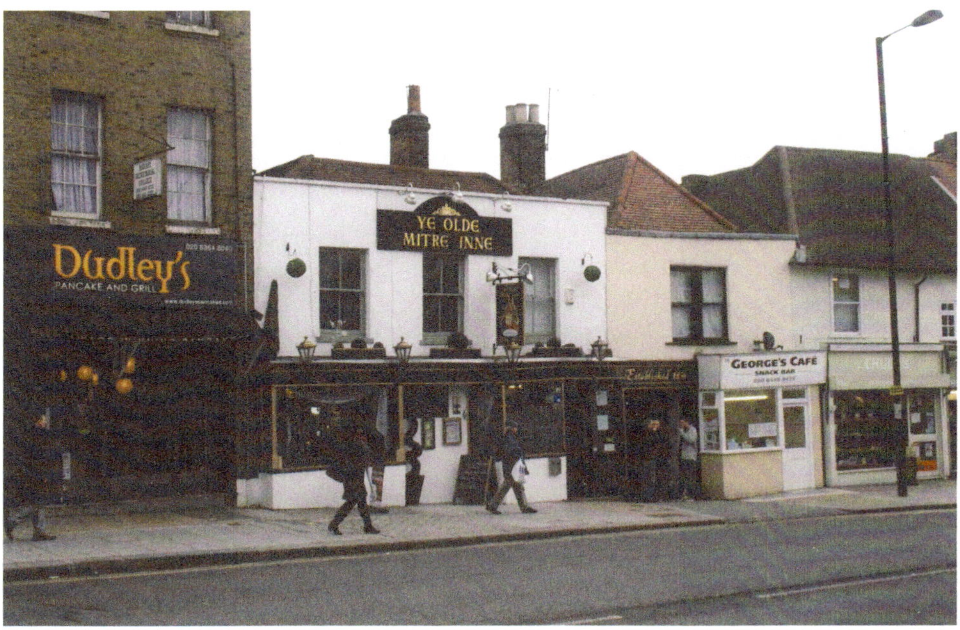

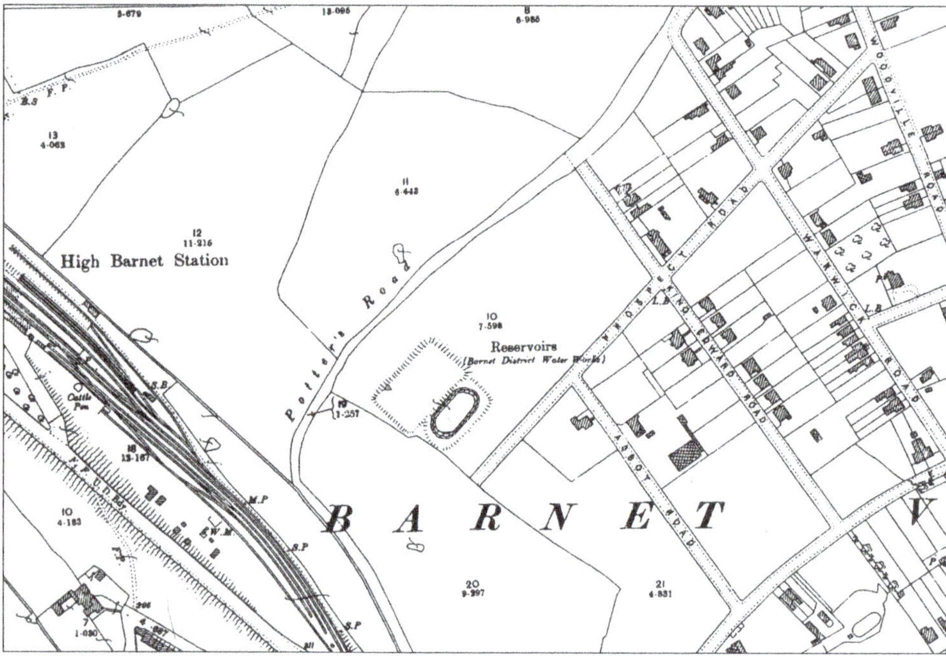

High Barnet Station

Above is a small section of the 1896 Ordnance Survey map showing High Barnet station and the still quite sparse nature of building in the vicinity. High Barnet station was opened in 1872 by the Great Northern Railway Company. Below, High Barnet station looking south around 1900.

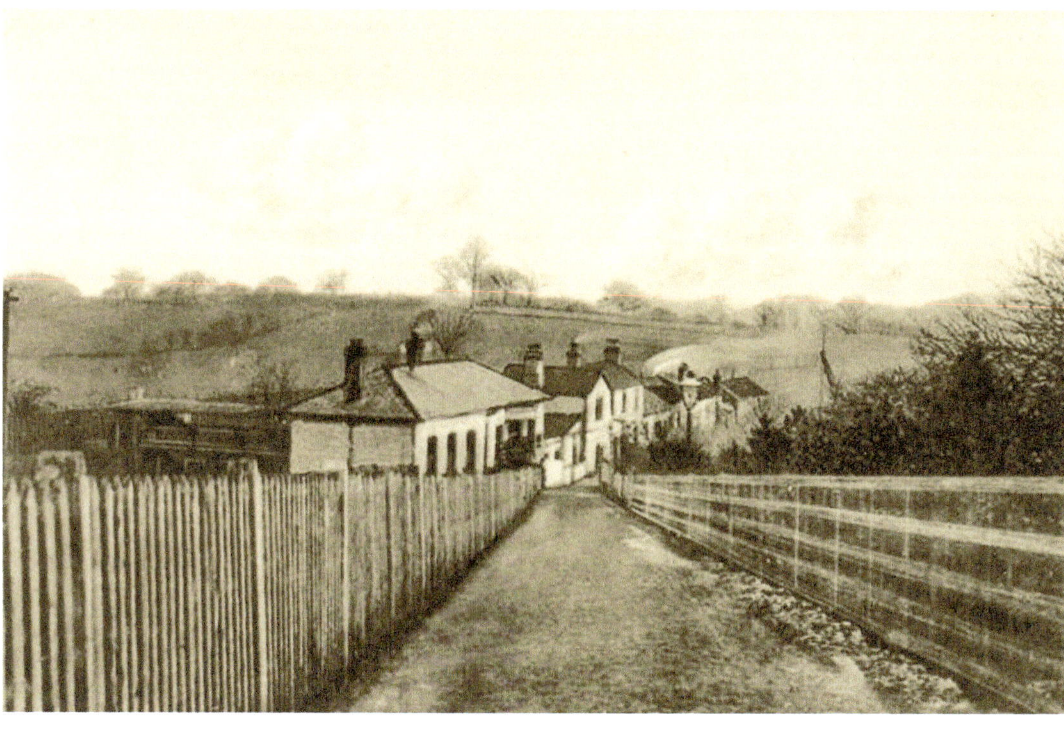

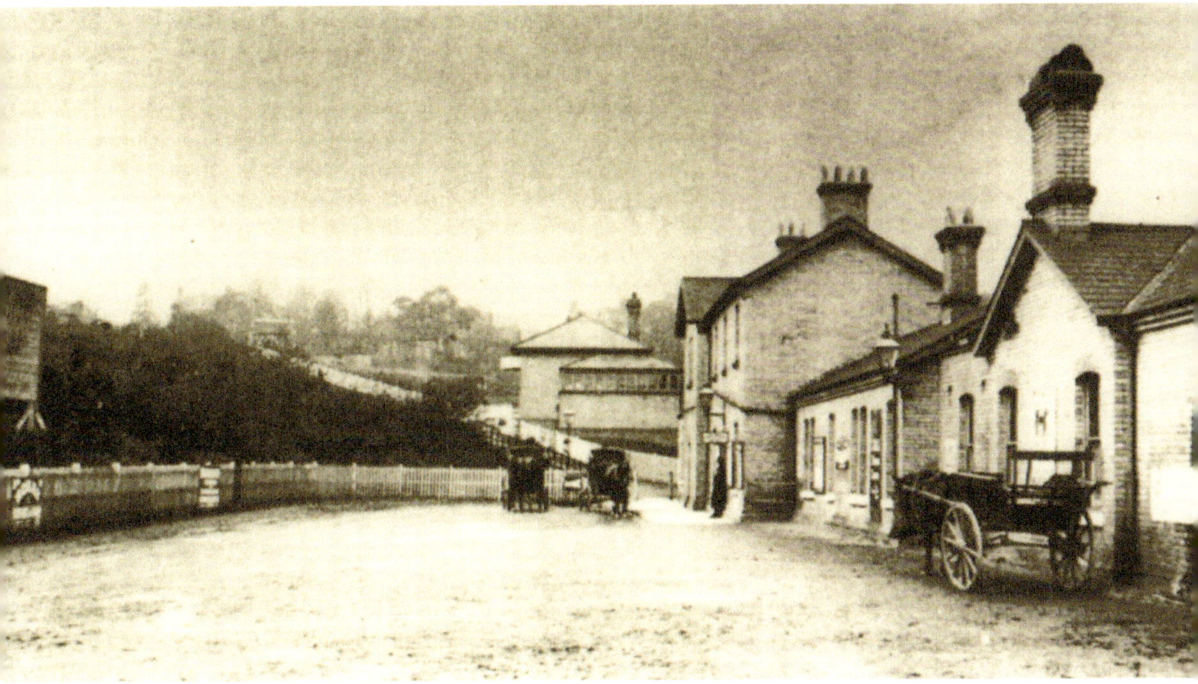

High Barnet Station

High Barnet station around 1900, looking north. The line was incorporated into the Northern Line via a new tunnel to Archway in 1939. Below, in 2013 the same view is almost still recognisable.

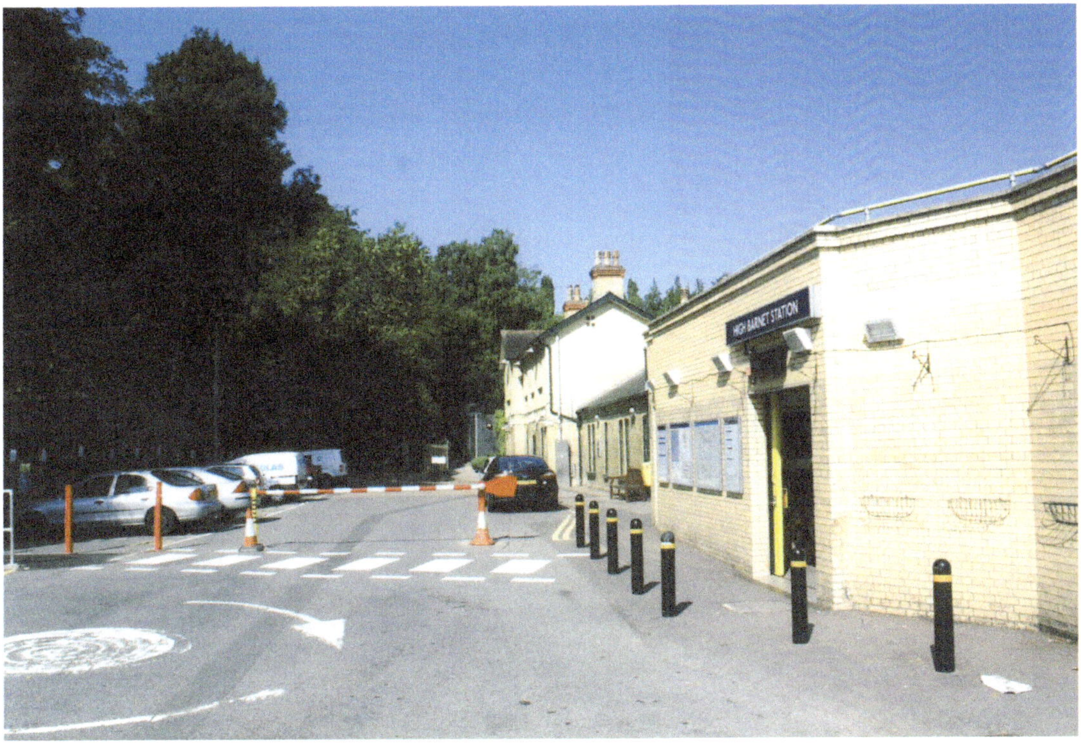

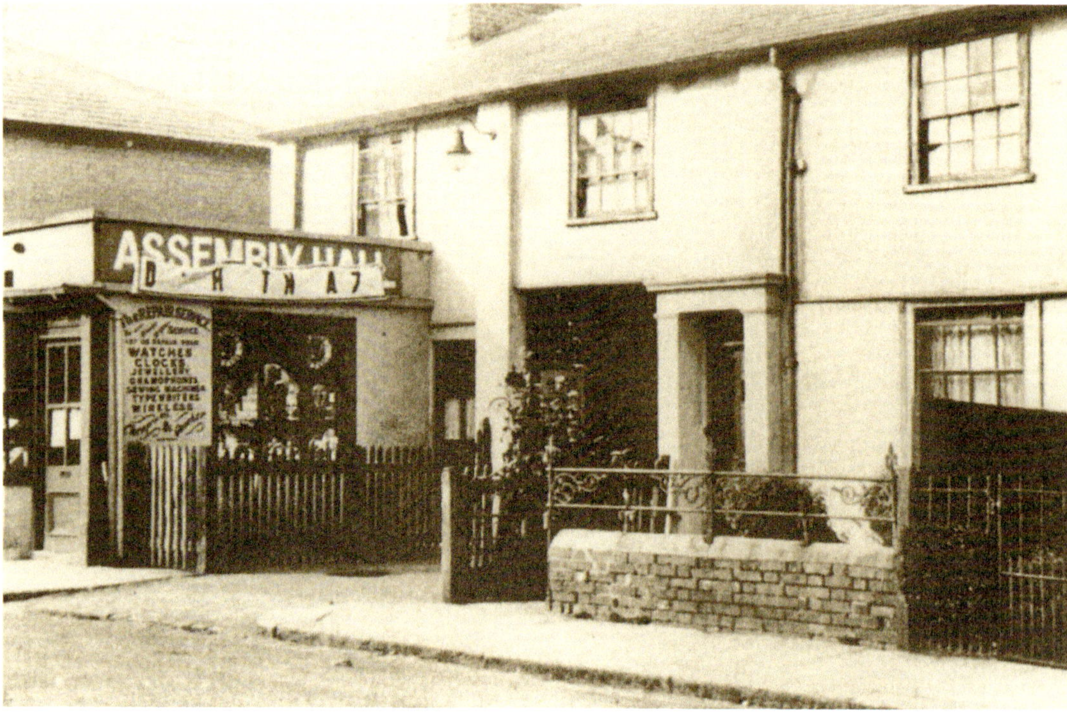

Assembly Hall

The above picture shows the Assembly Hall in Union Street, Chipping Barnet, in 1930. It started as a reading room in around 1888. It was later used as Labour Party headquarters, and was demolished around 2000. A doctor's surgery now stands here. Below, what was formerly the Albion public house in Union Street in 2013.

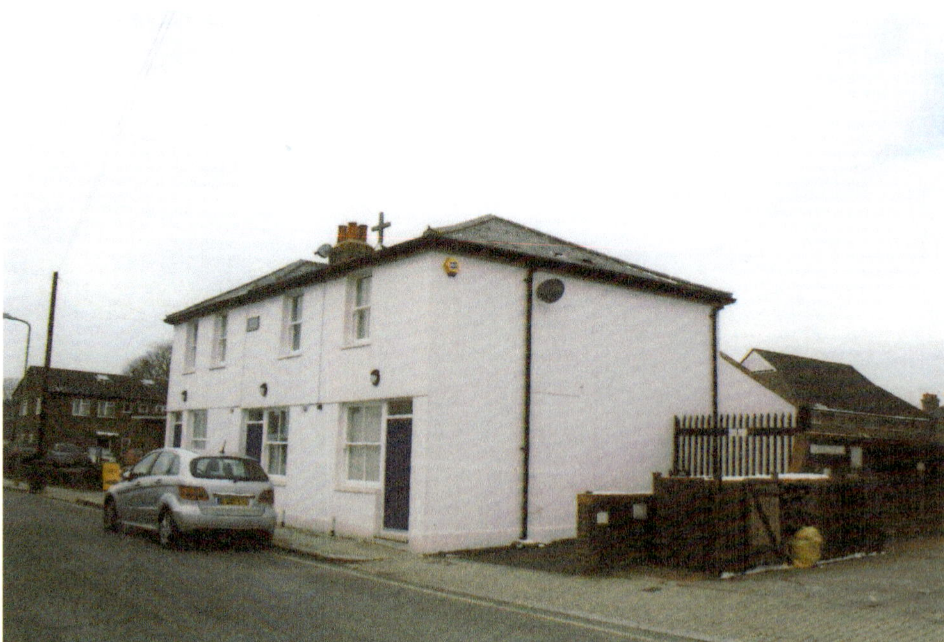

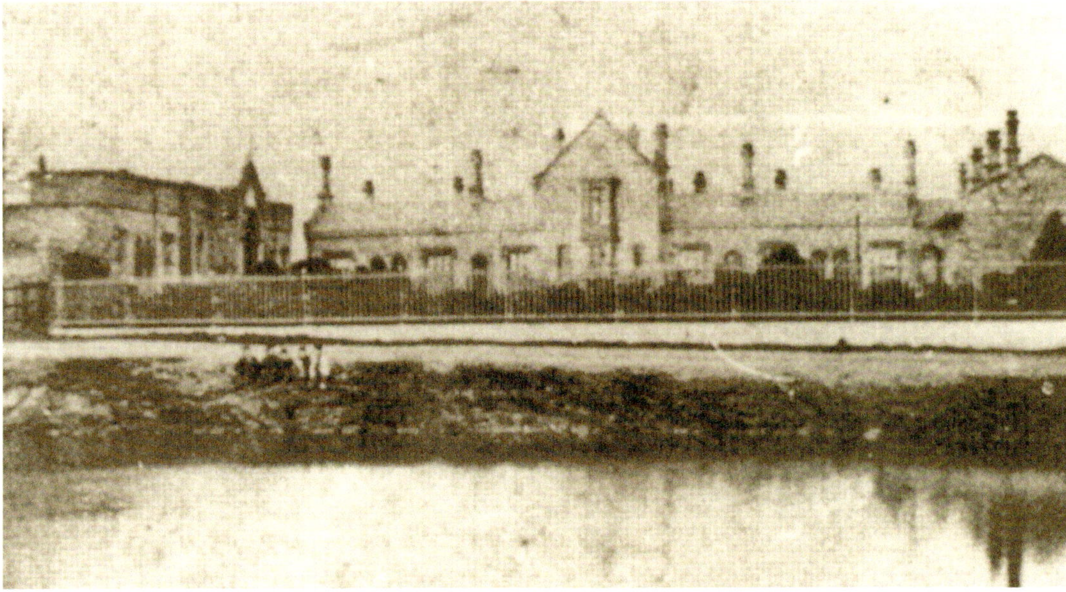

Wood Street Almshouses

The Leathersellers Company bought land in Wood Street in 1603, which was let for pasture until the 1830s, when they decided more almshouses were needed. The foundation stone was laid in 1837 and a series of additions were made during the nineteenth century. The iron gates were added in 1926. The variations in the old and new photographs are the result of rebuilding in 1964–66.

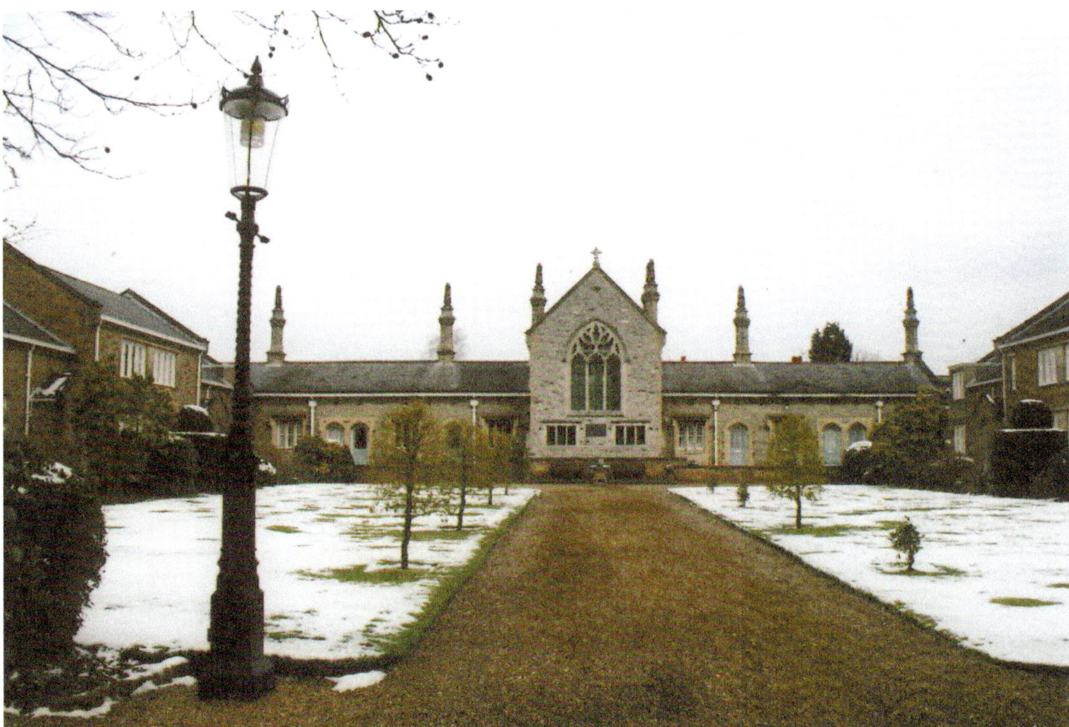

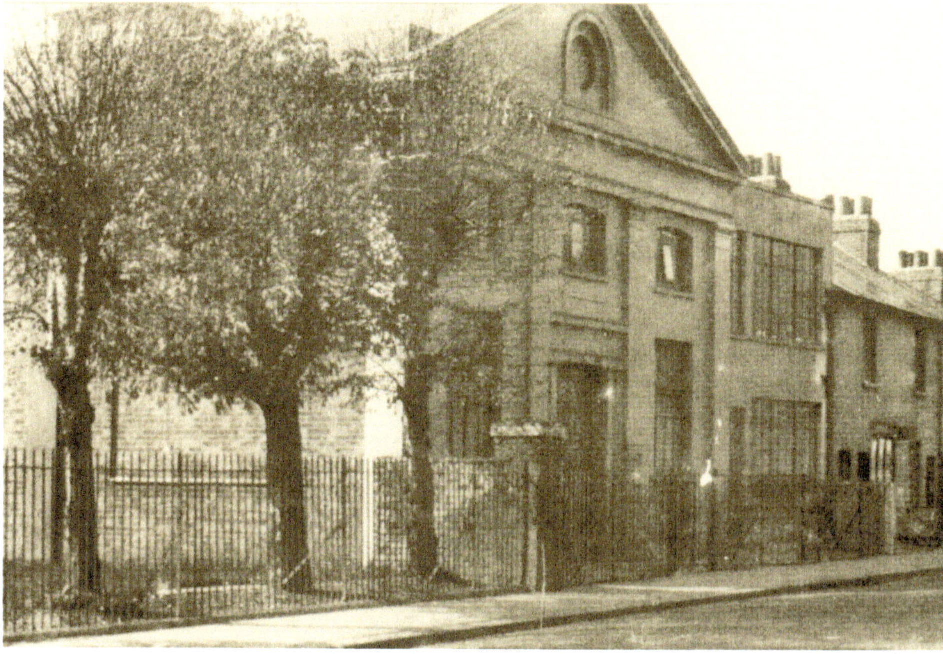

Barnet Town Hall

Union Street was built in 1837. From 1889 to 1912, Barnet Town Hall was in Union Street. The old picture above dates from around 1890. An early history describes the town hall as 'a brick building, of little or no architectural pretensions'. The building today is used as offices.

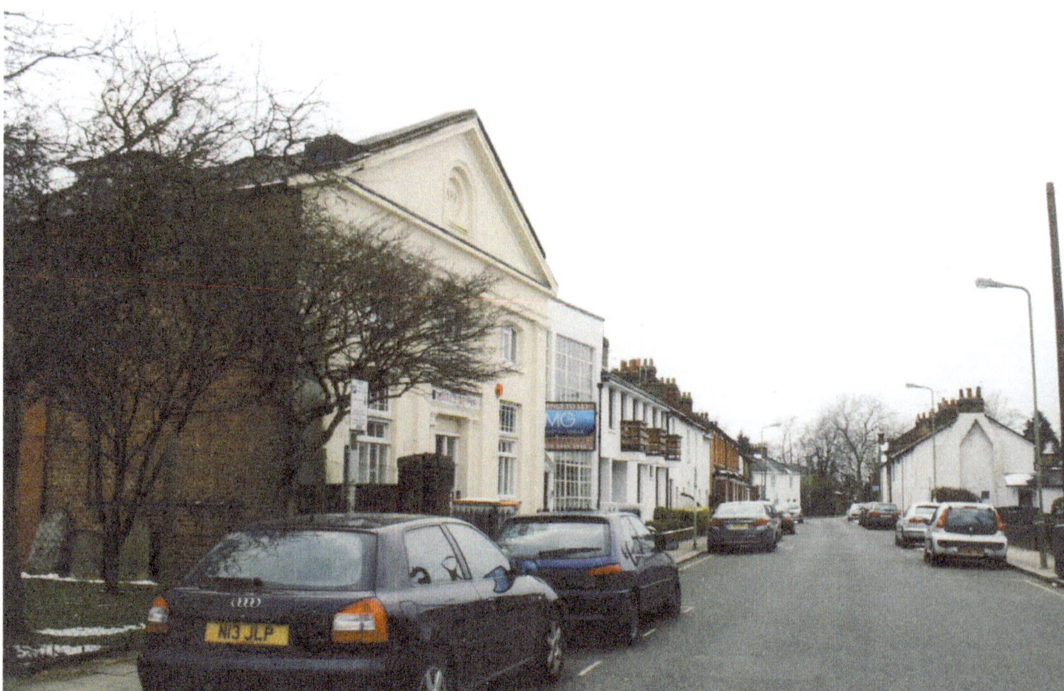

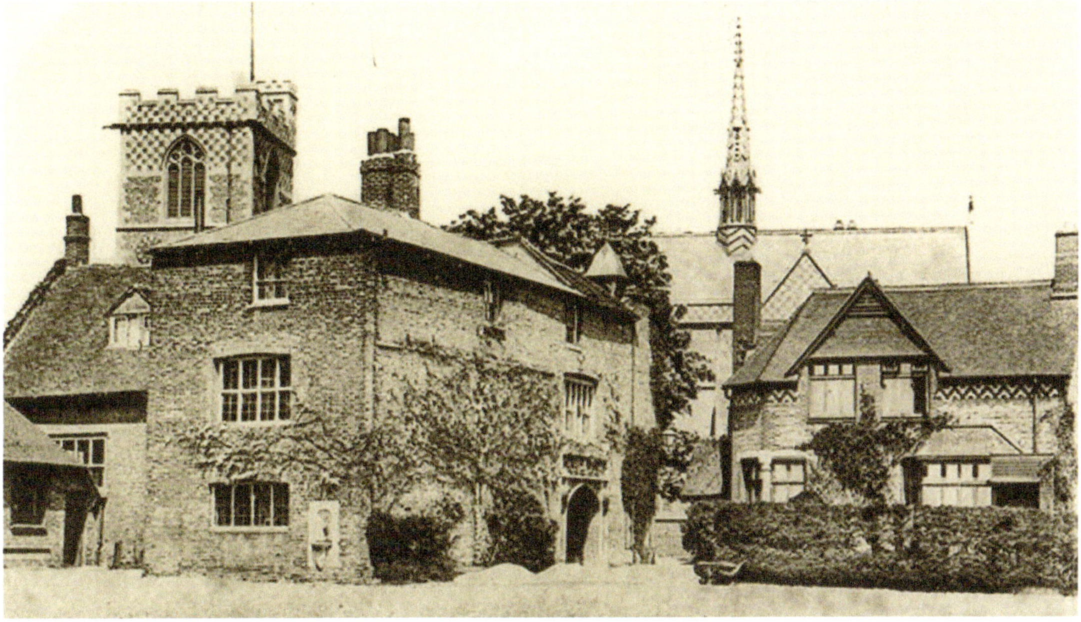

Barnet College

Probably the most eye-catching building situated on Wood Street opposite St John's church is the Tudor school, now incorporated into Barnet College. An 1880 description states, 'The Grammar School is in Wood Street; it flourishes under the shadow of the parish church. It consists of one large and lofty hall, which is as old as the reign of Elizabeth, dating from 1573, and has much of the Tudor style of architecture, with a turret at either end ... The dormitories above the large hall are almost coeval with the building itself and the eastern end once contained rooms, in which more than one of the masters lived, these being now removed, the hall now extends to fifty-five feet in length.'

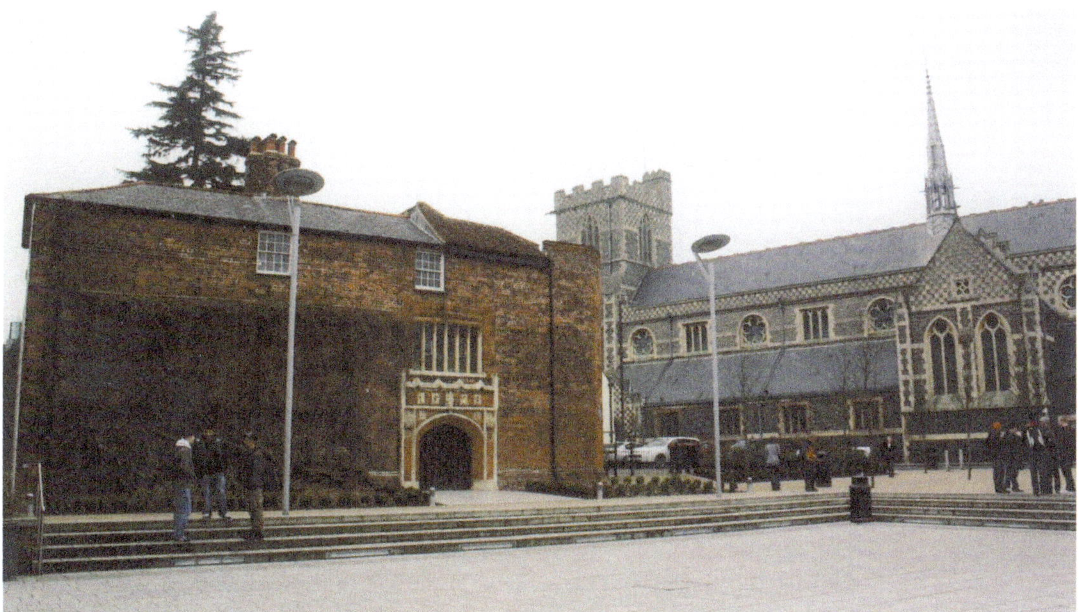

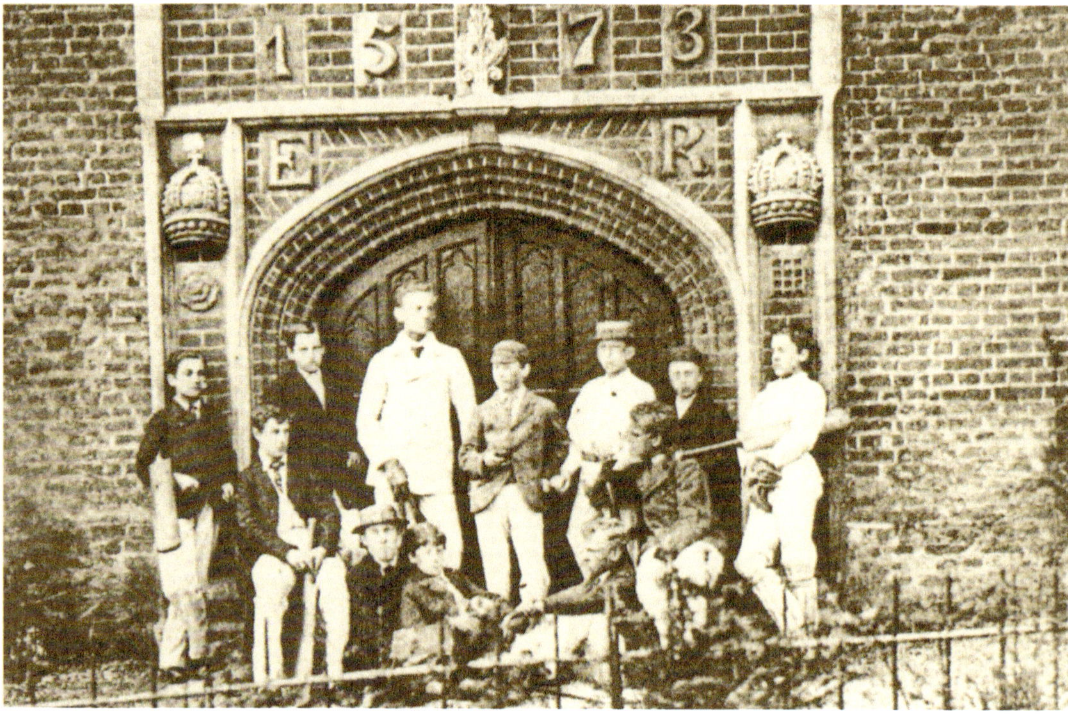

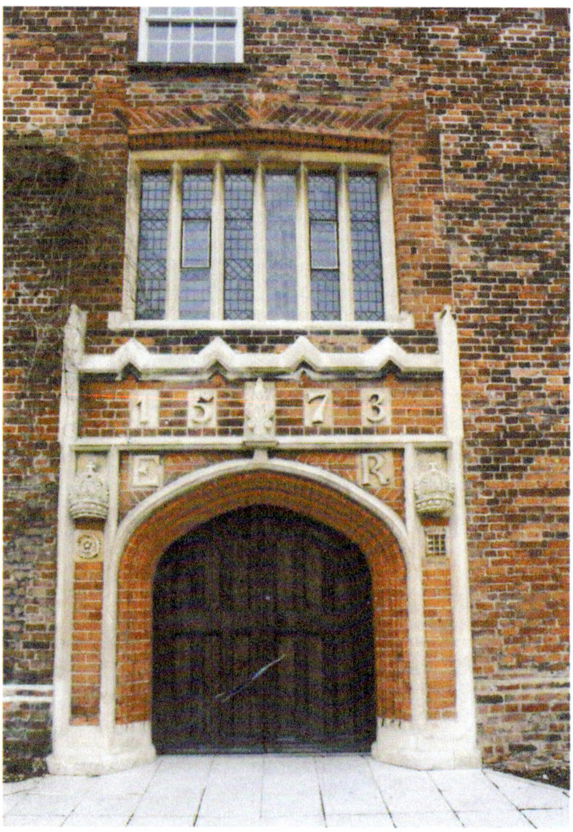

Barnet College

The 1880 history continues: 'The school contains over a hundred boys, and the course of studies is modern and practical rather than strictly classical, in the ancient sense of the term. Its pupils some twenty years ago had dwindled down to the most insignificant number, but a "new scheme" was proposed, and warmly welcomed.' Its reputation at one time sank to a low. Dickens, in 1851, wrote a barely disguised account: '... under Dr Laon Blosse, head-master, who, besides superintending the education of seven foundation or free boys, seeks private pupils of his own, who are to qualify themselves for admission by bringing with them silver forks and spoons. Under scarcely-veiled aliases, the writer describes the approach to the school from the railway-station, the general grouping and arrangement of the little town, and the ivy-grown school-room, with its dull, heavy entrance-court, and its flanking round, or rather angular, turrets at either extremity.'

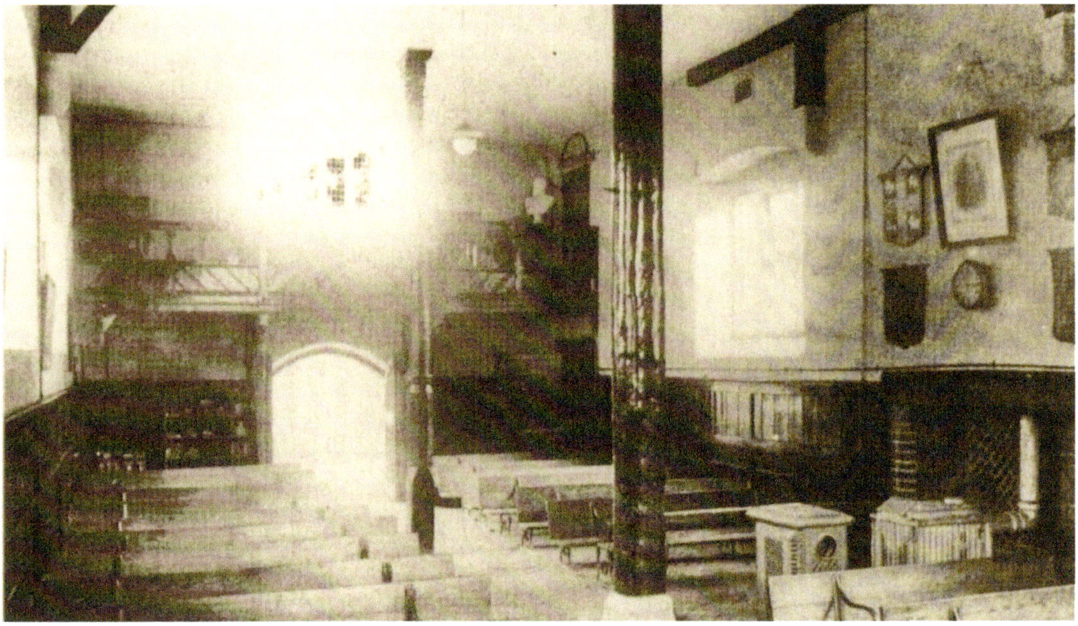

Barnet College

The upper picture dates from around 1900 and shows the interior of the building, of which Dickens wrote that he 'confessed to being somewhat affected at the notion of standing in a school-room built in the old days of Queen Elizabeth, not at all large, but tolerably lofty'. It remained a classroom until the 1920s. The class below, shown sitting by the main entrance, dates from around 1890.

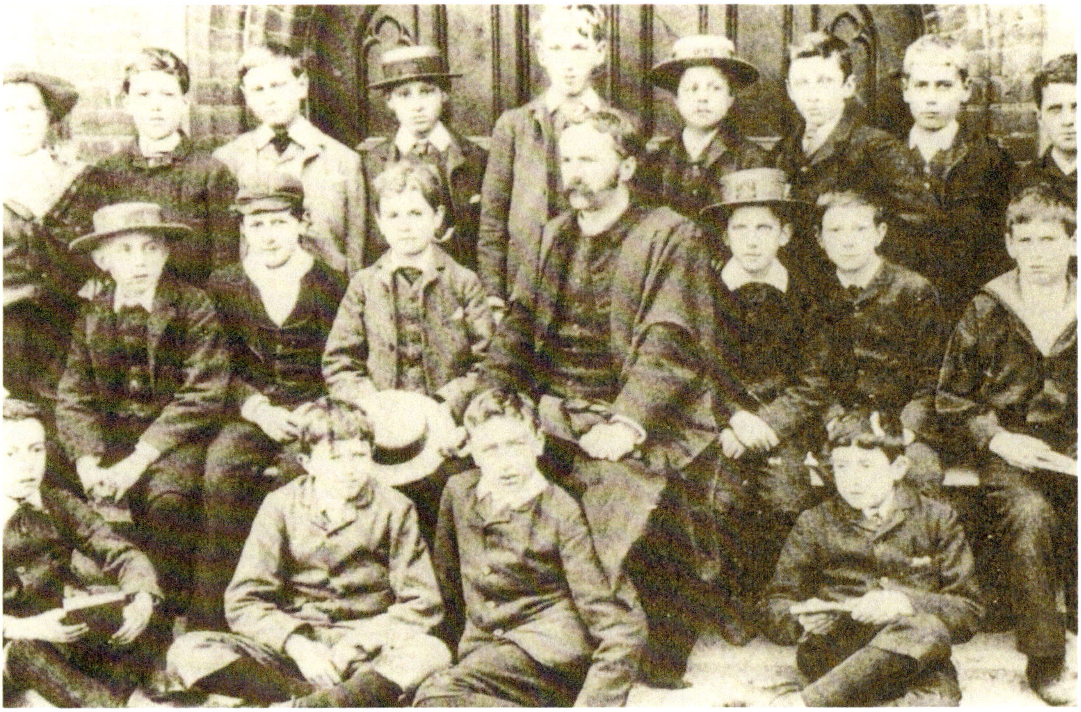

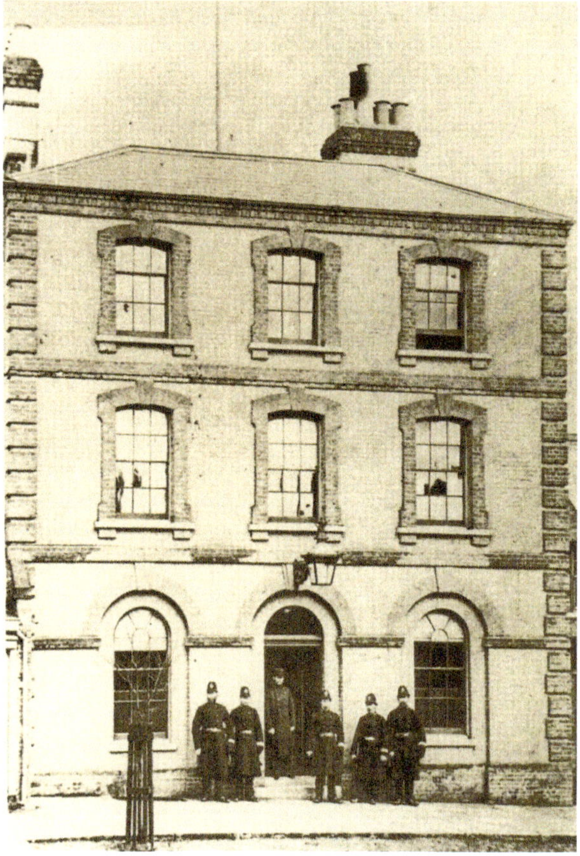

Barnet Police Station

Barnet was incorporated into the Metropolitan Police District in 1840. A visitor in 1854 to Barnet Fair wrote, 'On more than one occasion we met with drunken policemen who were rushing about where accidents occurred more calculated to increase than prevent injury.' The Barnet police station (*right*) was built in the 1860s. The picture dates from around 1880. The picture below is Barnet Hill, looking north towards the town centre. The police station stood approximately where the first lamppost on the right stands.

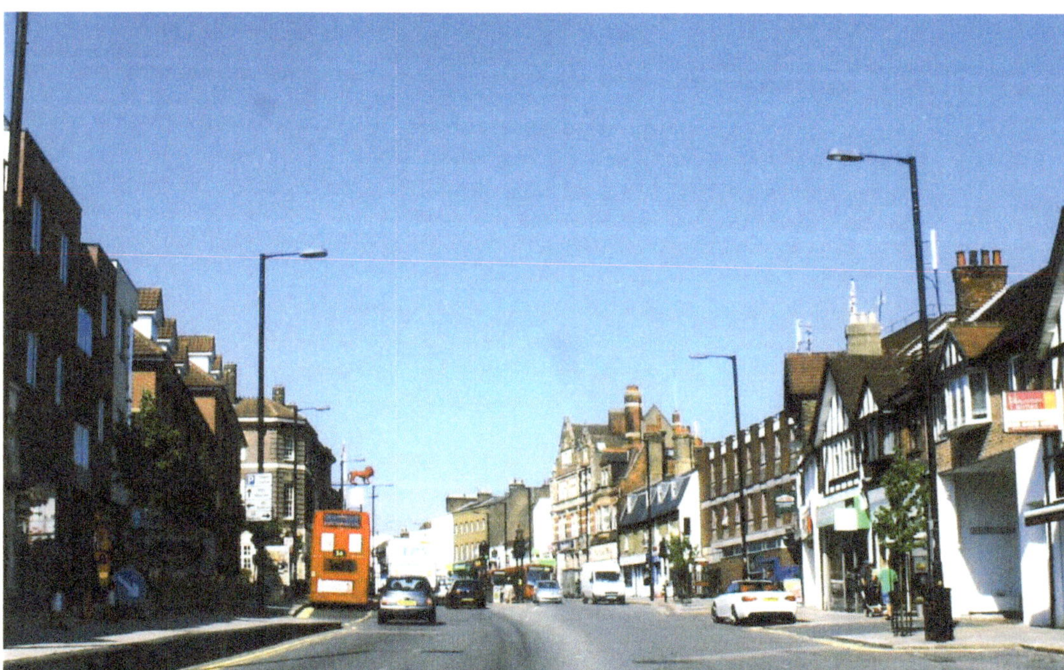

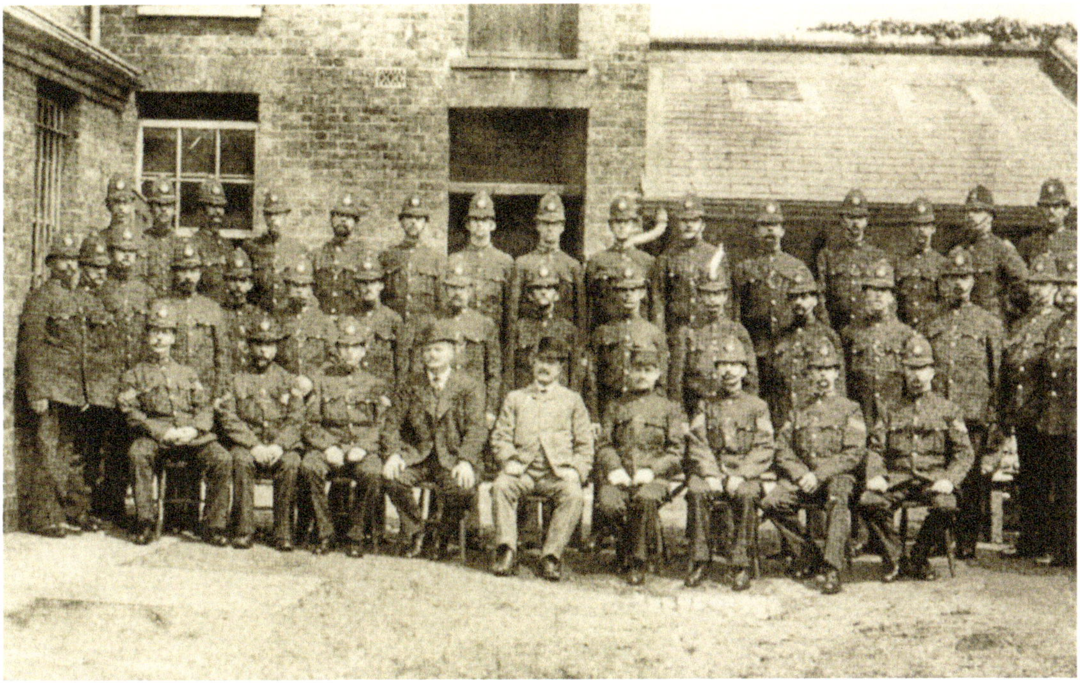

Barnet Police Force and Magistrates' Court

Above, the Barnet police force in around 1910. Below, the Magistrates' Court, which was sited strategically opposite the police station, and remained a court until very recently when cutbacks led to its closure.

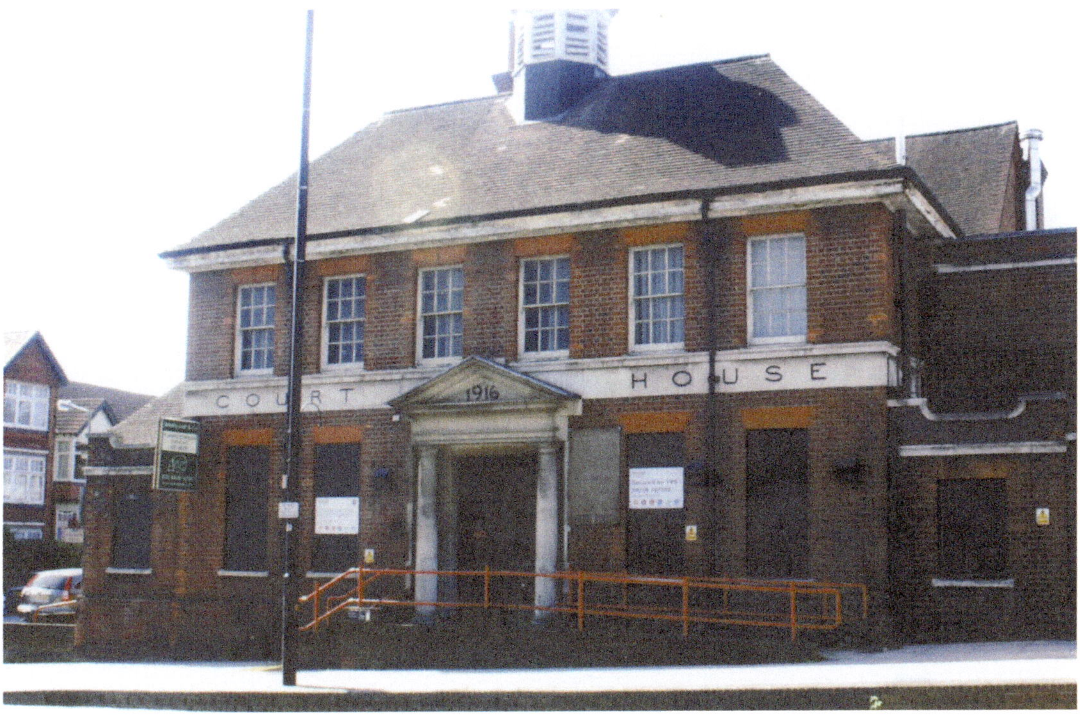

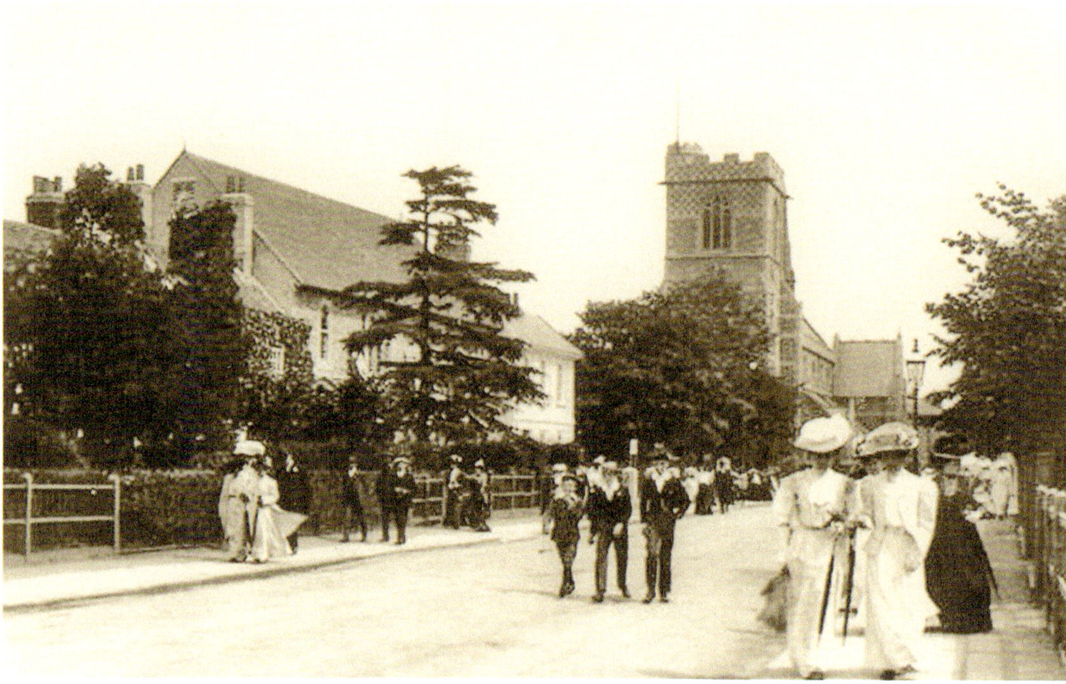

Wood Street

Wood Street in more relaxed times with St John's church in the background. The photograph dates from around 1905. Below is the same view in 2013.

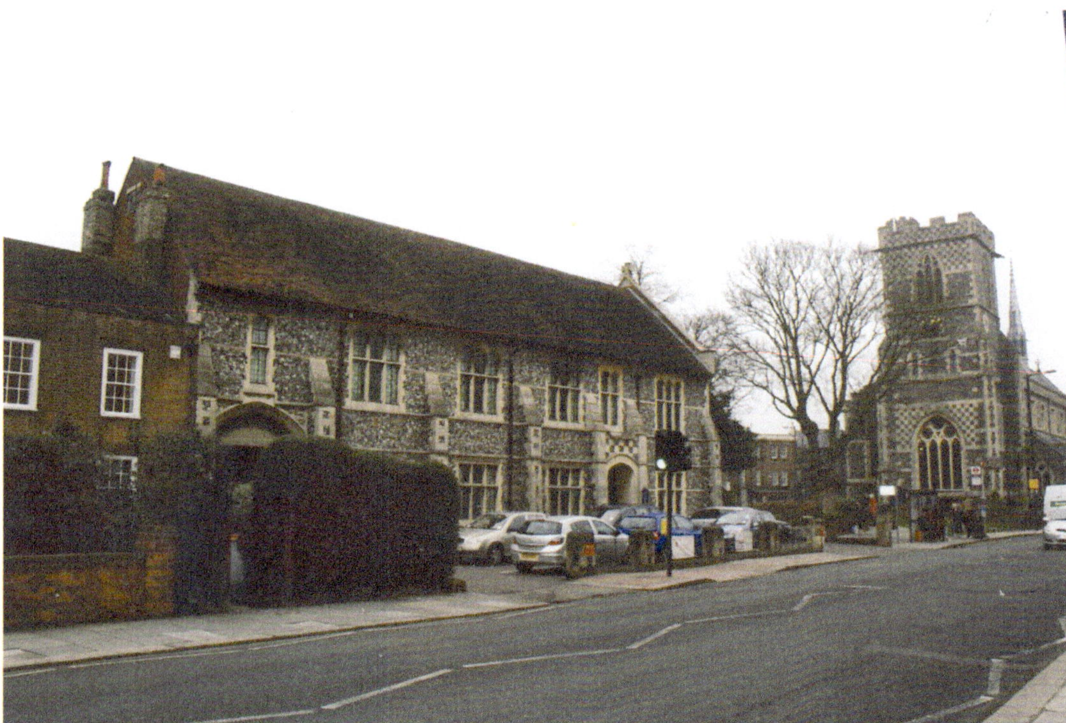

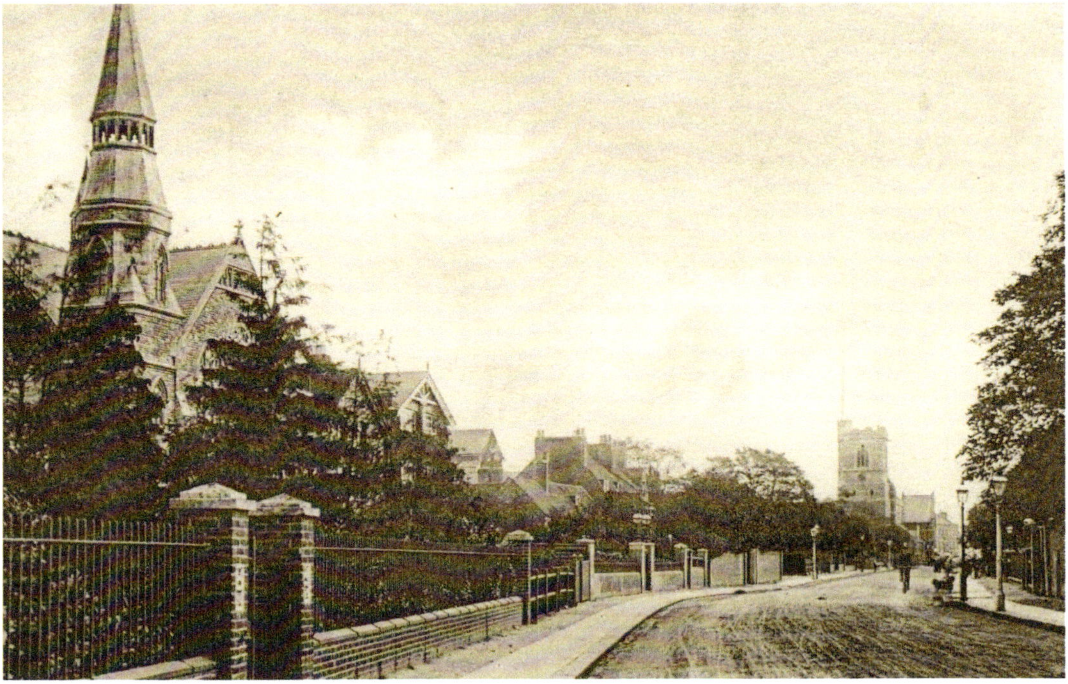

United Reform Chapel

The photograph above was taken outside the United Reform chapel. The picture probably dates to just after 1907, when the Ewan Hall, just visible in the lower photograph, was built.

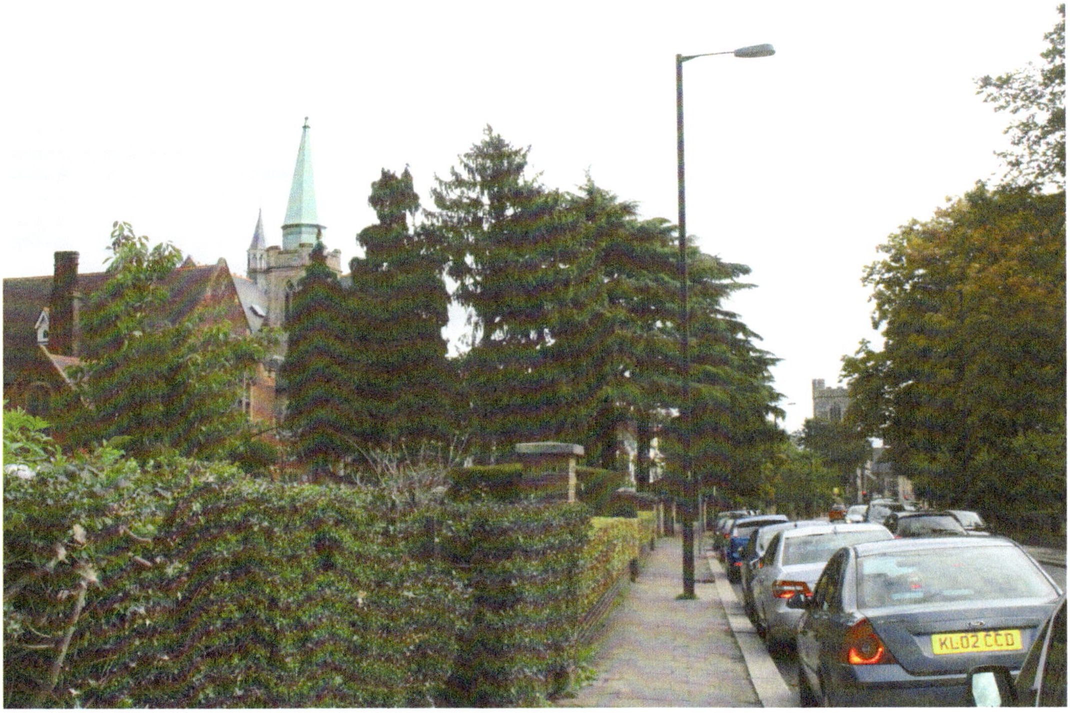

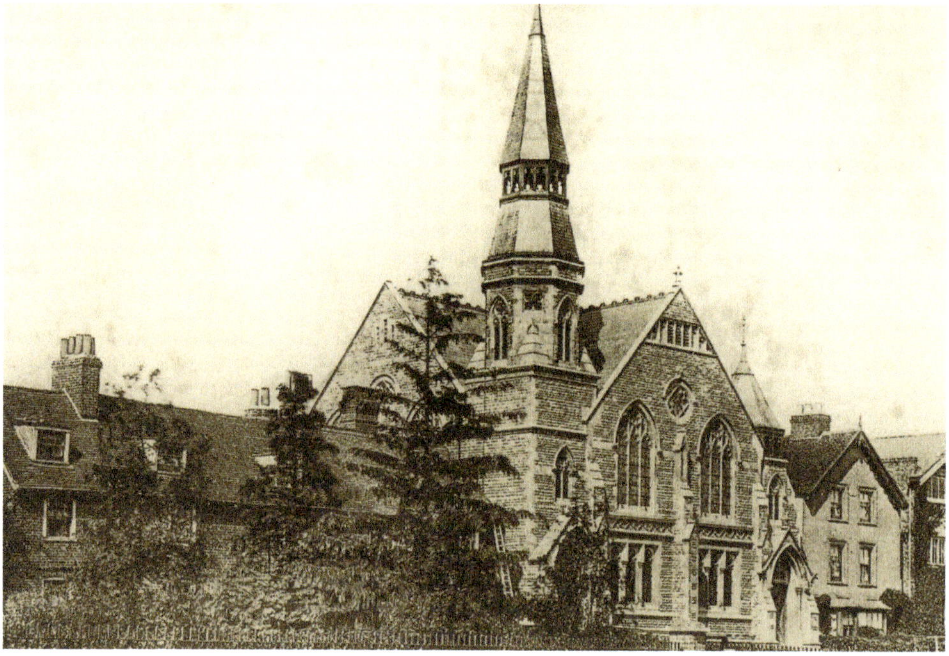

Ewan Hall

The cottages on the left (*above*) were replaced by what is now known as Ewan Hall in 1907, the land having been purchased by the adjoining United Reform church in 1900. The hall was used as a Sunday school, and classrooms were opened. This building was also used as a hospital during the First World War. Below, the church and hall in 2013. The church dates from 1893, having replaced the church built in 1824.

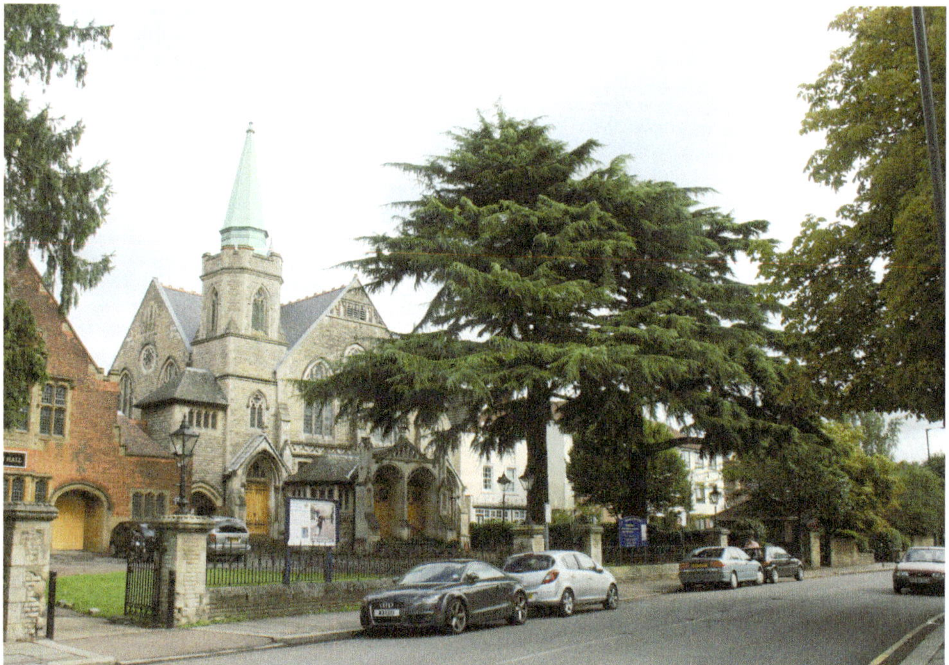

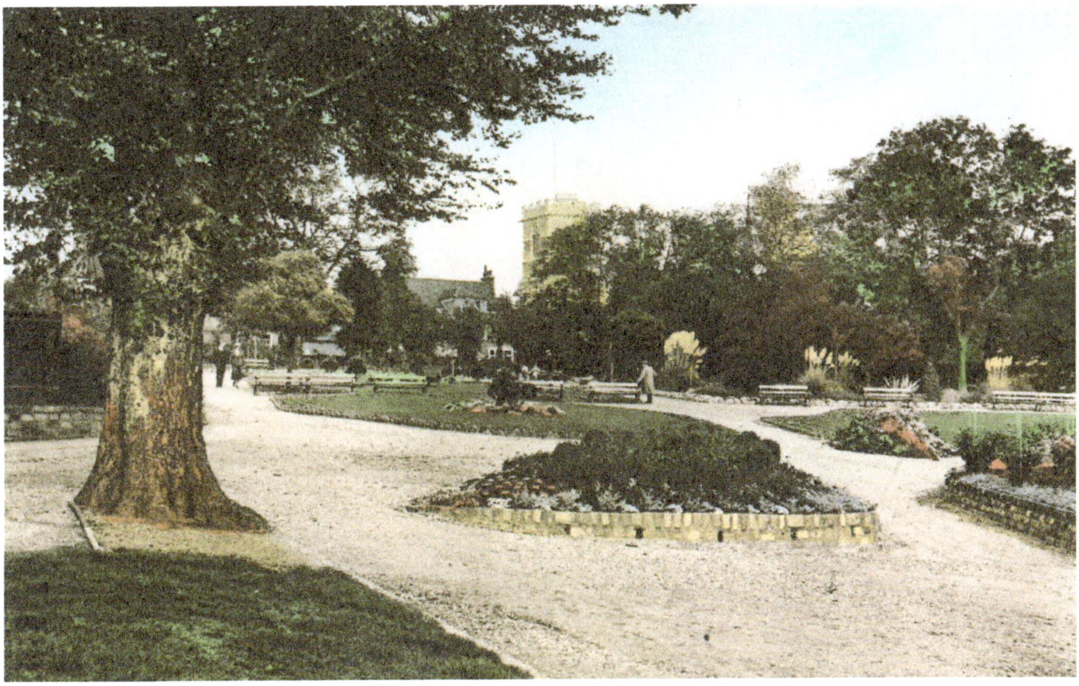

Wood Street View

A view from behind the Old Court House in Wood Street, looking towards St John's church, seen in the centre of both images. The above view is dated 1905, while below is the same view today.

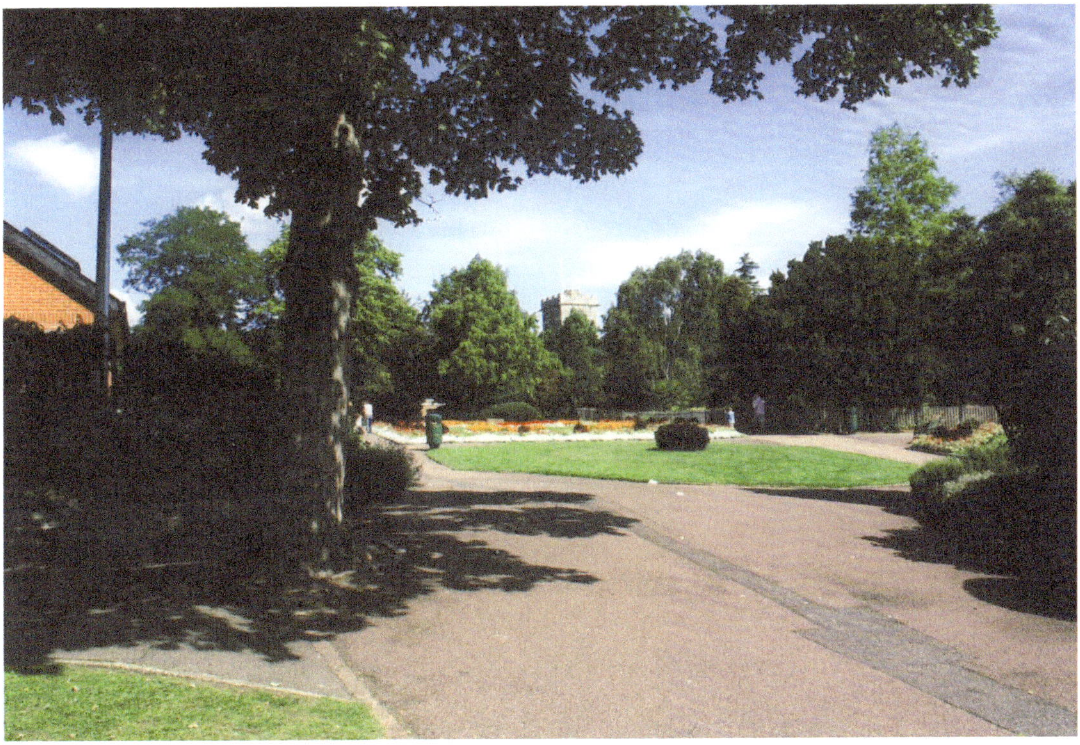

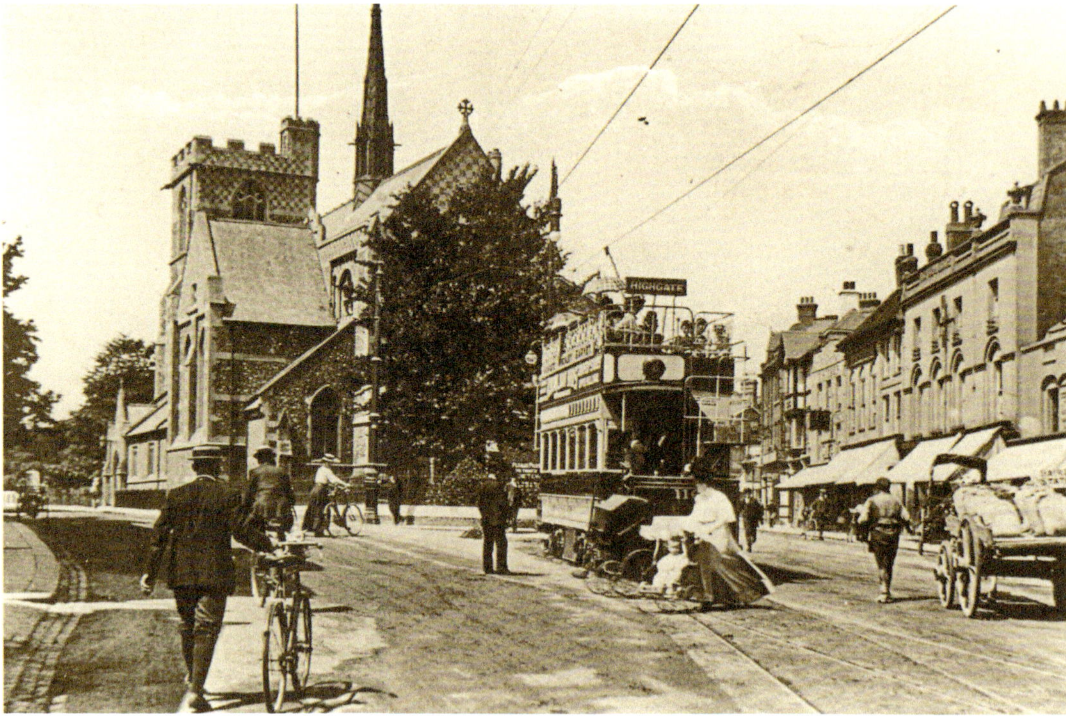

Barnet Hill

Barnet Hill was initially a problem for trams and they finally arrived on 28 March 1907. The terminus was just south of the church, as shown in the above photograph. The picture dates from around 1910 and is looking north, with Wood Street to the left.

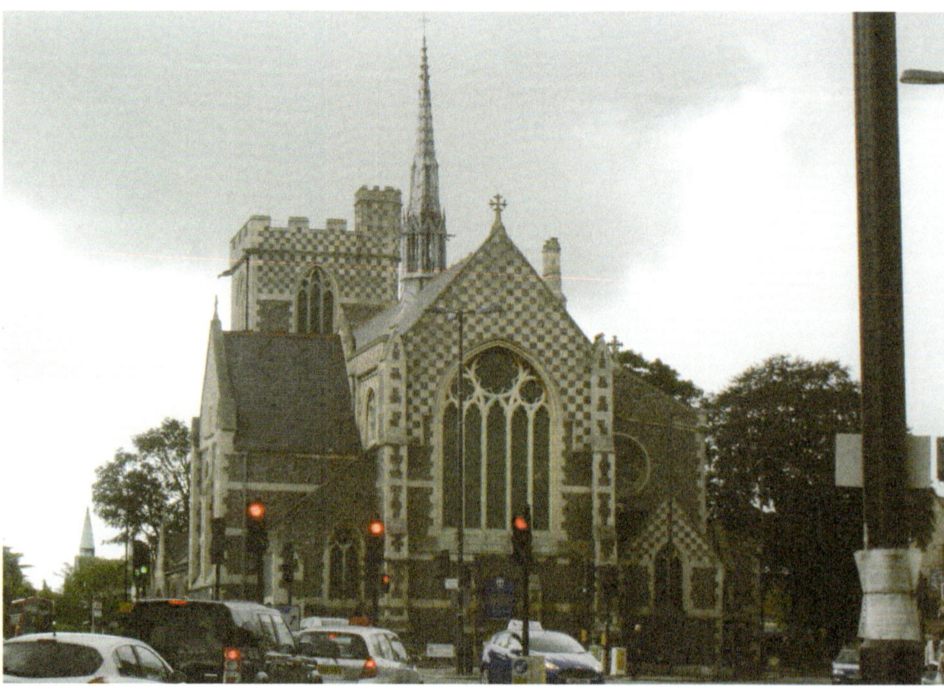

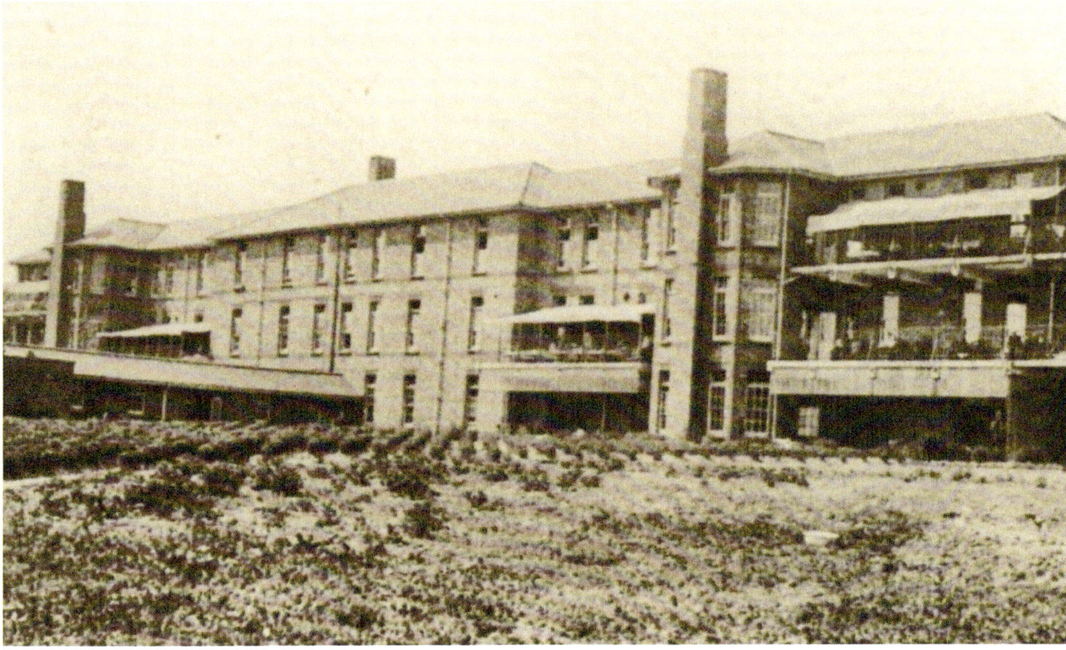

Barnet Workhouse

Chipping Barnet had its own workhouses from 1729. The Barnet Union workhouse was built in 1836/37 at the end of West End Lane and at the south side of Well House Lane. The main building, backing onto Well House Lane, had a T-shaped layout with deep wings containing back-to-back wards. A chapel was added at the south-west of the workhouse, probably in the 1920s. The site was taken over for use as a military hospital during the First World War and now serves as Barnet General Hospital.

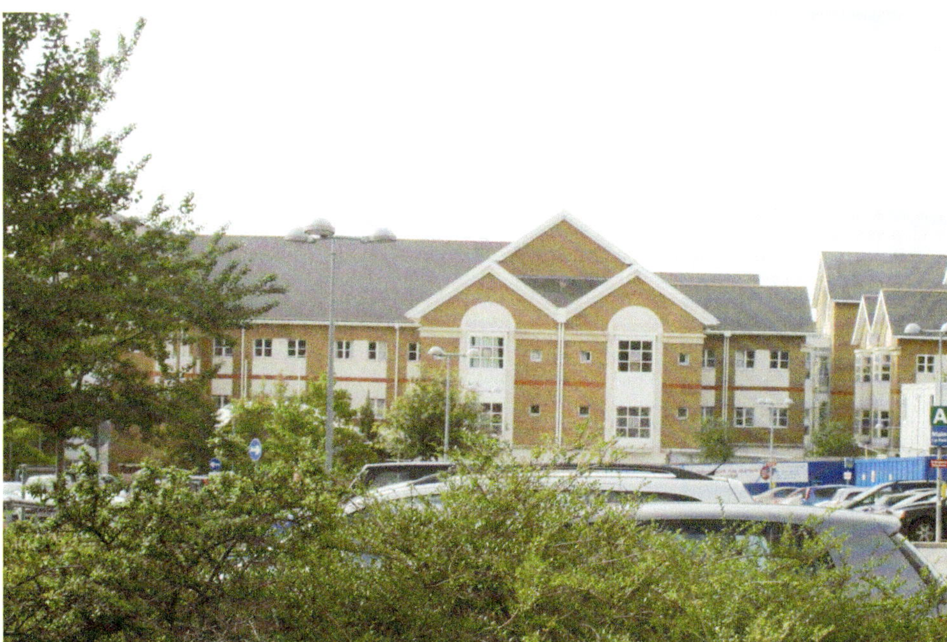

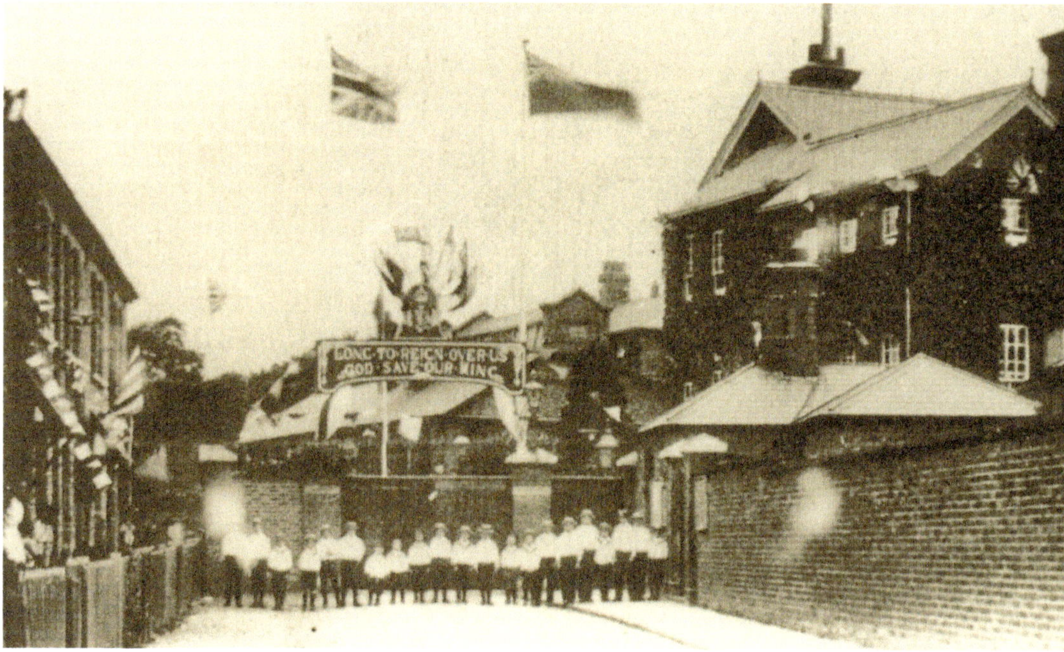

West End Lane

The inmates of the workhouse are probably celebrating the accession of Edward VII in 1901. West End Lane (*above and below*) was the entrance to the Barnet workhouse. It is said to have been the inspiration for the workhouse in the Charles Dickens' novel *Oliver Twist* after a friend of Dickens' paid a visit to the establishment and heard one its young inmates 'ask for more'. In 2002, the hospital authorities announced plans to demolish the workhouse and to use the site as a car park.

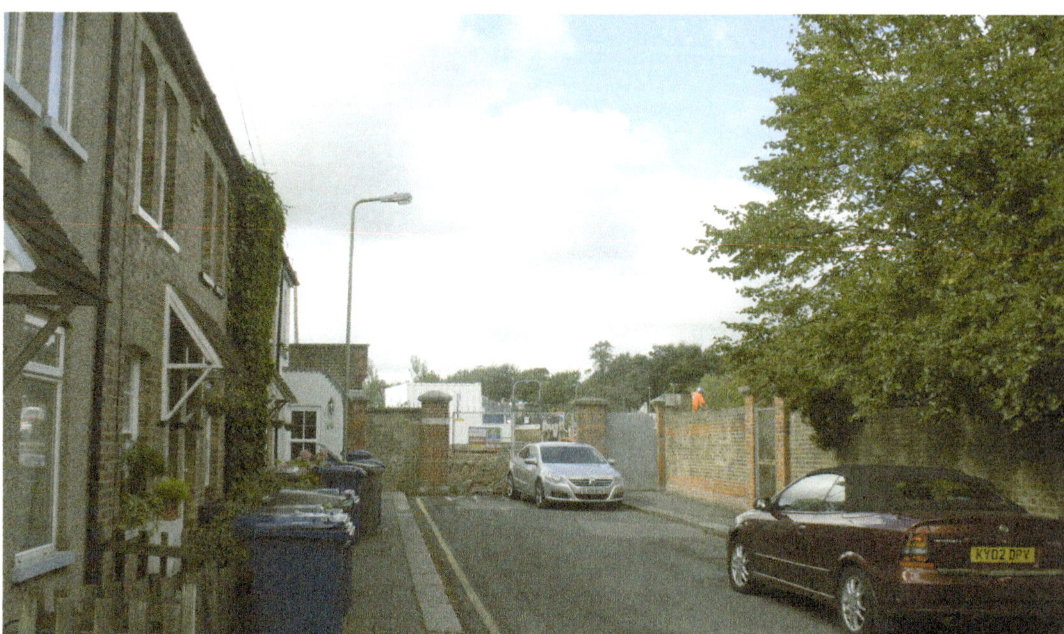

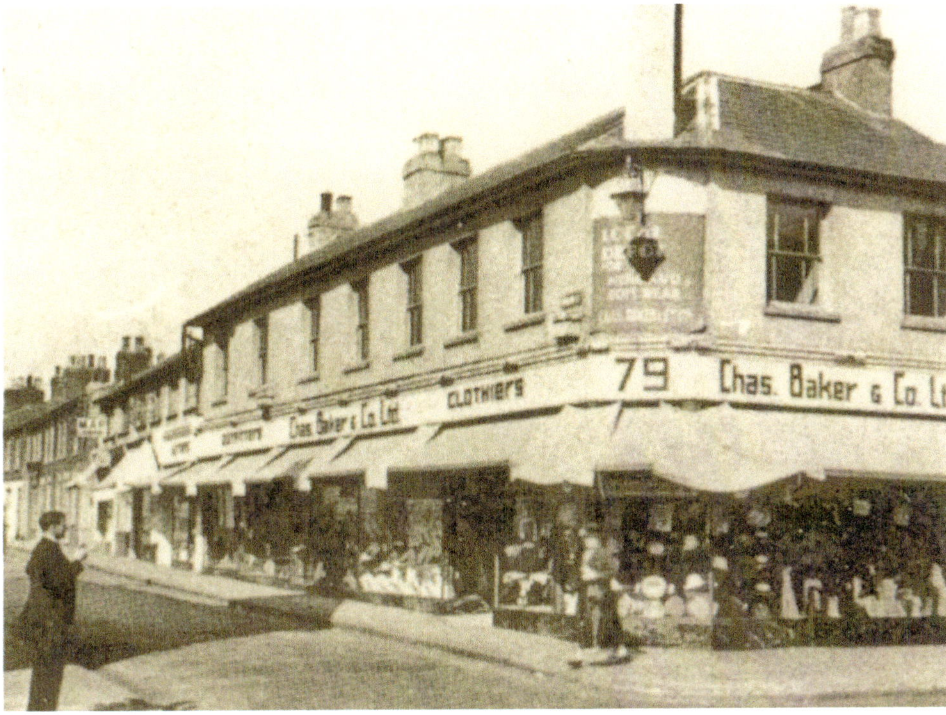

Union and High Street

Above, the extensive unit on the corner of Union Street and High Street in 1934. Below, the unit in 2013.

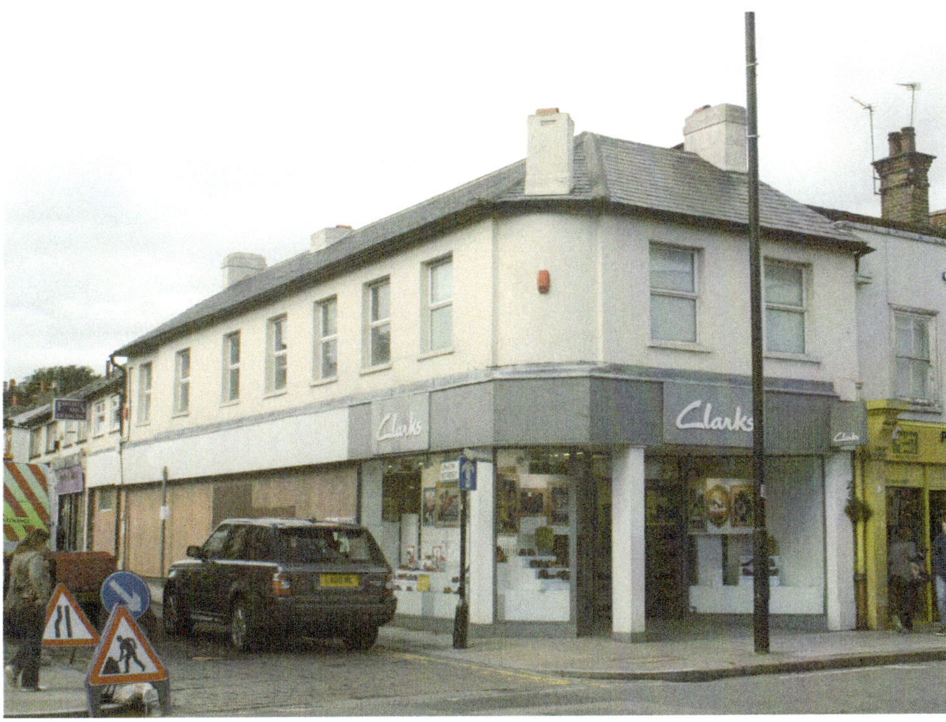

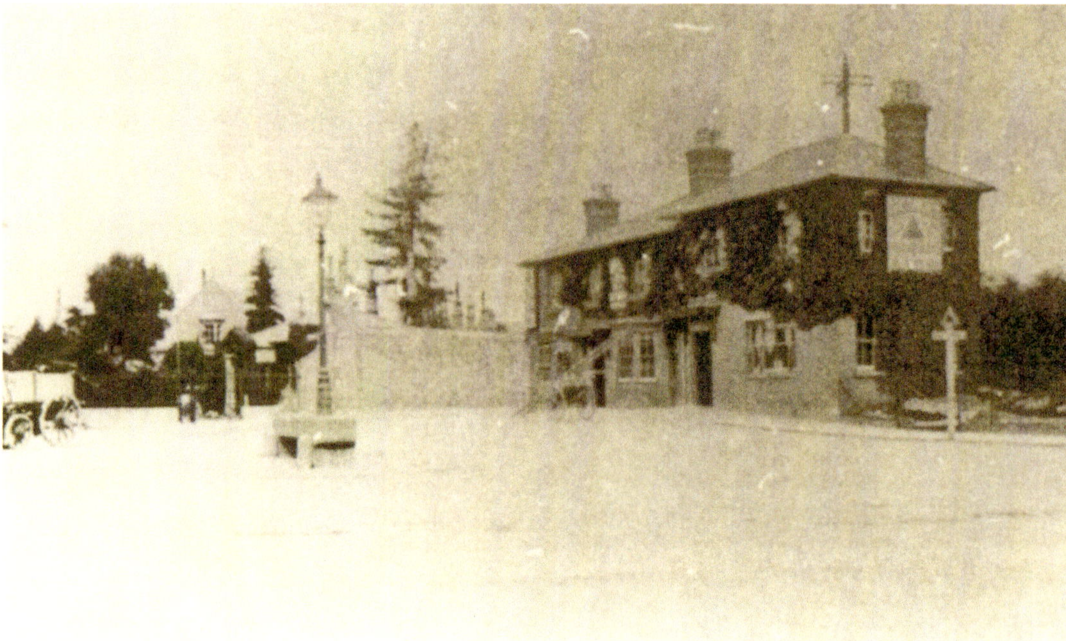

The Black Horse

The Black Horse public house around 1890, located just off Wood Street at the Barnet end of the Barnet Lane. The pub claims a ghost, and is easily recognisable over a century later, backing onto the Leathersellers Almshouses, which can be seen in the distance. Below, the Black Horse in 2013.

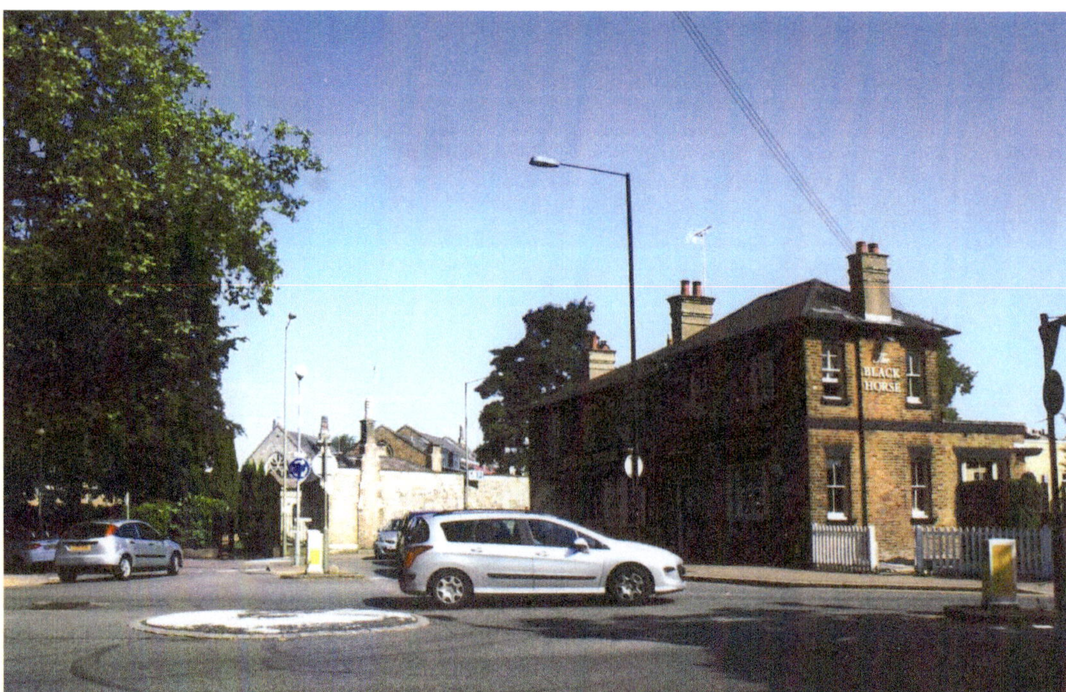

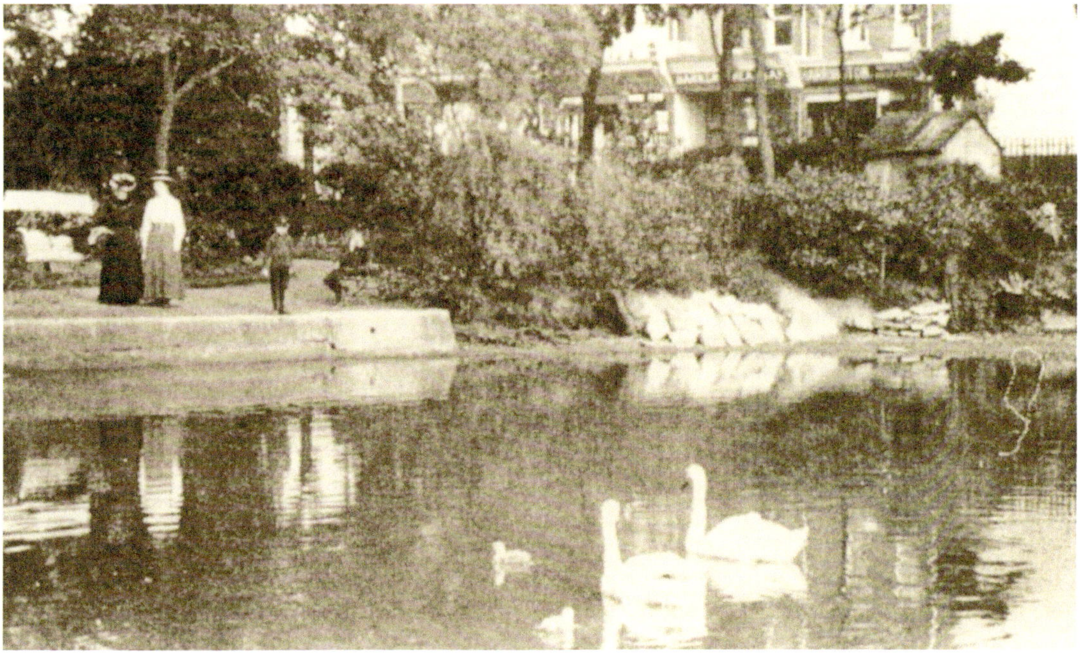

Ravenscroft Pond

Ravenscroft Pond with Wood Street in the background. The above photograph dates from around 1905. This was once within Barnet Common. In the 1880s, houses and a new road were being built and the remaining open land with a pond was converted into this public park. It was later named after James Ravenscroft, a great benefactor of Barnet. It was laid out with serpentine walks, shrubs and bedding. There were two ponds, both drained in 1992, and sunken areas now mark their previous location.

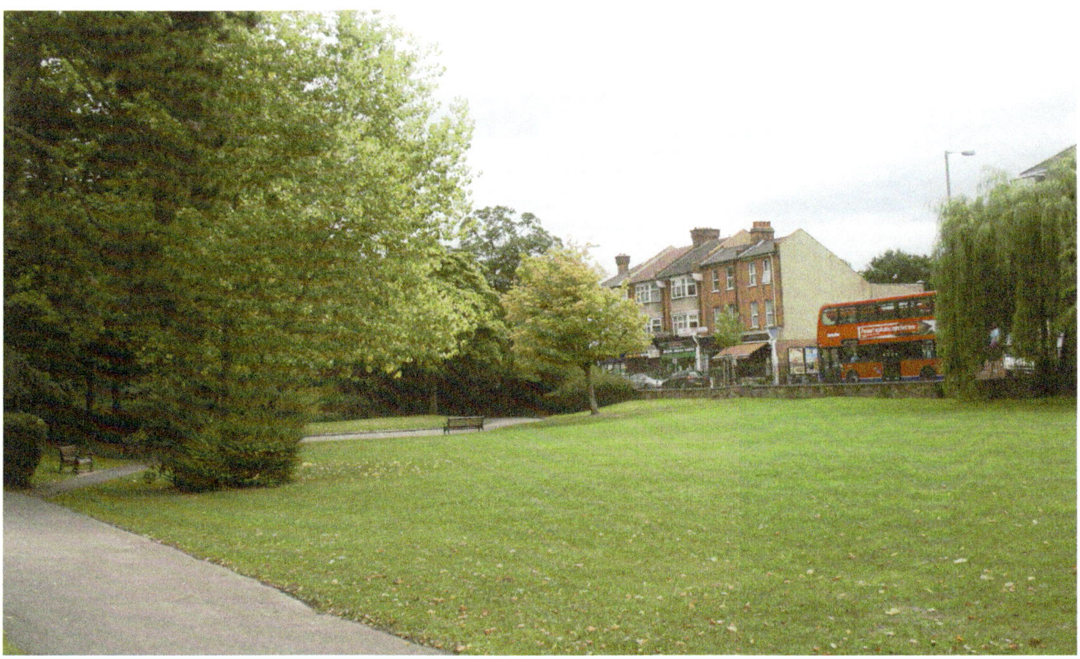

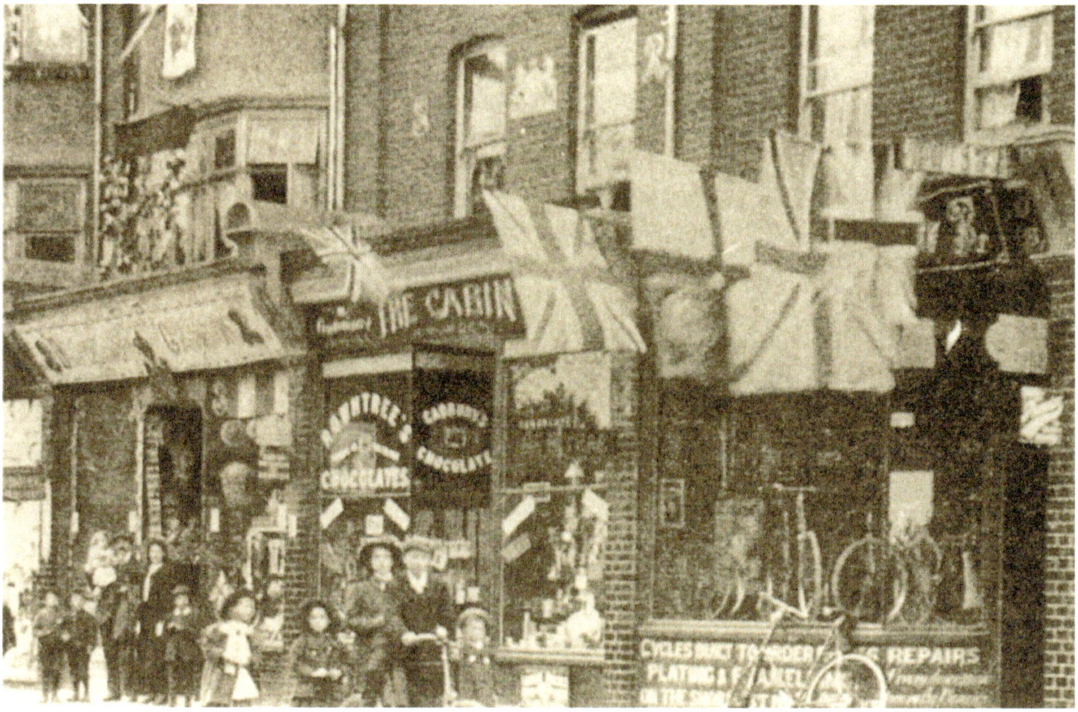

Ravenscroft Park

Shops in Wood Street opposite Ravenscroft Park in 1911, at the time of George V's coronation. Little has changed in over a century.

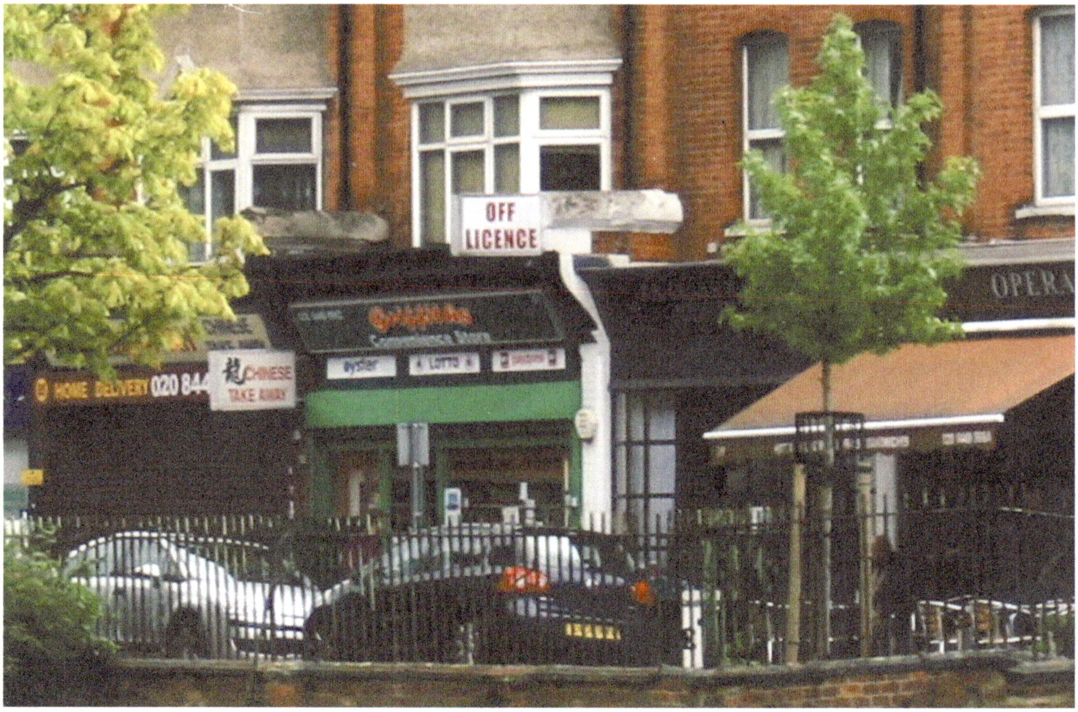

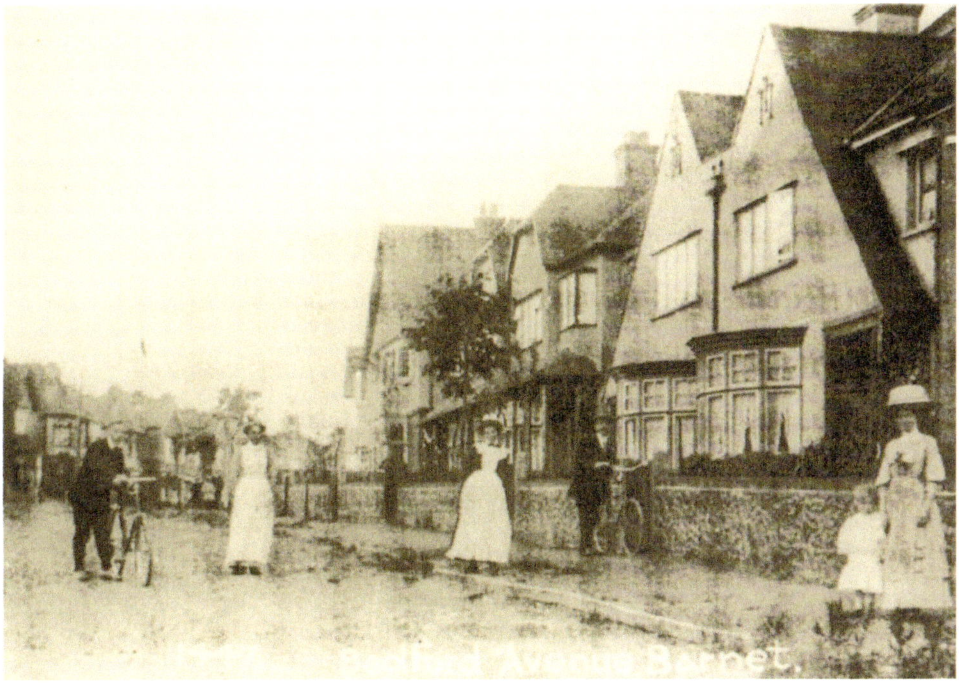

Bedford Avenue

Bedford Avenue near Barnet Hill came into existence after the arrival of High Barnet station. Apart from cars, little has changed since the photograph above was taken in around 1910.

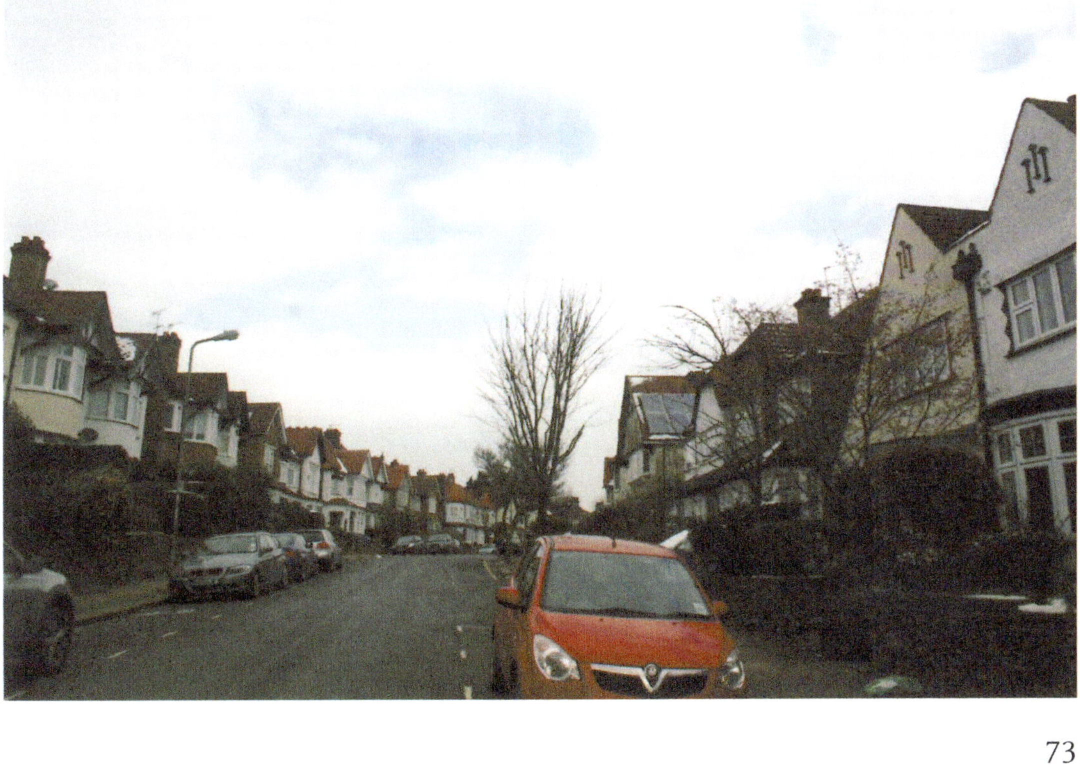

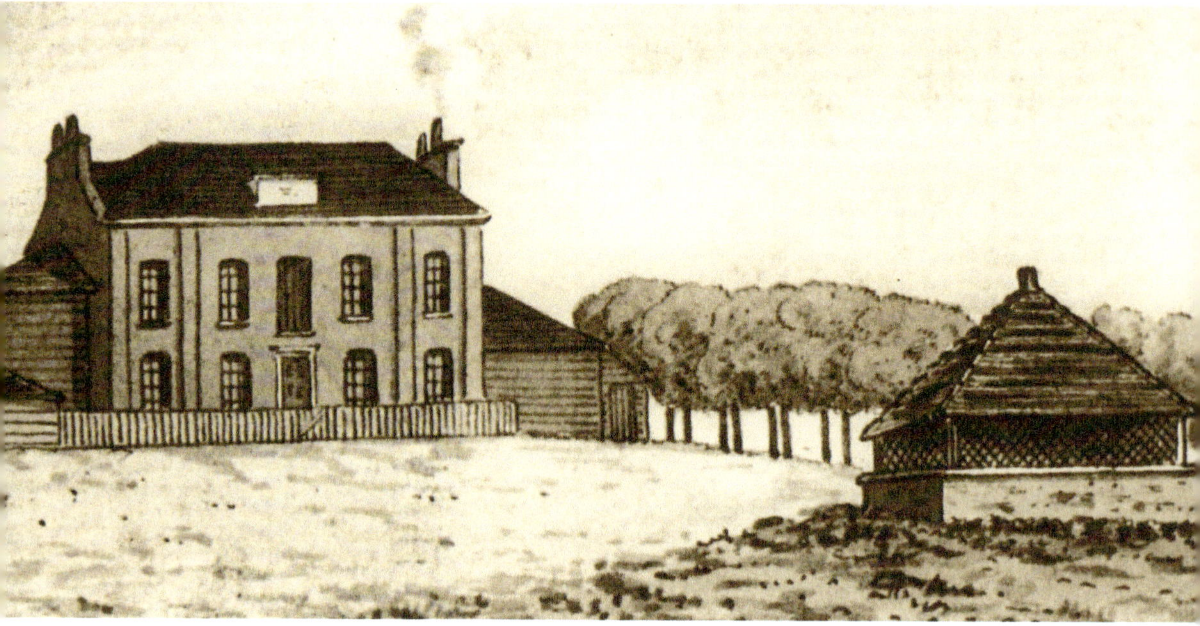

Barnet Common

Barnet was once famous for its mineral water, drawn by a well on what was known as the Barnet Common. It was referred to in 1586. Samuel Pepys wrote in his diary of 11 July 1664 that he had swallowed five glasses of water. The illustration above probably dates from around 1800. The 2013 photograph below shows the present mock Tudor building, erected in 1937.

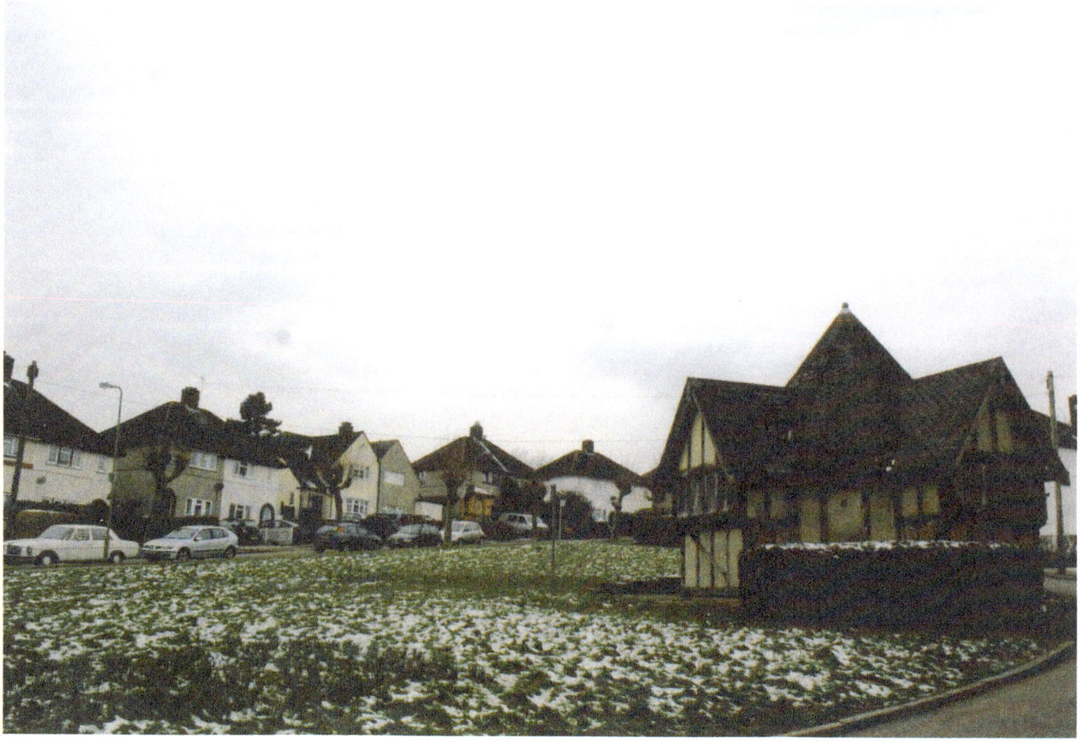

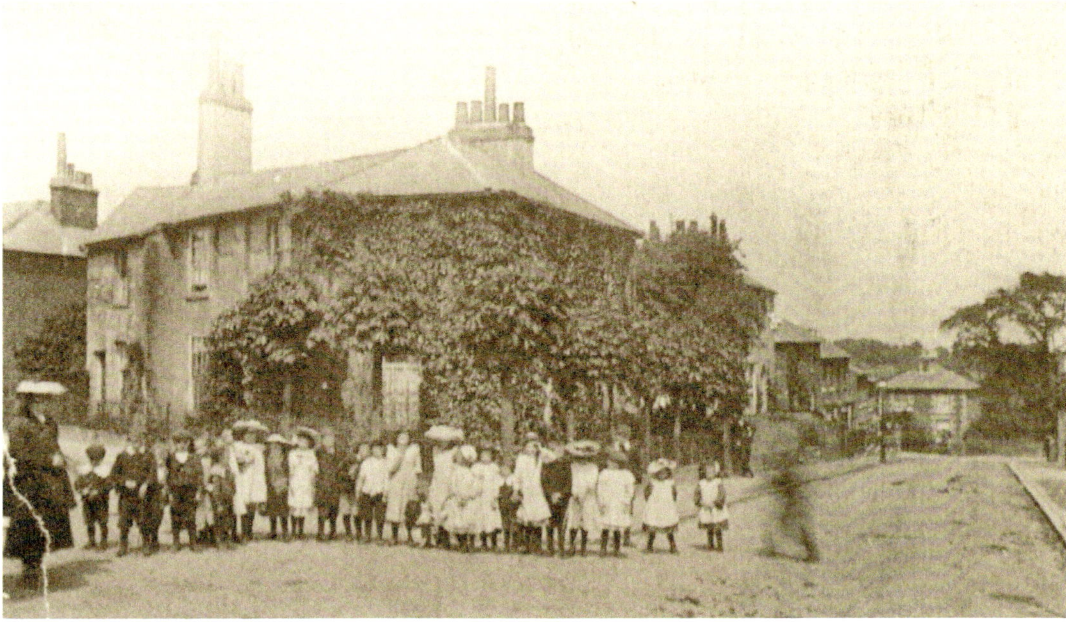

Moxton Street

The building in Moxon Street, which runs off Barnet High Street and once housed Moxon Street School, still stands. The picture above dates from 1903. Below, the same view in 2013.

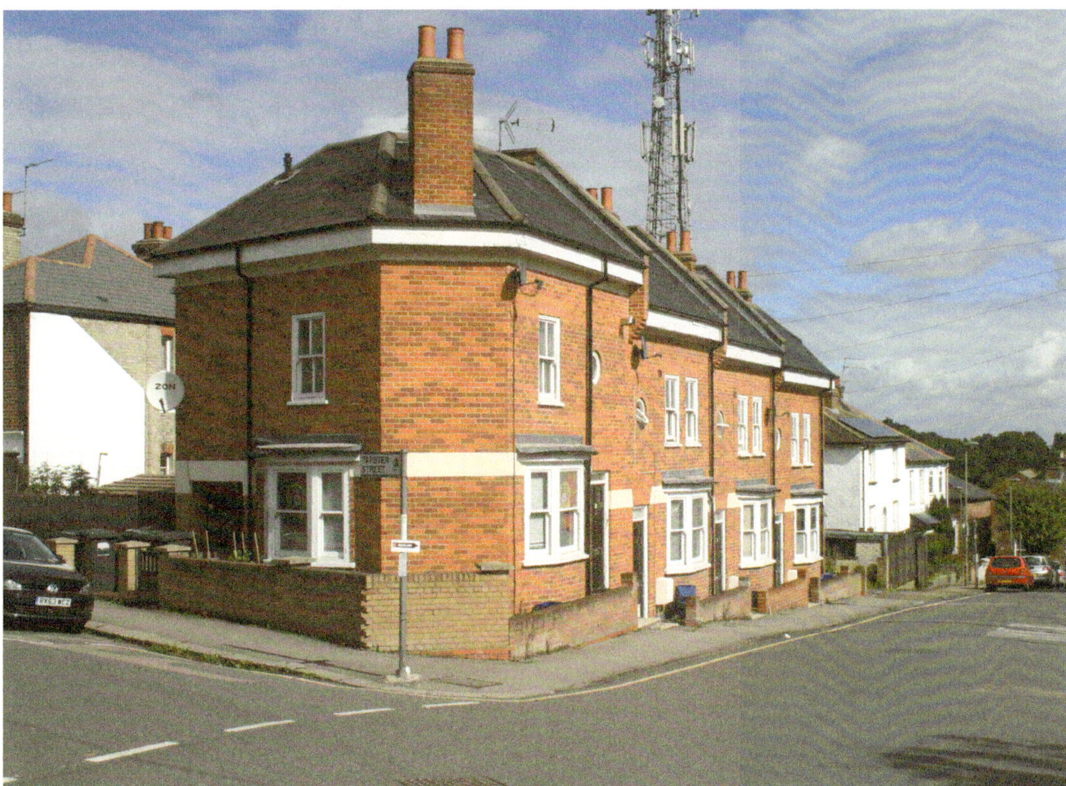

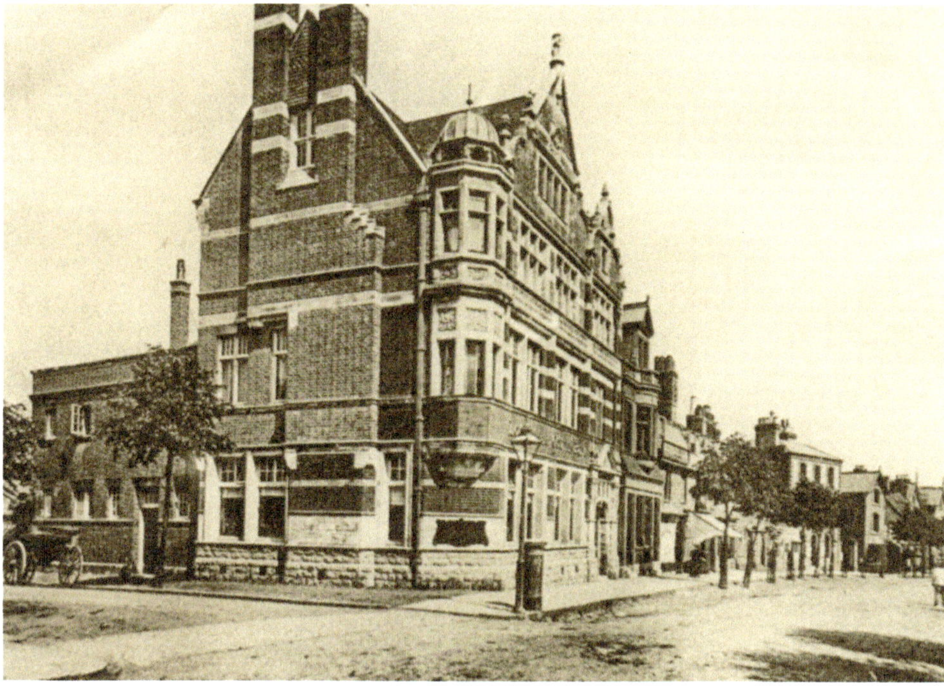

High Barnet Road and Park Road

The building on the corner of High Road Barnet and Park Road is still immediately recognisable. At the time of the photograph above, it was the London & County Bank.

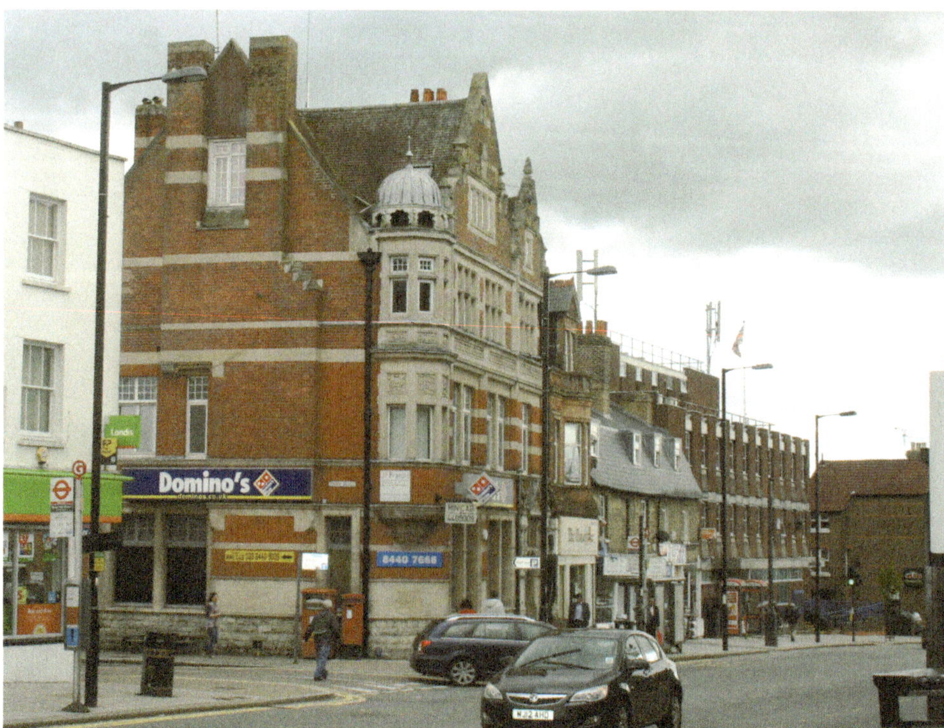

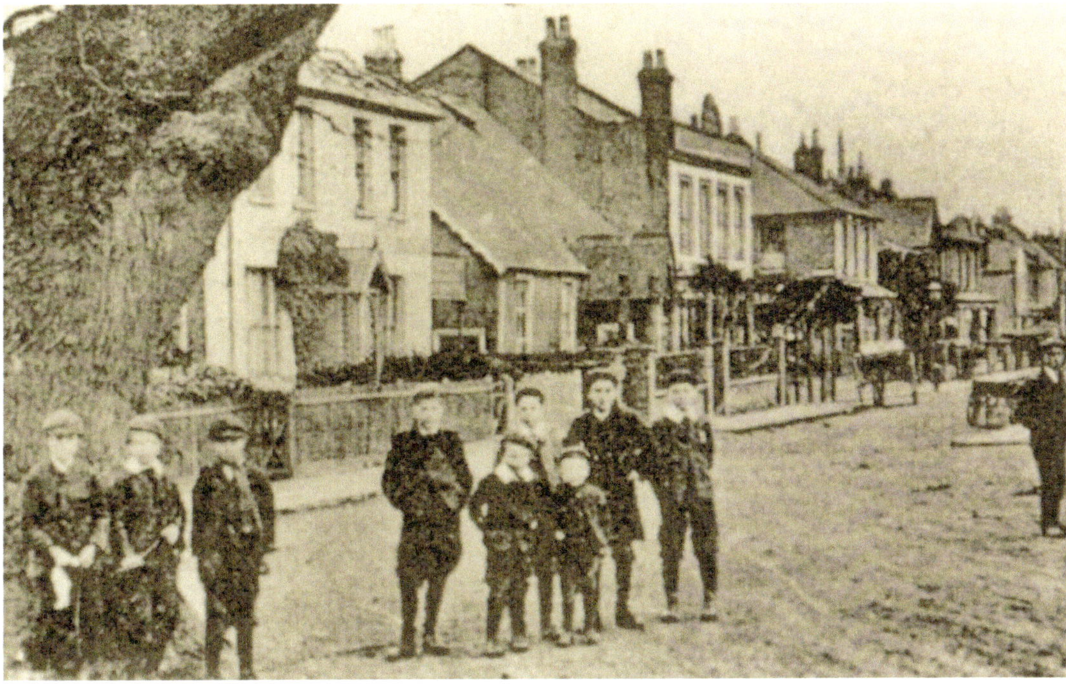

Alston Road

The children above in Alston Road in Barnet were probably photographed around 1890. The tree has gone in the 2013 view, but otherwise many of the buildings are the same.

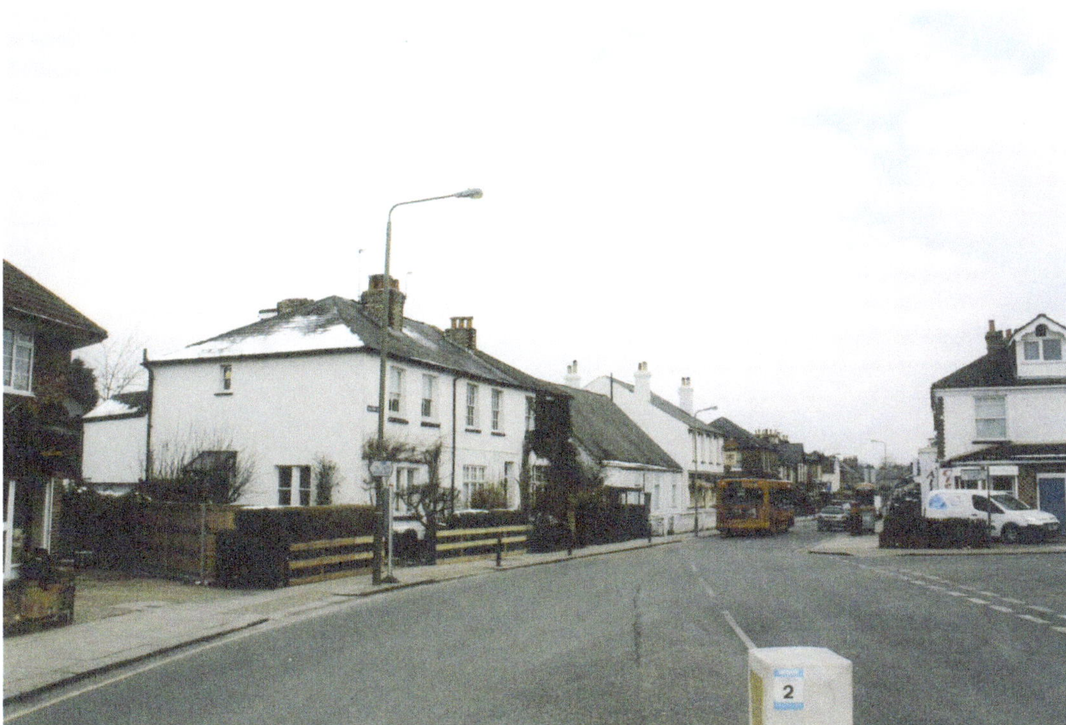

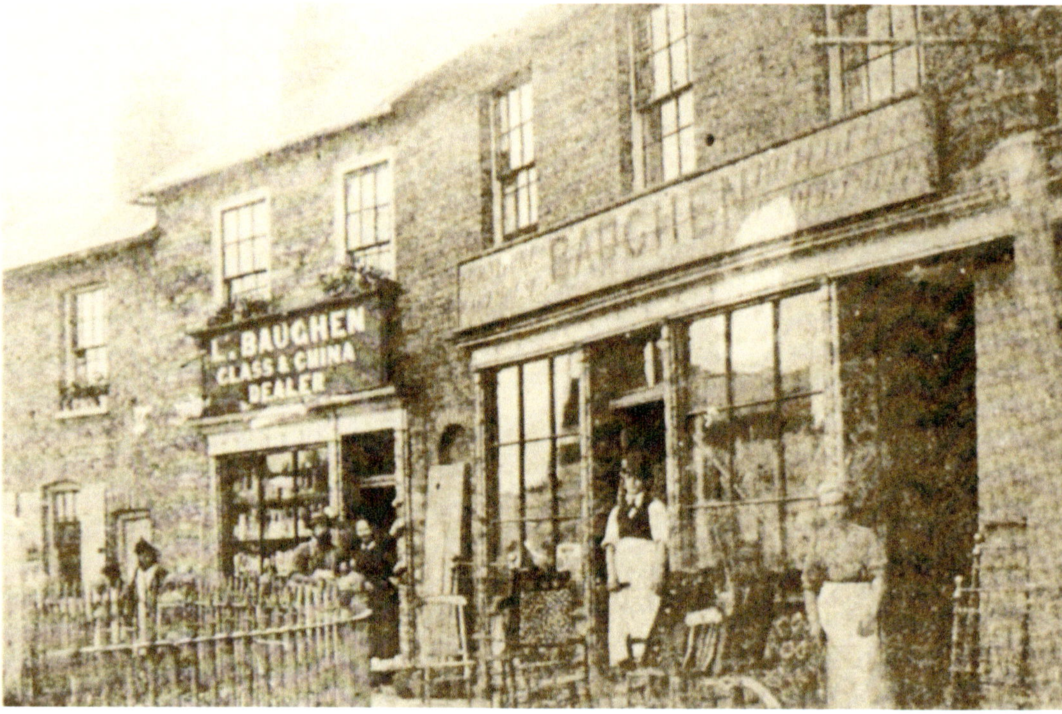

The Church Passage

Above, the church passage adjoining St John's church around 1900. The shops shown have since been demolished.

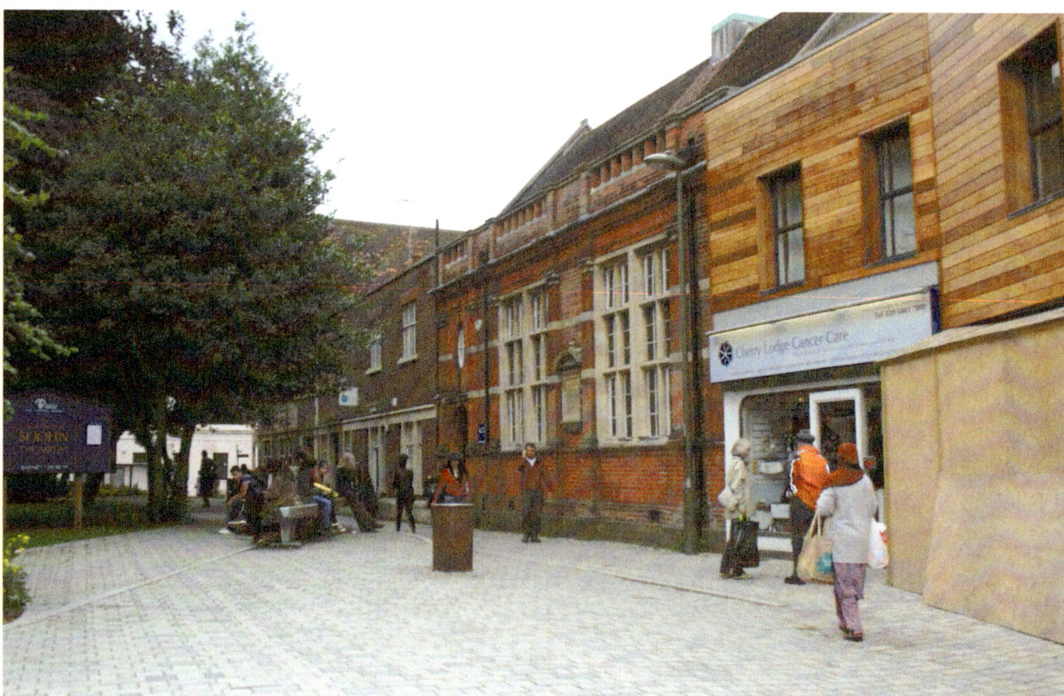

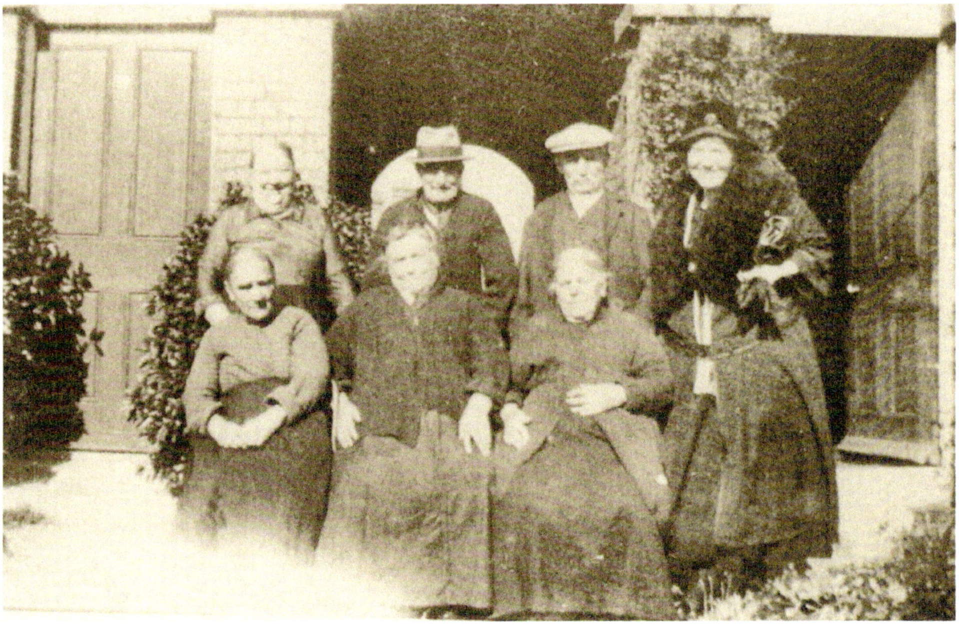

Eleanor Palmer Almshouses

Above, the residents of the Eleanor Palmer Almshouses, Wood Street, 1929. The *Victoria County History* tells us, 'The almshouses known as Palmer's almshouses, situated in Wood Street, were built in 1823, and are maintained in part by two-thirds of the rents of three acres of copyhold land known as the Fortess Field Estate in St Pancras, given, as appears from an inscription on a tablet in the church, by Mrs Eleanor Palmer, who died on 29 February, 1558, for the use of this town and Kentish Town for ever.' Below, the almshouses in 2013.

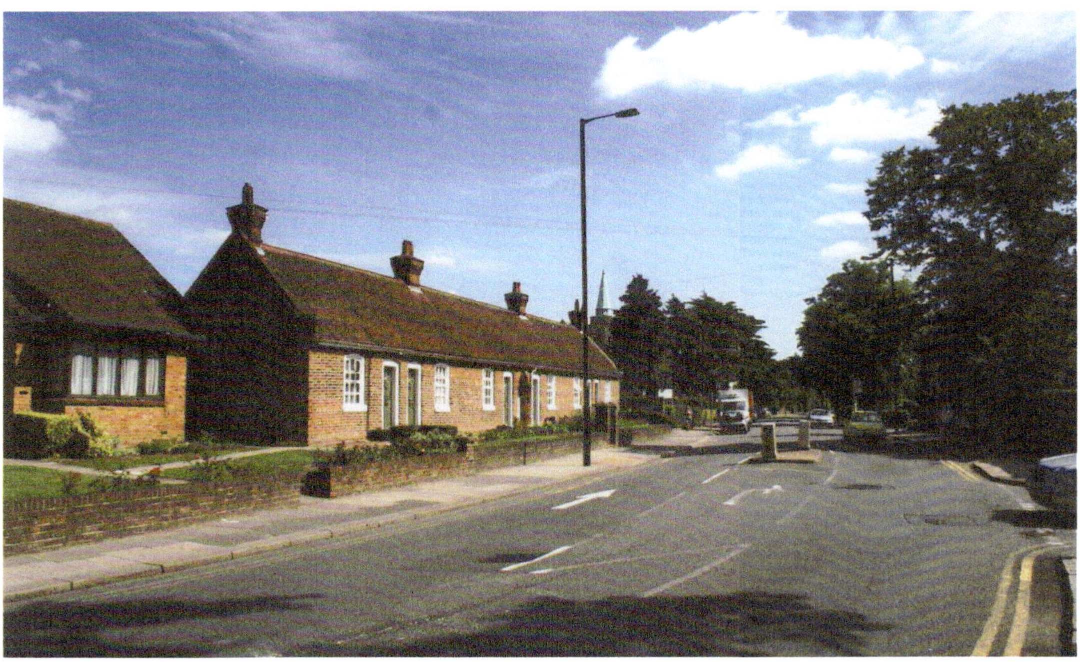

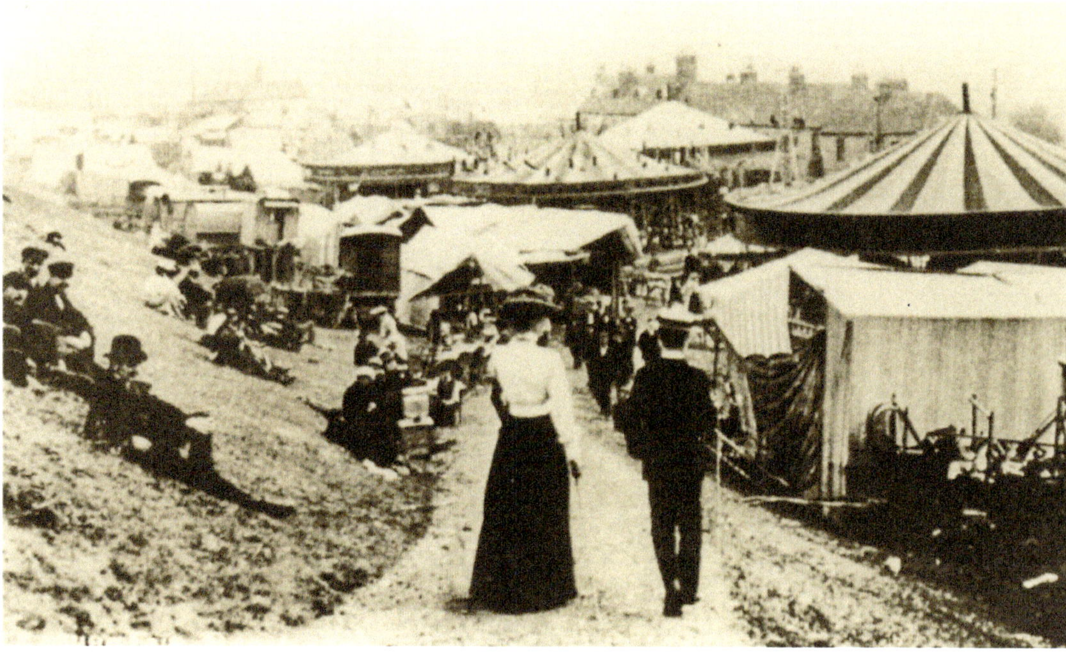

Barnet Fair

Barnet Fair covered the roads and fields along the slope around Underhill, situated at the bottom of Barnet Hill opposite where High Barnet station stands. The fair was vital to the local economy. The *Daily Telegraph* in 1881 wrote that 'the high road in the immediate vicinity of Barnet Station commands an almost uninterrupted view of the broad spread of hill and dale, where the hundreds – thousands I should think it might safely be said – of horned cattle and horses are collected for buyers to pick and choose from, the cattle being separated from the horse.' Below, the pathway still remains in 2013.

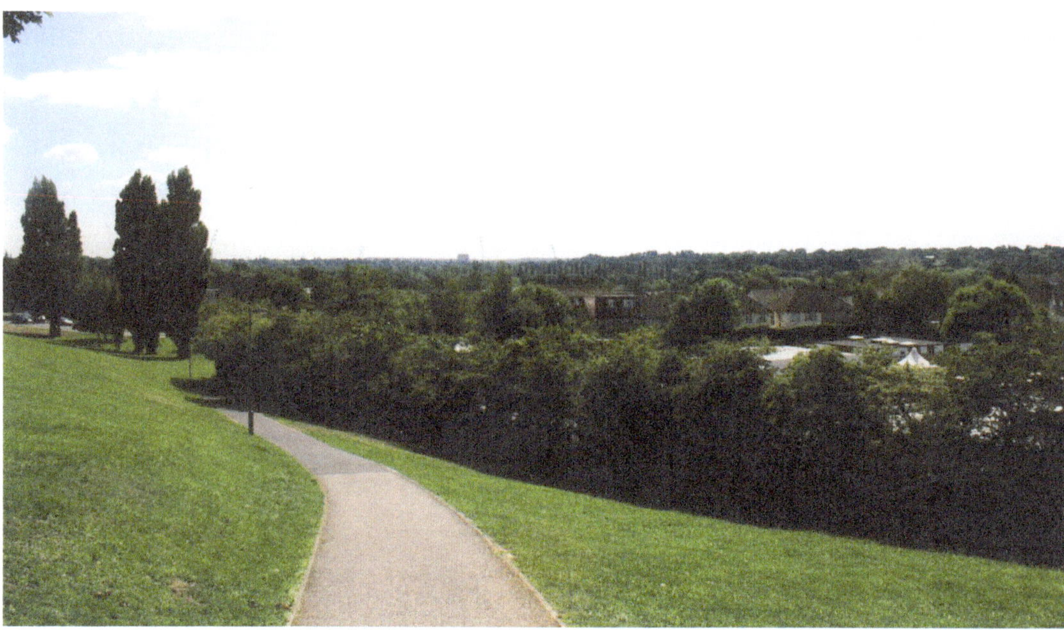

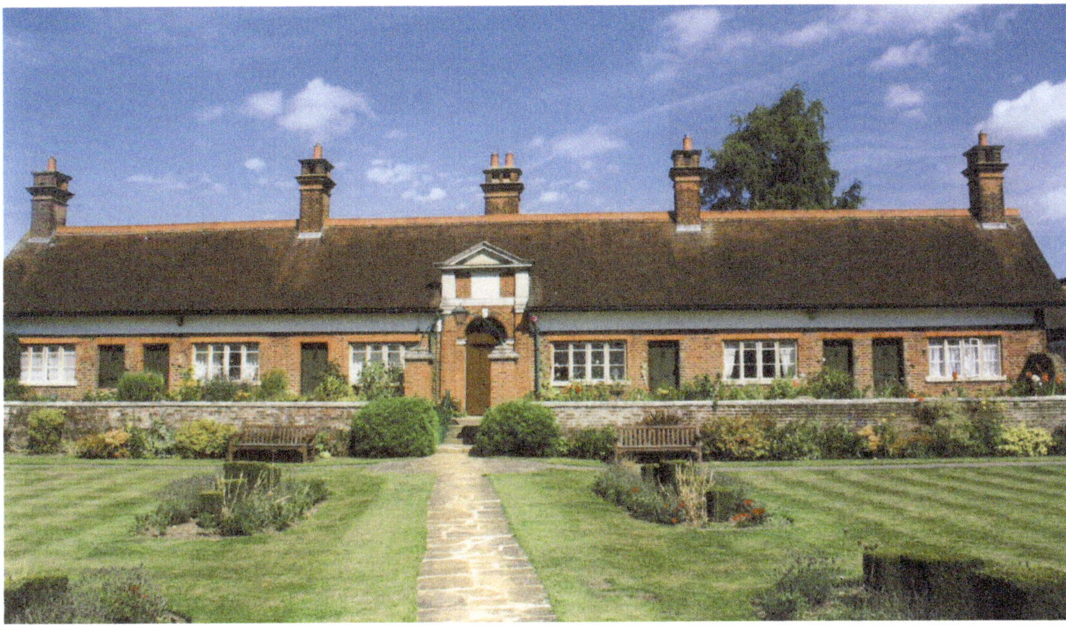

Jesus Hospital and Elizabeth Allen School

Above, the Jesus Hospital, situated in Wood Street, which was founded by James Ravenscroft by deed dated 28 April 1679, as a 'hospital or almshouses for six poor and impotent women (widows or maids), one of them to be the governess. The institution was to be a body corporate, and the said James Ravenscroft thereby granted to the governess and sisters the hospital site and buildings erected by him' (*Victoria County History*, 1908). Below, the Elizabeth Allen School 1824–1973 (now a rest home) in Wood Street. Elizabeth Allen died in 1727, leaving this land for the building of a free school for boys and girls of Barnet to learn reading, writing and arithmetic.

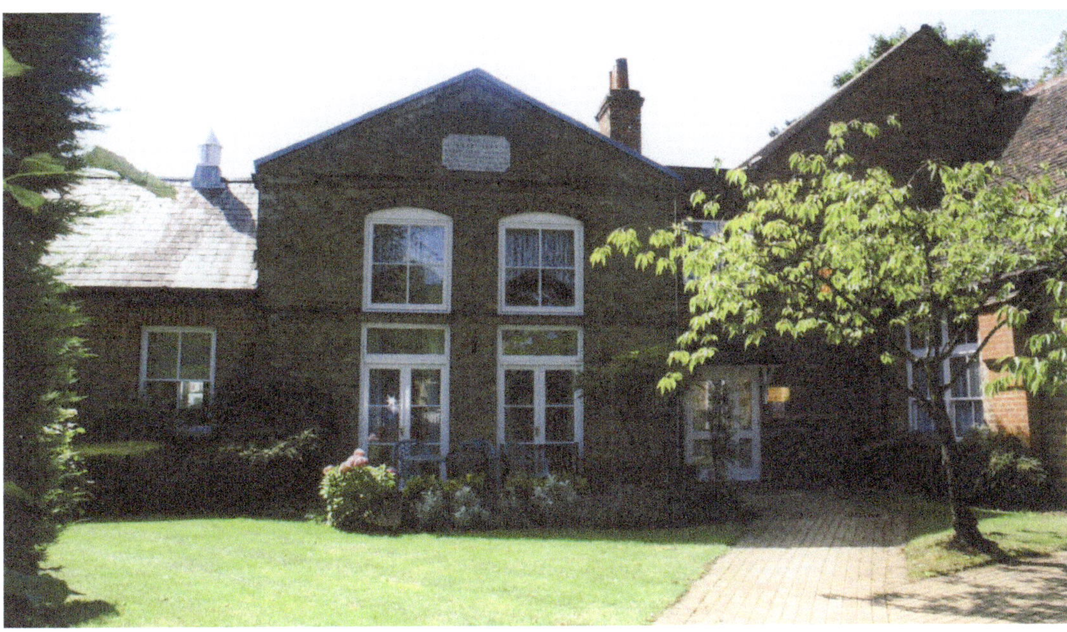

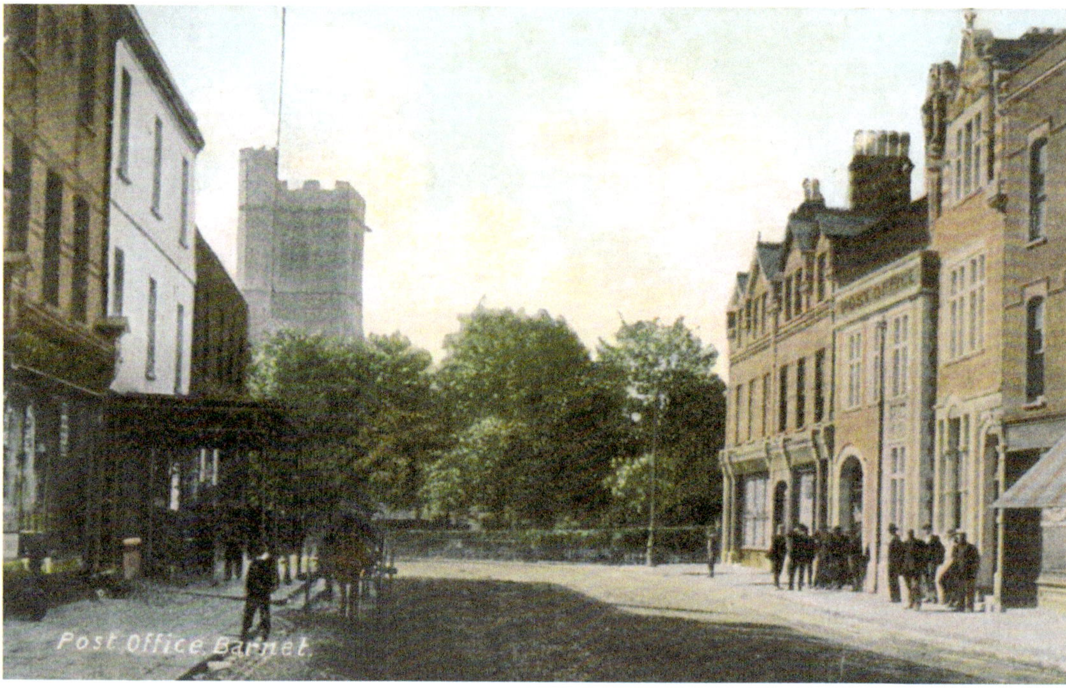

Barnet High Street Post Office

Above, the post office in Barnet High Street, 1905, looking south. Below, the same view in 2013, which is still recognisable.

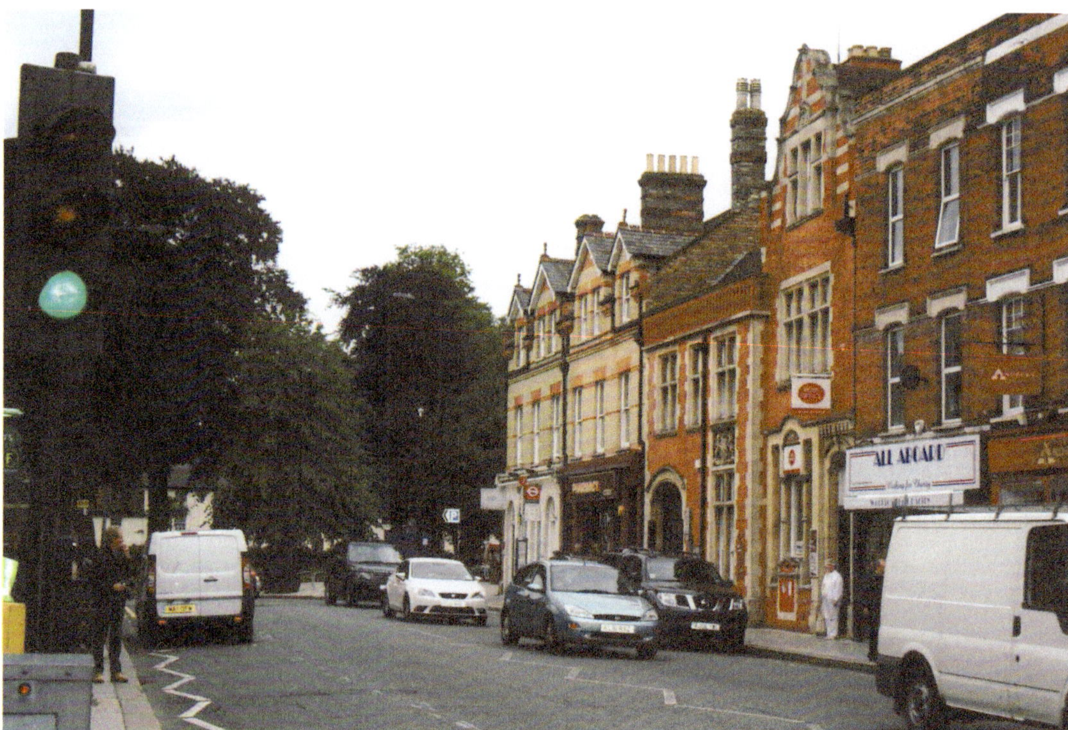

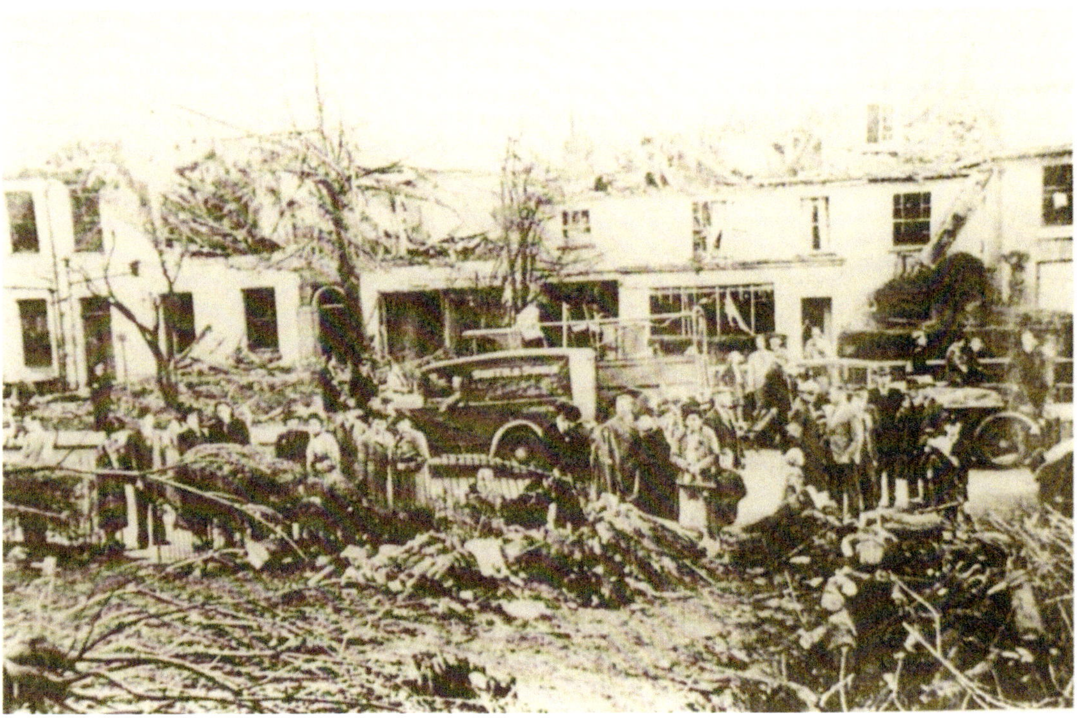

Wood Street Bomb Damage

Bomb damage in Wood Street, 18 October 1940. Among the damaged buildings, now restored, were the Barnet Museum and Bow House. Below, the restored buildings in 2013.

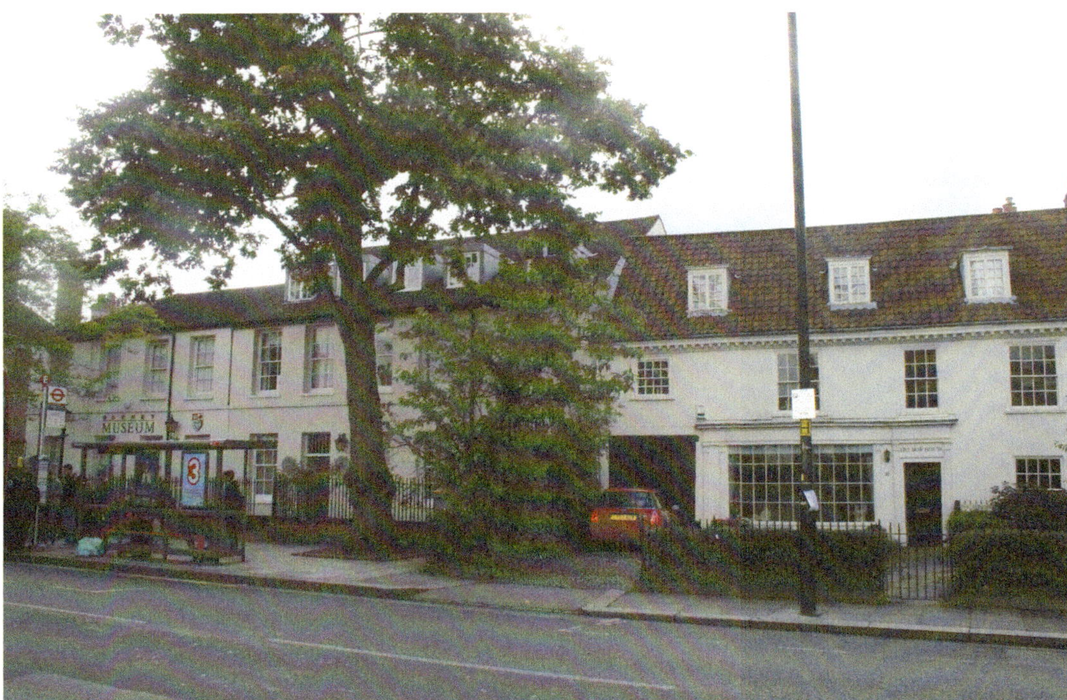

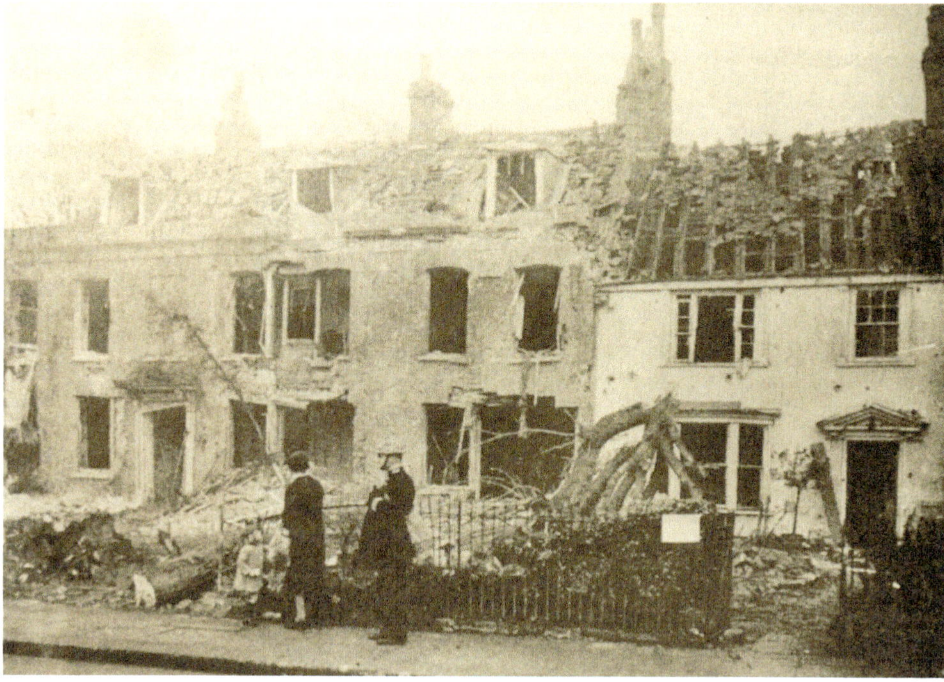

Wood Street Bomb Damage
Bomb damage opposite the Barnet Museum and Bow House from the same bombs that fell on 18 October 1940. Below, the same buildings in 2013.

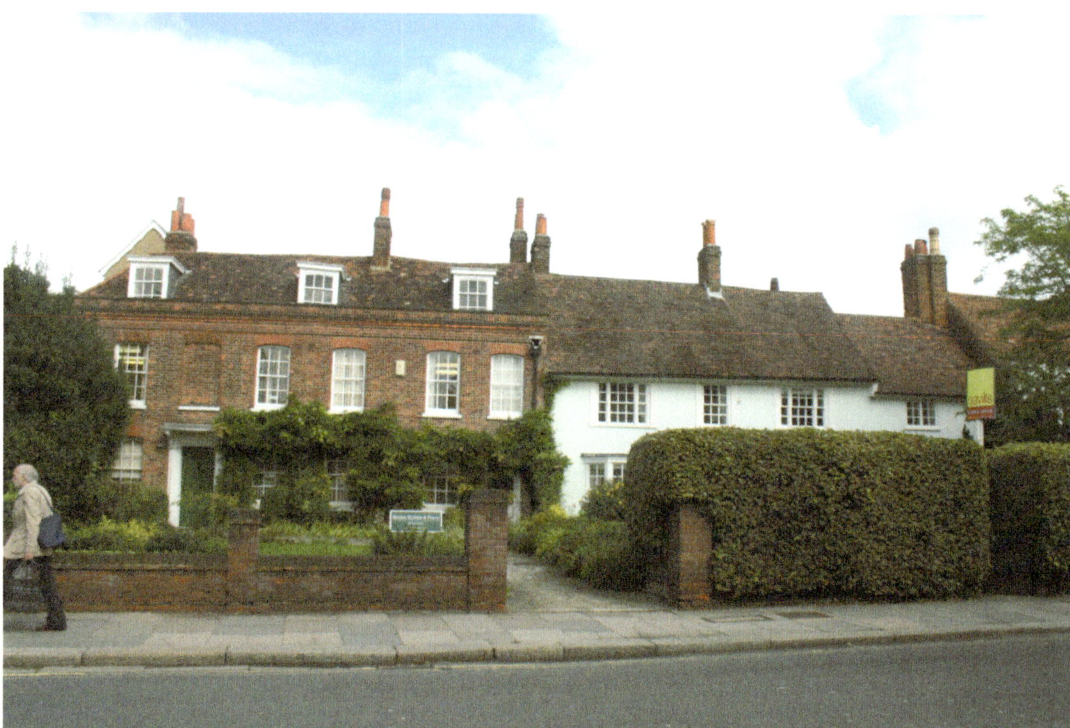

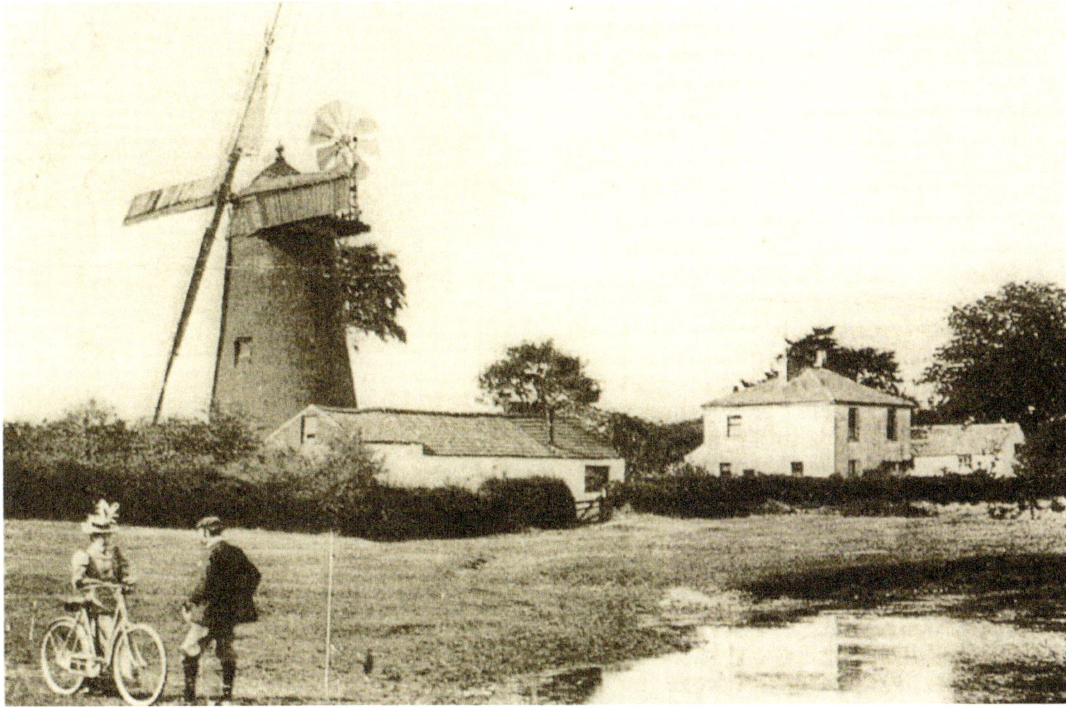

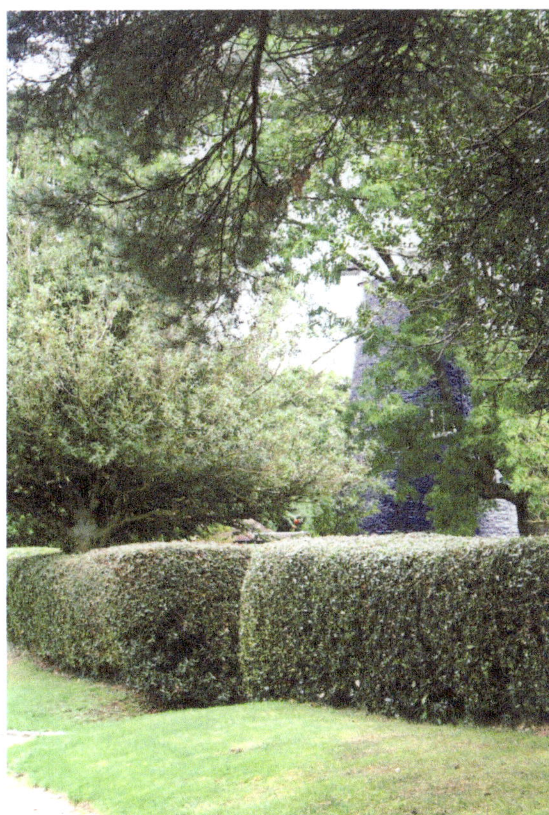

Barnet Gate Mill

Barnet Gate Mill was built in 1826. Although steam had been added in 1895, it was powered by wind until 1918, latterly on two sails. The mill was restored in 1930. It is situated on the north side of Barnet Lane near The Gate public house, but is only open to the public one day every year.

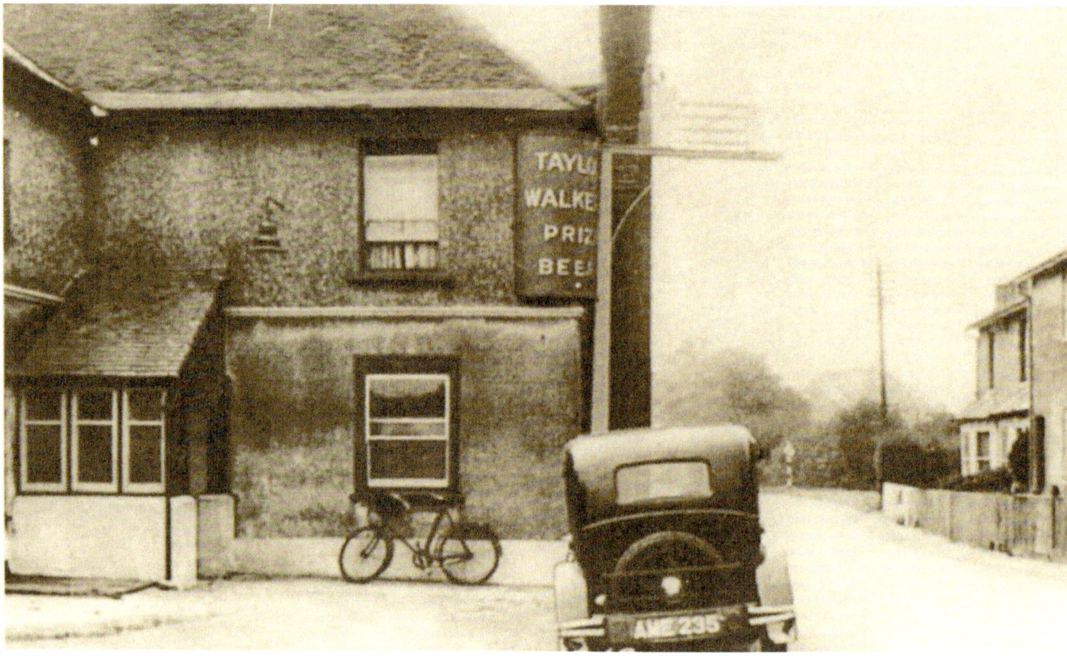

The Gate Inn

Above, The Gate Inn at Arkley in around 1925, looking towards the A1 roundabout; the gate hangs over Barnet Lane. The extensively altered Gate public house is of Victorian origin, and was originally called The Bell. The message on the gate reads, 'This Gate Hangs High And Hinders None, Refresh and Pay And Travel On.' There was never a toll gate or turnpike here – just a barrier that prevented cattle from straying onto Barnet Common. Below, The Gate in 2013.

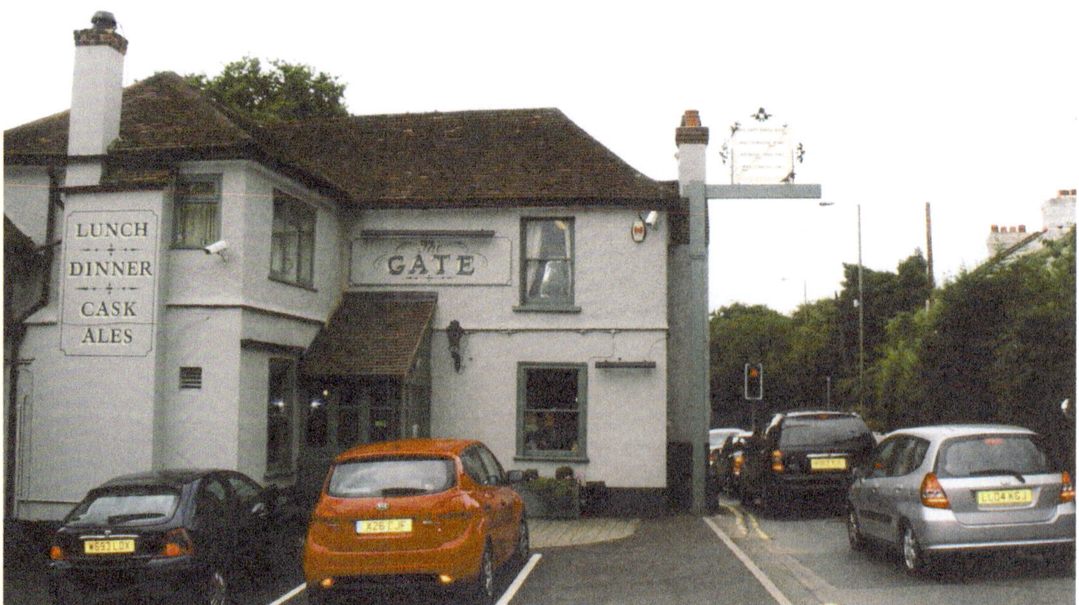

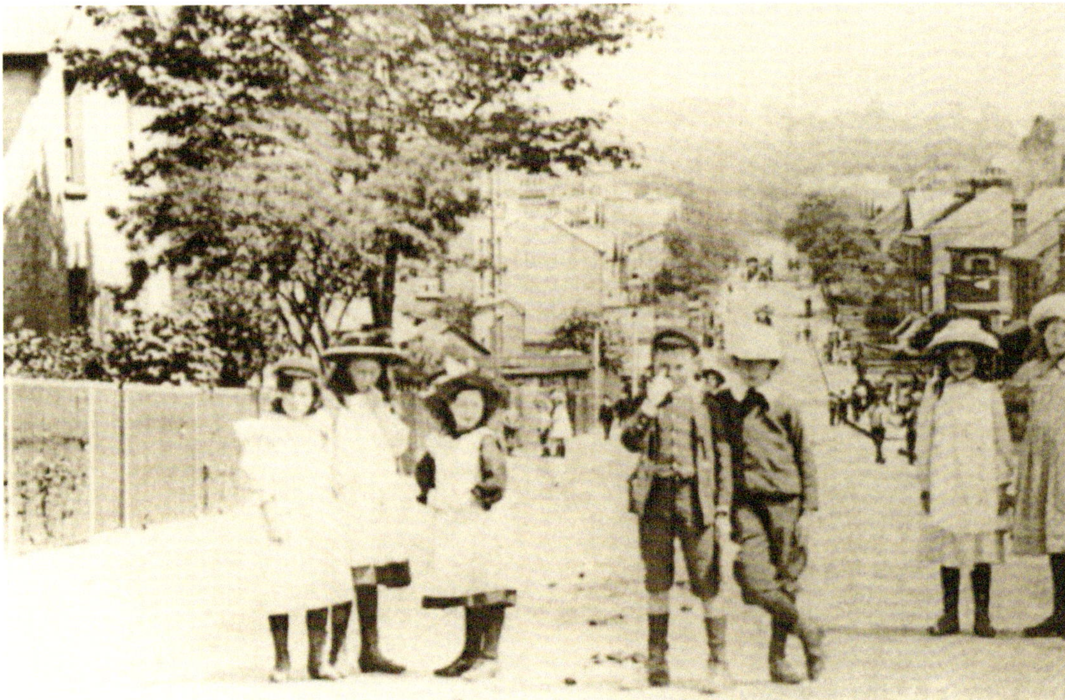

Margaret Road

Above is Margaret Road in New Barnet, near the junction with Lancaster Road. The picture dates from around 1900. The same view in 2013 is shown below.

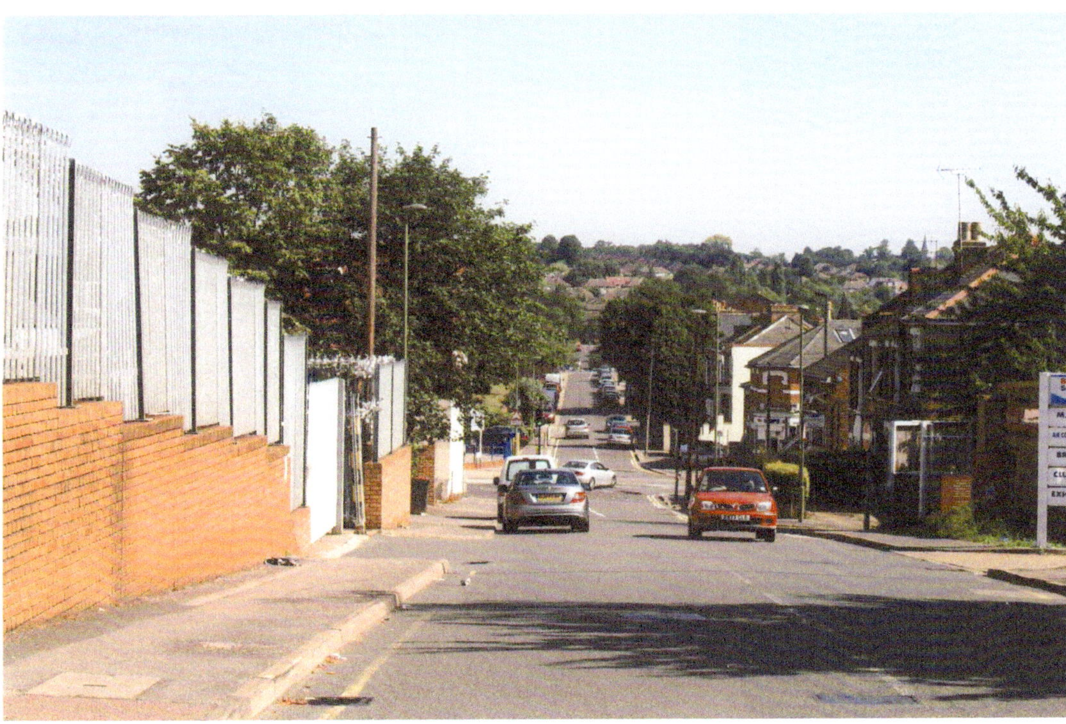

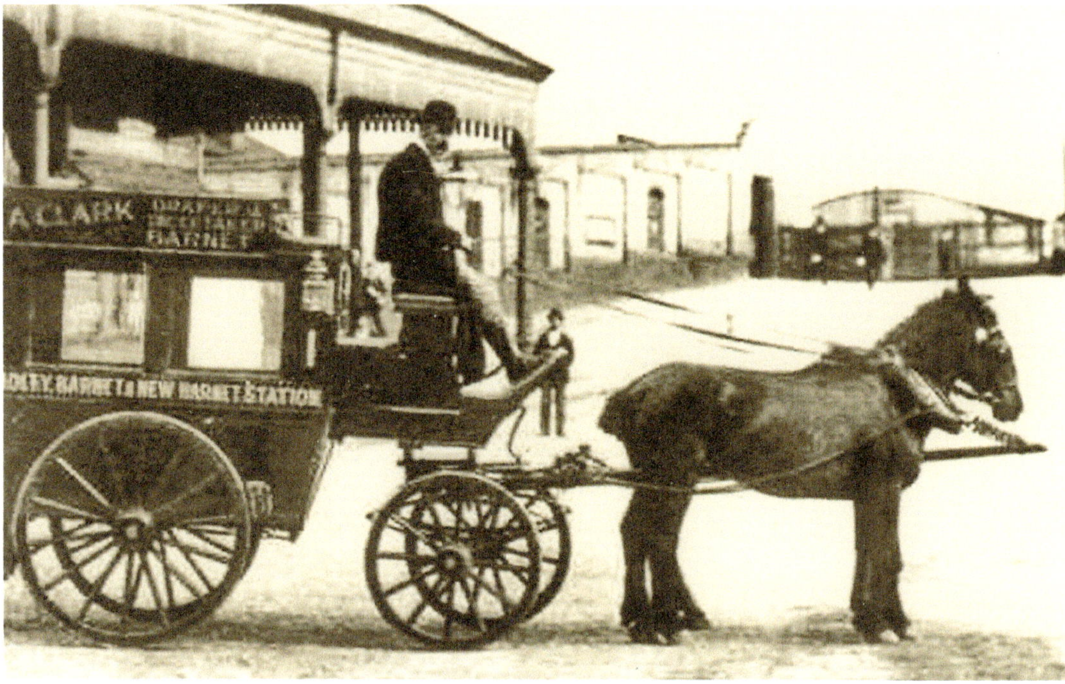

New Barnet Station

New Barnet railway station is seen here in around 1900. Originally Barnet station, it was renamed New Barnet station in 1884. Below, little remains from the original station in 2013.

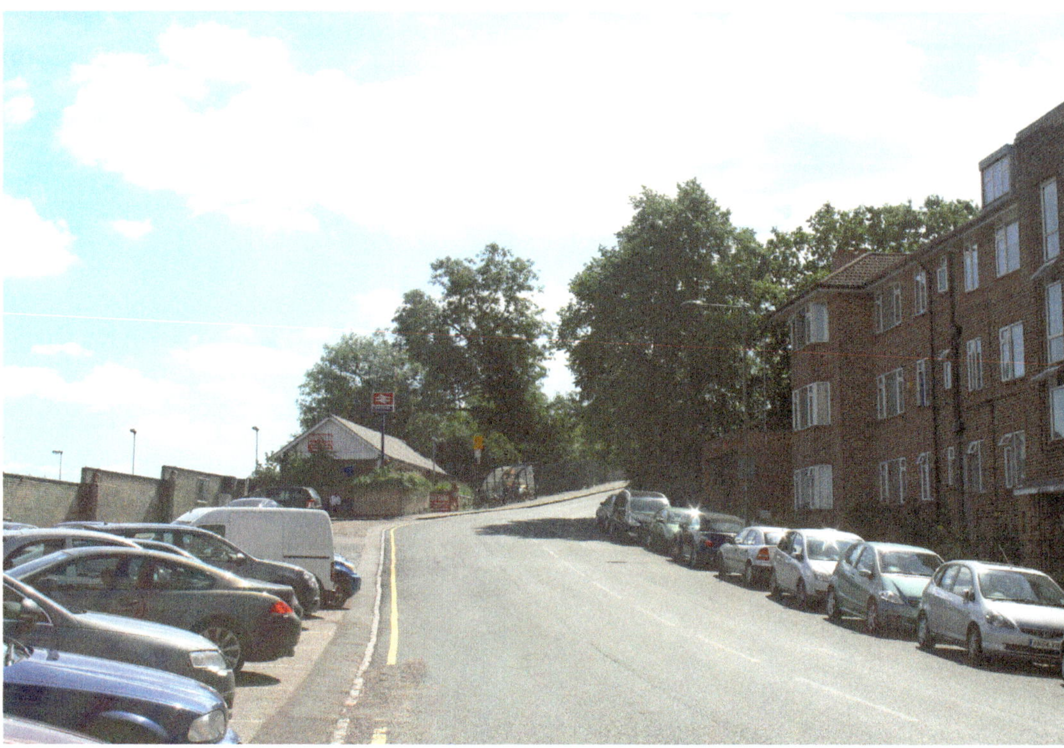

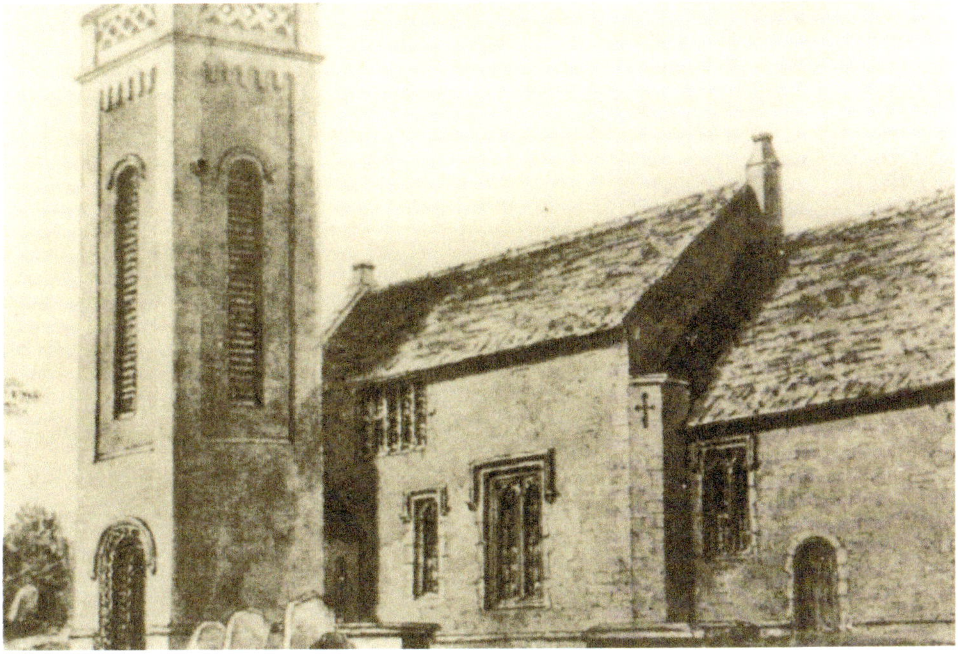

St Mary's Church

The church of St Mary's is one of Barnet's treasures. Enough remains of the original Norman church and its brooding, atmospheric churchyard to take one back to earlier times. The church originally belonged to the abbey at St Albans, and was possibly built in the 1140s. The small tower connected to the church was put up in 1829. The church stands at the top of Church Hill Road overlooking Oak Hill Park. The road and park have a reputation as being England's most haunted area.

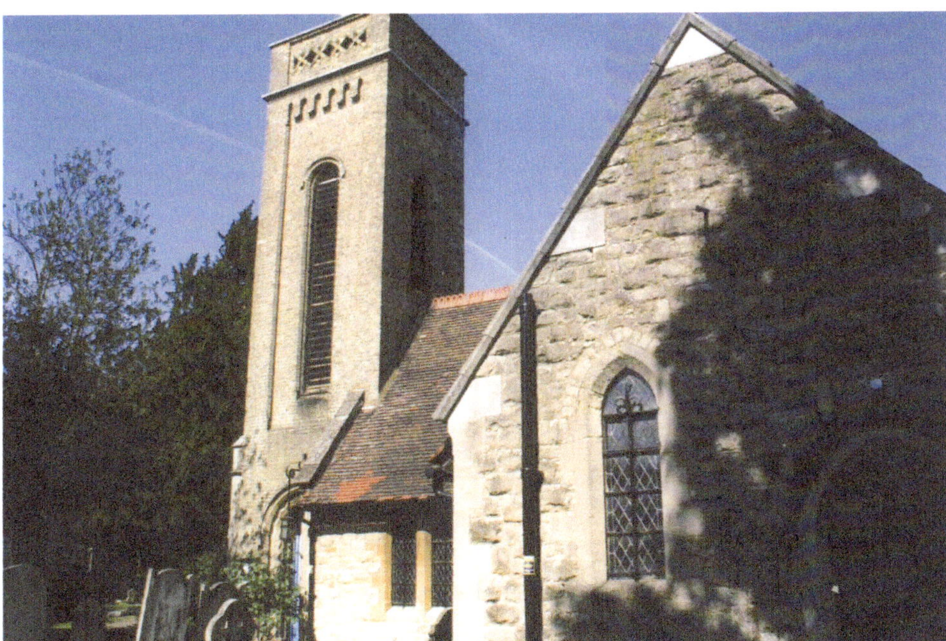

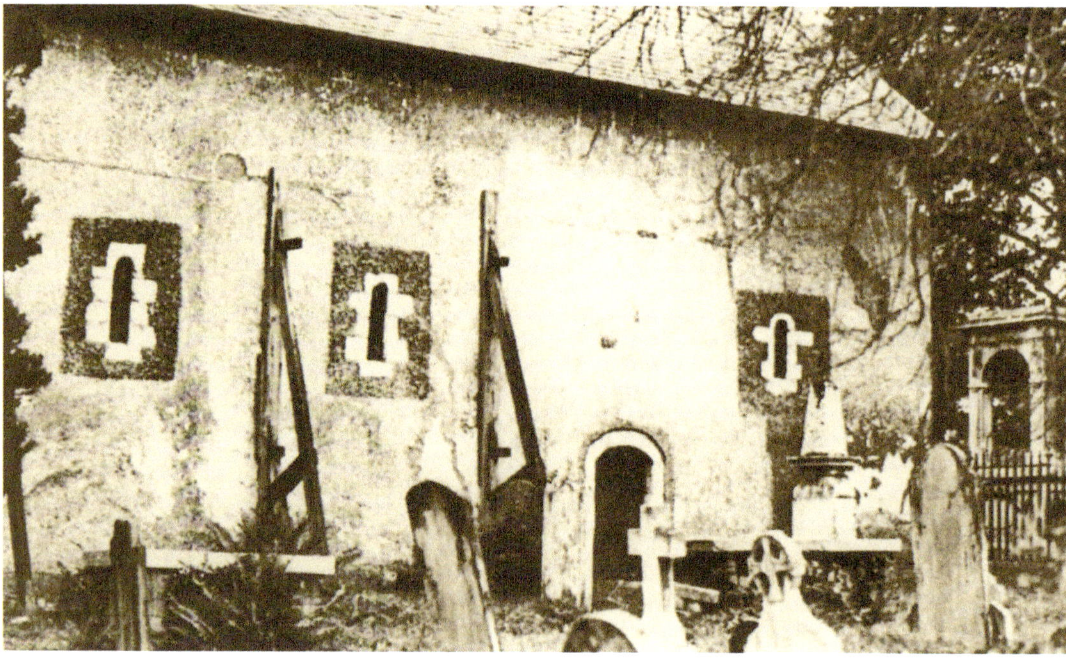

St Mary's Graveyard Ghost

One of the more prominent ghosts in this area is that of Sir Geoffrey de Mandeville, 1st Earl of Essex. He was besieged by King Stephen in 1144, and died from a wound sustained from an arrow during a skirmish. He had also been excommunicated in 1143, so was denied a Christian burial. Sir Geoffrey is said to appear in full armour on horseback, galloping across Oak Hill Park and disappearing behind St Mary's church, through the graveyard.

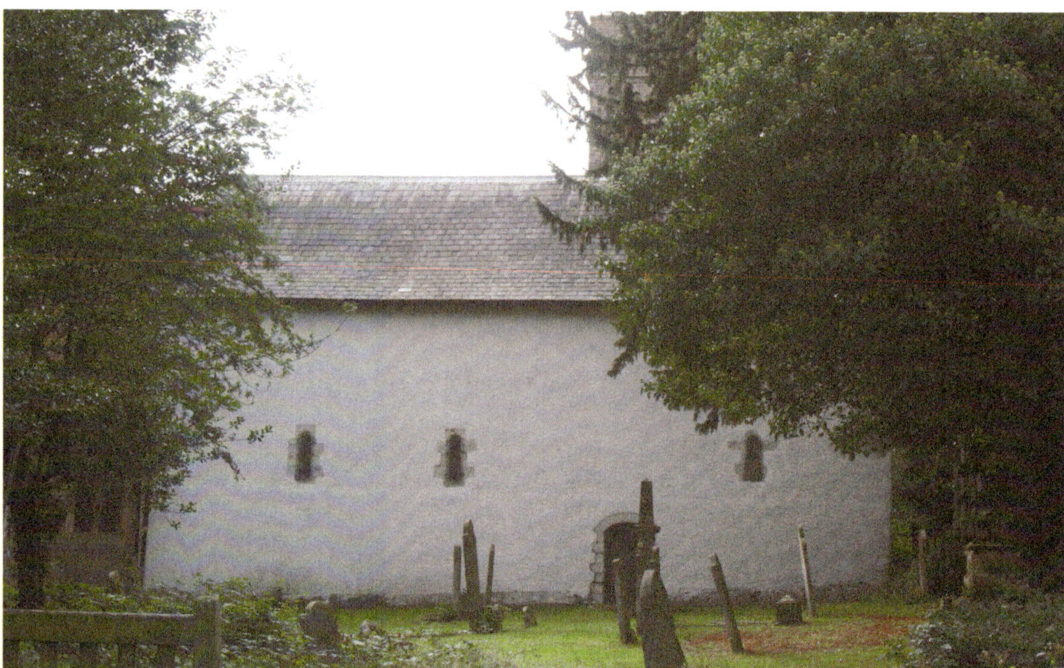

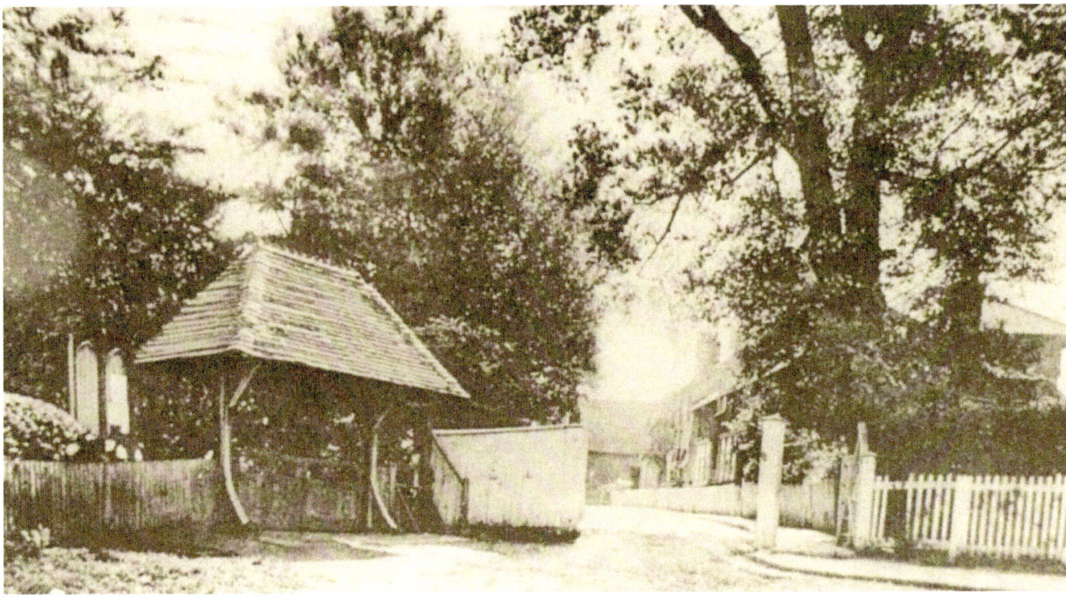

St Mary's Church Lychgate

Above, the lychgate at St Mary's church, around 1890. It was originally erected in 1872, but was rebuilt by Barnet Council in 1991. Lychgates were originally built when churchyards were first enclosed, and allowed the pallbearers at funerals to rest and shelter outside the church until the priest arrived to receive the body into church. The adjoining stile was installed to allow access when the gates were closed to prevent animals entering the churchyard and becoming ill from eating the leaves of the yew trees that line the church path. These trees are about 300 years old. Below, the lychgate in 2013.

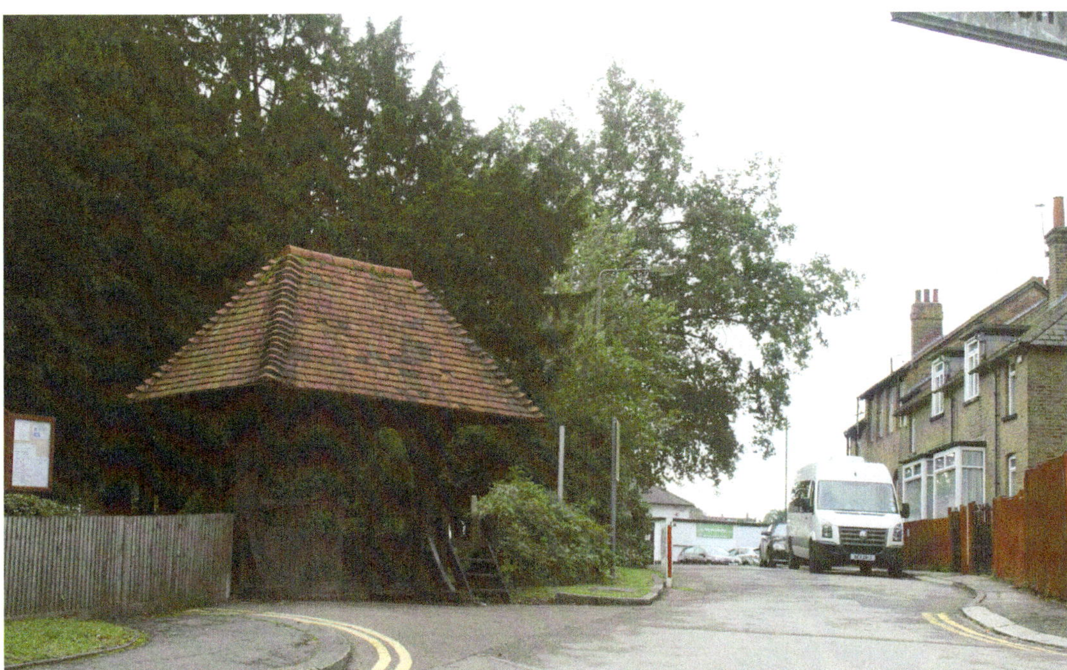

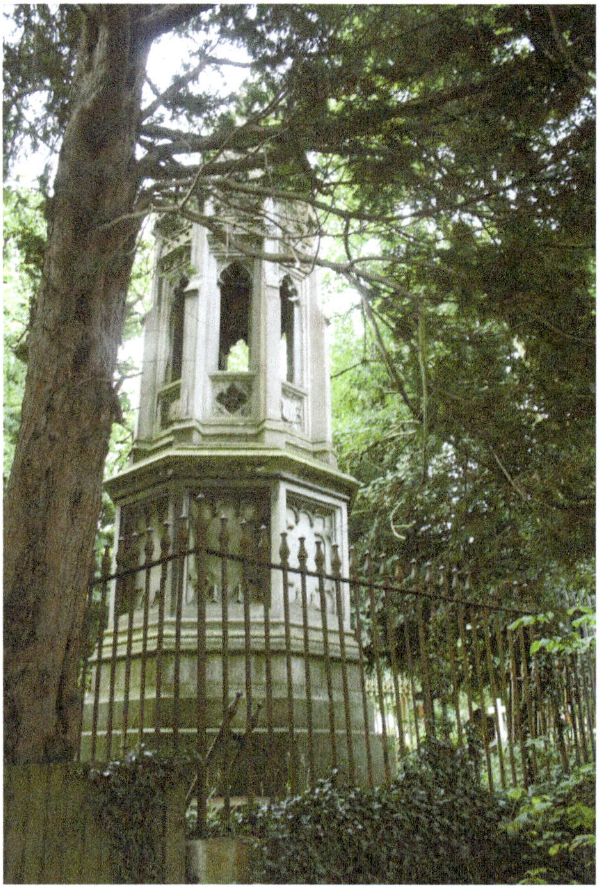

Oak Hill House

In the graveyard of St Mary's is what has been described as an extraordinary gothic monument to Sir Simon Haughton Clarke (*left*), who lived at Oak Hill House and died in 1832. The monument, foliage allowing, puts his final resting place in a direct line of sight of his former home. Below, the white building on the other side of Oak Hill Park is Oak Hill House. Oak Hill House was built around the 1790s. The house was described as having twelve bedrooms and farmland with a herd of cows when it was sold in May 1890. In 1928, the house and gardens became a theological college. The farm was sold to East Barnet Council in 1930, who converted 70 acres of it into a park that opened in October 1933. Cows were still grazed on the small amount of land at Oak Hill House into the 1960s.

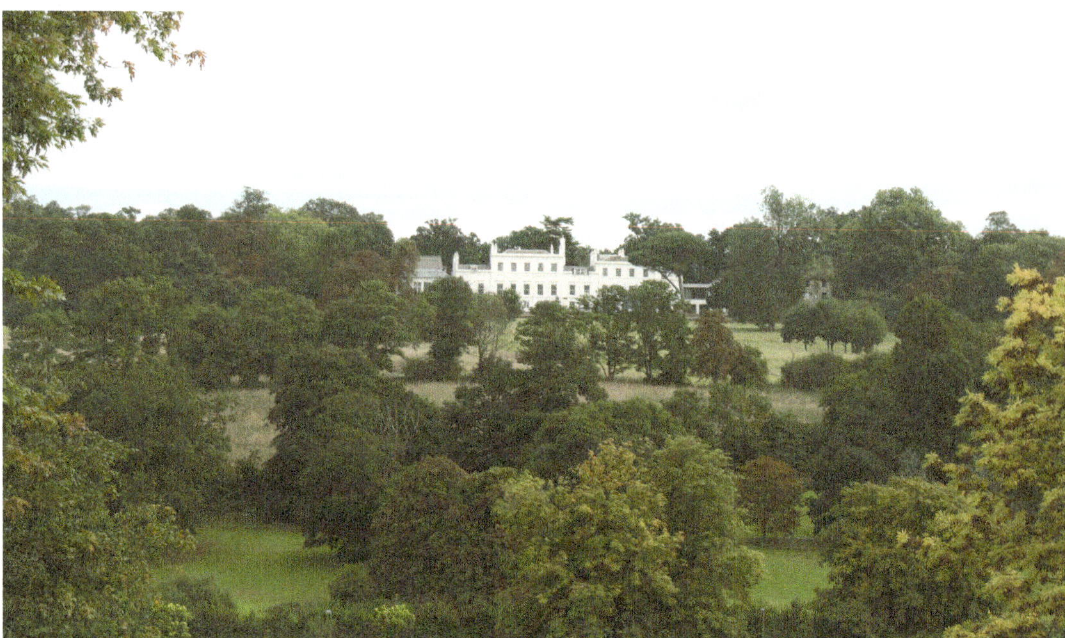

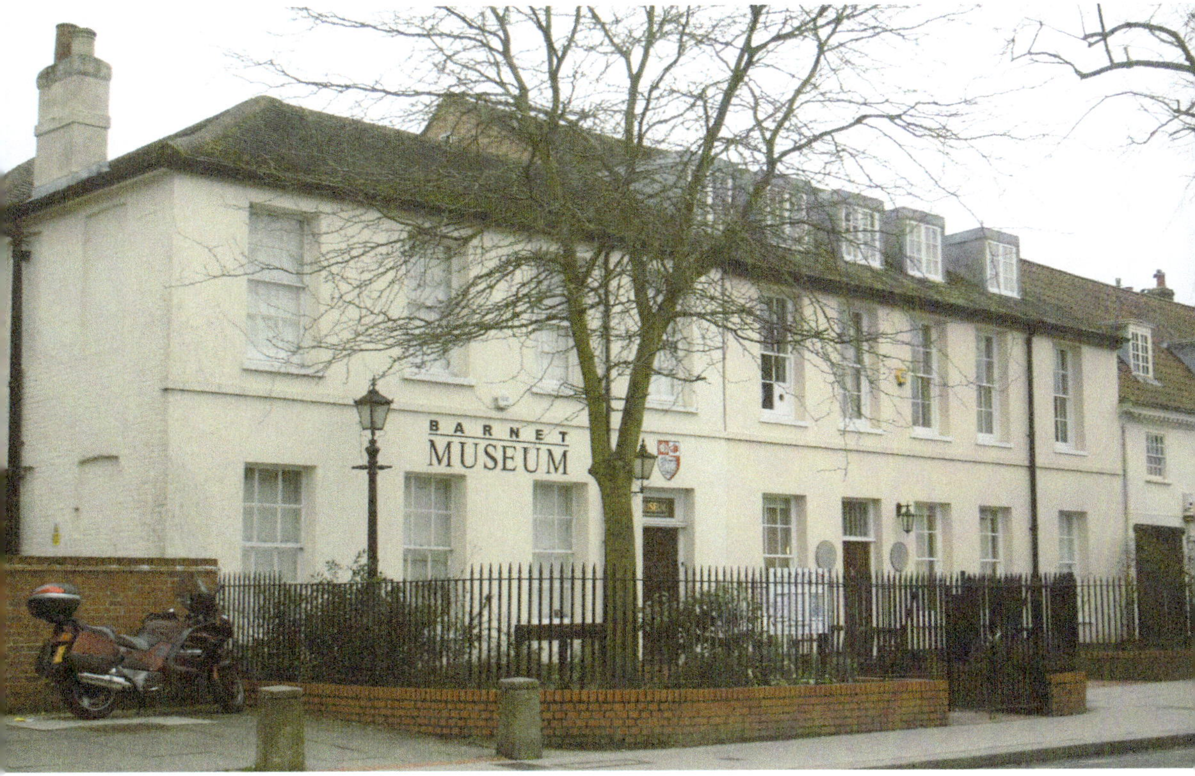

Barnet Museum

Barnet Museum at No. 31 Wood Street is run by volunteers of Barnet Museum and the Local History Society, which is a charity. The museum holds a fascinating collection of many aspects from Barnet life. It houses everything from archaeological remains to a padded cell door, a collection of domestic paraphernalia to paintings of Barnet pubs, and a fine costume collection. The museum has free admission and is open Tuesday through Thursday, 2.30 p.m. to 4.30 p.m., and Saturday, 10.30 a.m. to 12.30 p.m. and 2.00 p.m. to 4.00 p.m.